Modern Halakhah
For Our Time

Modern Halakhah For Our Time

by

Emanuel Rackman

KTAV Publishing House, Inc.
Hoboken, New Jersey

Copyright © 1995 Emanuel Rackman
Library of Congress Cataloging-in-Publication Data

Rackman, Emanuel.
    Modern Halakhah for our time / by Emanuel Rackman.
        p.   cm.
    Includes bibliographical references.
    ISBN 0-88125-295-6
    1. Jewish law--Philosophy. I. Title.
BM520.6.R33 1993
296.1'8--dc20   93-35397
                                                                           CIP

Manufactured in the United States of America

Dedicated to

Our Sons

משה, ישראל ברוך, מרדכי ויוסף רבה

who, with their loved ones—ours too,

have blessed their parents with great nachas

and forced their father to think harder

when studying Talmud with them.

Contents

Acknowledgments

For more than sixty years I have been engaged in the teaching of Jewish law. Whether as a congregational rabbi or in academia I have sought to cultivate interest in the subject and especially to gleam insights, more than rules, that can enrich Jewish life now and forever. Often I was critical of colleagues who failed to do this but I was rewarded when occasionally one student or another would thank me for this very engaging and edifying pursuit. Jewish law was the one force that insured Jewish continuity for millennia. I am committed to the notion that it can still serve that purpose. Not only were democratic ideals a part of it but those very ideals had no more enduring foundation than the religious faith which is the source of Jewish law.

I am very grateful to Mr. Bernard Scharfstein, of KTAV Publishing House, Inc., who undertook to publish a sampling of the essays that appeared in learned journals over a long period of time. I hope that, as with an earlier book of mine, *One Man's Judaism*, it will cause readers to ponder the greatness of a legal system that ought not be permitted to die.

It is impossible to list the many to whom I owe thanks for all that I am, all that I have, and all that I may have achieved. But I owe them an apology because their generous effort warranted more spectacular results. For my failures I shall have to account to our *Maker*.

Halakhah: Orthodox Approaches

The Analytical Approach

Most halakhic authorities regard the Halakhah as a body of rules handed down by the Divine Sovereign to enable the Jew to live according to His will. Some of these rules were transmitted by Moses in writing, while others were transmitted orally by him, together with a methodology for creativity within the revealed rules. Disobedience to some of the rules may be punished by authorities to whom God delegated that power, while for other breaches of the Covenant He reserved unto Himself the power to punish.

In such a simplistic conception of the Halakhah, the rationale of the rules is rarely, if ever, an integral part of the rules themselves. Man simply lives to obey these rules—and in obedience lies his salvation. To the extent that creativity is possible, it must be without reference to social or economic conditions, unless such considerations are implicit in the rule. Such instances are very few. The process of Halakhah is discovering what God had said. This is what the law is. Such an analysis must be strictly logical, arrived at deductively or inductively from existing rules and texts, without reference to ideal ends or social facts.

Thus, when in modern times the question arose as to whether light produced by an electric current does or does not constitute fire, and consequently whether it falls under the biblical prohibition on making fire on the Sabbath, the approach of many who made reply was purely analytical. The words and the applicable rules were carefully studied on the basis of textual distinction between hot coals and hot metals. The philosophical rationale of the biblical command was not relevant to the issue.

In modern jurisprudence this approach is known as "analytical" or "imperative." It distinguishes sharply between the role of the legislator and the role of the jurist. Whereas the legislator may promulgate new rules, the jurist limits his activity to the analysis and exposition of established rules and recognized authorities.

It was in line with this juridical approach that Rabbi Moses Feinstein, when asked about bat mitzvah celebrations, discouraged them since there was no source for such celebrations in halakhic literature, and thus festive meals marking such occasions could not be deemed *se'udot mitzvah* (banquets in fulfillment of religious obligations). He even forbade the use of synagogue premises for such ceremonies.[1]

In the absence of a text or precedent he had no role to play as a jurist in the halakhic tradition. On the other hand, Rabbi Isaac Nissim, former Chief Rabbi of Israel, did find a precedent for such banquets in a collection of unpublished responsa by a Sephardi scholar, and he consequently permitted them.[2] But neither rabbi chose to take into consideration contemporary pressures for the equality of the sexes.

Similarly, halakhic experts refused to consider granting equal status to sons and daughters in inheriting estates of their parents. There is no authority whatever for such a move in either biblical or rabbinic literature, especially with regard to the father's assets, although with regard to a mother's assets there was such a minority view in favor of daughters inheriting equally with the sons in both the Babylonian and Palestinian Talmuds.[3] As a result, a determined effort by the late Chief Rabbi Isaac Herzog to legislate equality ended in failure. Those committed to the analytical approach cannot act in the absence of well-accepted texts and authorities in halakhic literature.

Because of their total commitment to what the law is, as it has come down from the past, halakhic authorities are especially intransigent with regard to many problems of modern medicine. The old texts simply did not envision the developments that the Halakhah must now face. The question of the permissibility of organ transplants can serve as an example.

In certain cases an organ must be removed from the donor before the moment of death as the latter is defined in the Halakhah, that is, before the cessation of respiratory and/or cardiac activity. A talmudic source (Yoma 83a, 85a) dealing with the desecration of sacred days in order to save a person's life states that so long as there is some respiratory or cardiac activity he is presumed capable of being revived, and no effort must be spared to save him. Total, irreversible, brain damage is not a factor; it has been assumed for millennia that a person is alive no matter how dead his brain is. Jewish law, for reasons that are cogent, tolerates no mercy killing.

---

1. *Iggerot Moshe*, Pt. Orah Hayyim. 1:104.

2. See *Tradition*. 14, 2 (1973). 126–7.

3. BB 111a; TJ. BB 8:1, 16a.

Notwithstanding the arguments of many ethical philosophers today, Judaism is opposed to any acts that would put an end to the misery of conscious patients or the helplessness of the unconscious.

However, if a man leaves instructions that, should he suffer total, irreversible, brain damage, his heart or kidneys are to be donated to a patient in need of them, are his wishes to be honored'? Two questions arise here. Is the surgeon permitted to "murder" one person to save the life of another who otherwise would die? May one deem a donor the master of his own body to the extent that he can authorize such "murder" to be committed against his own person? The position of the Halakhah with regard to killing a human being is well-nigh absolute. Whereas the killing of an attacker and the execution of a criminal are permitted, there exist no precedents for killing one person in order to save another; a talmudic maxim (San. 72b) enjoins one from preferring one person's life to another's. The Halakhah does specify priorities when the issue is whose life should be saved when a choice is possible, but the problem of organ transplants was never contemplated; a purely analytical approach can yield no answer, because the old texts never envisioned the new situation. The surgeon would indeed be a "murderer."

To return to the question of the donor: may he authorize the gift of his organs, even though consummation of the gift will involve his own death? Suicide is prohibited by the Halakhah. Nevertheless, one may risk one's life to save another, and one is even exhorted to martyr oneself to sanctify God's name; one must also engage in war to protect one's people and one's country. Thus there are precedents that permit what might be regarded as the equivalent of suicide. However, logical analysis demonstrates that these cases differ from that of the donor, who unimpulsively, after long premeditation, decides to be heroic and authorize his own death in order to enable another human being to live with consciousness, a blessing he himself will no longer have. Unless he applies a non-analytical approach to the Halakhah, a rabbi today cannot approve of this heroic decision; and even other approaches do not enable him to add one more instance to the list of situations in which taking one's life is a *mitzvah*—a noble deed. The texts and authorities that specify the situations in which one may fulfill *kiddush ha-Shem* by martyrdom do not include dying to save another from such a fate.

The late Chief Rabbi Abraham Isaac Kook did suggest—and he

is the sole authority to have done so—that the heroic sacrifice of one's life by submitting to certain death to spare another from a similar fate may be permitted. Often in Jewish history individual Jews did precisely that—they offered themselves to the enemy to save groups or communities or even other individuals whose lives they deemed worthier than their own. But there was no halakhic authority that permitted this. On the contrary, a talmudic maxim supports the view that one's own life has the highest priority; to meet this difficulty, Rabbi Kook suggested that this maxim may be permissive, rather than mandatory (Mishpat Kohen (1966²), No. 143, cf. ET, 10 (1961), 347). The Talmud (BM 62a) suggests that if one of two individuals traveling in a desert has just enough water to save his own life, he need not share it with his companion. The opposite view—that both shall drink and neither see the death of the other—is not the prevailing one. But may the owner of the water give it to his friend, and thereby sacrifice himself'? Rabbi Kook thinks that he may, but this too would hardly be an authority that would, for example, permit one to place one's body in the path of a bullet destined for one's son. And it certainly would not justify the donation of a heart or a kidney to be taken from the donor when he suffers irreversible brain damage. In these two situations one is destroying oneself by action rather than inaction. For, as stated, analytical approach is bound by texts and authorities, and permits virtually no consideration whatever of imperatives other than divine ones already established. The impulse of the heroic parent to save his child has no support in the literature and therefore may be halakhically objectionable.

The No-Risk Approach

An added factor which tends toward a rigid approach to the Halakhah derives from the fact that, because the halakhic imperatives are divine in origin, many authorities dread using even the analytical approach for anything other than broadening the prohibitions, since one should not incur any risk with regard to God's will. Since that will is indescribably sacred, one dare not risk acting in violation of it ! If in doubt about the permissibility of a particular deed, the best course is to avoid action.

For a devotee of the law, its prescriptions require at least as much caution as is exercised with regard to personal health or safety. One does not drink a potion that may be only doubtfully poisonous, and one does not cross a bridge which may be only remotely liable to collapse. By the same token, one does not marry a person about whose legitimacy there may be the slightest reservations. And one does not, for example, bring into being children by artificial insemination, with the donor someone other than the husband, because one rabbi or another expressed the view that such offspring may suffer the taint of bastardy, even though the overwhelming majority of authorities hold the contrary view. (There can be no bastardy according to the Halakhah unless there has been literal sexual intercourse.) But when one distinguished halakhic authority in the United States published this view he was mercilessly attacked as rash and brazen by the followers of one hasidic rabbi, even as he himself subsequently attacked Chief Rabbi Shlomo Goren of Israel for his opinion regarding the competency of the Langer sister and brother to marry. The "no-risk" approach has much to commend it when it is invoked to determine one's own course of action. However, it is certainly not approved by the halakhic tradition as a suitable approach when others are involved. Indeed, the Talmud lauds those authorities who have the courage to permit rather than prohibit.

Especially with regard to the development of Jewish family law in the modern era, the "no risk" approach is stifling. Jewish family law is presently palpably unfair to women. For them to enjoy complete equality in the area of divorce it is necessary once again—as in the distant past—to renew the exercise by rabbinical authorities of their power to annul marriages. In this way also the *agunah* problem can be solved, whether it is caused by the husband's disappearance without trace, or the refusal of the recalcitrant brother-in-law to release his brother's childless widow. The annulment of marriages is a great power which only courageous rabbis will undertake; those who shun risks will avoid it like the plague.

The Legitimacy of Diversity in Interpreting Divine Law

Persons unfamiliar with halakhic literature often wonder how there can be so many different Orthodox views when the analytical and no-risk approaches enjoy such overwhelming support. After all, if logic rather than history and experience is the life of the Halakhah, can logic yield so many contradictory answers to the same question? Moreover, they question whether a revealed religion can ever evolve. Given that God's will is timeless and eternal, can man arrogate to himself the right to change it?

In general, a pat negative is assumed to be the correct reply to such questions; as a result, many Jews have come to regard Orthodox

Judaism as monolithic—as having a fixed philosophy, and a completely inflexible approach based on Jewish Law. The very term "Orthodox" conjures up the image of a central authority, comparable to that of the Pope, who makes ultimate decisions binding upon the faithful. This is, however, not even true of Roman Catholicism, and far less so of Orthodox Judaism. There have always been, and still are, different modes of Orthodox Jewish thought and practice, and Orthodoxy has always admitted a great measure of innovation. It is a fact that Orthodox Judaism has more splinter rabbinic groups than either Conservative or Reform Judaism. While Conservative and Reform rabbis are predominantly American, Orthodox Judaism has substantial rabbinic groups all over the world, their number and diversity often reflect ideological as well as national and geographical differences, and members not infrequently espouse ideas that are atypical for the particular groups to which they belong.

A few examples from contemporary Jewish life will show that not all Orthodox Jews think alike or act alike. Orthodox rabbinical seminaries disagree as to the propriety of studying non-Jewish culture. New York's Rabbi Isaac Elchanan Theological Seminary, by far the largest, advocates the mastering of all Western thought in order to create an ultimate synthesis with Jewish learning, and it was with this aim in mind that it founded Yeshiva University. Others hold that secular studies endanger faith, and that if a rabbinical student wants a baccalaureate degree, it would be better for him to major in a subject that would not impinge upon his religious convictions—mathematics, for example. Others simply forbid their students to study anything other than Torah. This is the position of most yeshivot in Israel. In the United States, one large group of Orthodox rabbis today cooperates with their Conservative and Reform colleagues in whatever areas their programs are similar, whereas others even refuse to address them as "rabbi."

There is also a wide spectrum of opinion with regard to the re-establishment of the Sanhedrin. Even proponents of the idea are not in agreement: some want a central authority solely to impose uniformity in Orthodox practice throughout the world, whereas others wish to effect changes in at least rabbinic, if not biblical, law. Opposition to the Sanhedrin among Orthodox Jews includes both "rightists and "leftists." The "rightists" oppose a Sanhedrin on the ground that the present generation is not pious enough to make any changes whatever in Jewish Law. The "leftists" are in dread of what those who controlled a Sanhedrin could do; they prefer that freedom that still prevails in Orthodoxy because of the very absence of a central authority.

Consideration of Psychological Data

There are in the Talmud at least two instances in which the sages were at a loss on the interpretation of biblical commands. The verses involved lent themselves to different interpretations which, according to the analytical approach, could be regarded as equally valid. The problems were resolved on one basis only. The sages favored the interpretations which people would find more acceptable, for they held that the Torah's ways must be "ways of pleasantness."[4] Thus they yielded exclusively to a psychological factor—the greater aesthetic appeal of the procedures which they ordained, and they rejected alternative possibilities which seemed repugnant.

A number of responsa in modern times reveal that psychological data are not altogether ignored. Thus on the Sabbath one may do many things otherwise prohibited merely in order to allay the mental anguish of the sick even if there is no real danger to life. A distinguished modern halakhist has laid it down that husbands should travel to the hospital on the Sabbath when their wives are in labor, not only in order to provide added peace of mind to the prospective mother, but also to draw public attention to the fact that life-saving in Judaism is of supreme importance, and thereby to enhance respect for the tradition as a whole.[5]

Similarly for the education of the young it is permitted to disregard certain requirements about the presence in a minyan of ten Jews who have reached their majority, and to include minors in this quorum. Moreover, for educational goals even the biblical command not to take the name of the Lord in vain can be ignored. As yet, very few rabbis have been equally liberal with regard to the same issues insofar as women are concerned. The argument in favor of males who are minors is that they are being trained for their later performance as adults, while women will never have those obligations; however, it could be claimed that by indulging women the same privileges one is helping to train future mothers who presently bear the greater burden of training children in Judaism.

---

4. TJ. Sukkah 32a–b. See also Yevamot 15a and 87b.

5. *Iggerot Moshe*, Pt. Orah Hayyim, 132.

However, it is especially in family law that the use of psychological data should and can play a greater role than is now the case. In certain circumstances of levirate marriage where a woman might be expected to be released from the obligation to marry a surviving brother-in-law, the Talmud rules against such release, arguing that all women will accept even a bad marriage in preference to living alone. But in the twentieth century such a presumption can scarcely be said to fit with contemporary social conditions. Nowadays with the changes brought about by the women's liberation movement, the vast majority of women would certainly be happier to remain single than to enter into a dead marriage. Nevertheless, rabbis are reluctant to make decisions and either reinterpret old rules or legislate in the light of such well-known psychological facts.

Furthermore, while rabbis have taken physiological facts into consideration in connection with the annulment of marriages, only rarely do they reckon with psychological disorders of the husband (except for homosexuality) to arrive at the same result. In one interesting case.[6] Rabbi Moses Feinstein did precisely that, and again he was made the butt of fierce criticism. However, halakhic literature indicates that the early masters were as conscious of the psychological as they were of the physiological in all areas. Maimonides might almost be regarded as an expert in psychosomatic medicine. The reluctance to exploit this method to administer justice to those who seek it is not due to the dearth of halakhic authority, but rather to a psychotic fear that all that is modern is taboo.

Consideration of Sociological Data

The social and economic needs of Jews were always considered in halakhic literature. Rules pertaining to man's relationship with God, such as rules of cleanness and uncleanness and rules involving the Sabbatical year, were often either suspended or strengthened to accommodate such needs.

During the Middle Ages Jews found that several rabbinic rules prevented them from engaging in business with non-Jews. For instance, it was prohibited to enter into business partnerships with them, the reason being that in the event of a disagreement between the partners, the gentile would be required to take an oath by his god. In the Middle Ages the prohibition was relaxed by the decision that Christians were not to be regarded as idol-worshippers. The

---

6. *Iggerot Moshe*, Pt. Even ha-Ezer, No. 80,190–2.

analytical approach would have sufficed to justify the change—Christianity had also outlawed paganism, and the rabbinic rule was directed against pagans. But for seven or eight centuries no official pronouncement was made on this point, and the prohibition continued to apply to Christians as well. However, cooperation between Christians and Jews in business had not yet attained the dimensions that prevailed in the days of Rabbenu Tam (12th century), when the prohibition was relaxed, and apparently the social and economic needs of the time precipitated his modification of the rule and common practice.[7]

The rabbis today may not be as courageous as their forbears, but nonetheless this approach is still used occasionally, and is very much to be encouraged. Thus, for example, Rabbi Menahem M. Kasher dealt extensively with the problem of the international date line and its effect upon the Sabbath. According to the presently effective international agreement, when it is the Sabbath in Israel it is Sunday in certain parts of the Pacific. Now, when shall Jews in these Pacific islands observe the Sabbath—on the seventh day by their local calendar, or on Sunday, on the theory that it was God's intent that the Sabbath day be computed with Jerusalem as the center of time?

The problem is reminiscent of the great medieval dispute as to whether the earth or the sun was the center of the universe. The Church chose the earth and any other opinion was declared heresy. Similarly, many rabbis argued that Jerusalem was the center for the computation of time, and that no other place would satisfy the requirements of Jewish law. Against this view Rabbi Kasher marshalled all the sources, and he was upheld by Israel's Chief Rabbinate when he asserted that the international date line was binding on Jews. Actually Rabbi Kasher has been anticipated by earlier authorities but what makes his decision particularly interesting is that one of his arguments is sociological. He stated, for example, that if "the nations of the world in years gone by used their own capitals" for the purpose of measuring time, it reflected their concern for national pride and honor. We should not imitate them . . . particularly when they have waived their honor and agreed upon a more reasonable approach. His decision was also influenced by the practice with regard to the Sabbath already prevailing among Jews in the areas affected by the date line. Thus an awareness of what is good for humanity at large

---

7. E. Berkovits. "The Role of the Halakhah," *Judaism*, 19,1 (1970), 68.

played an important role in his decision.

Those familiar with the few responsa that Rabbi Joseph B. Soloveitchik has written are also aware of his great concern not only for halakhic sources but also for social facts. Thus, for example, a generation ago there arose a halakhic problem that involved the armed forces of the United States, which required Jewish chaplains. The three largest rabbinic groups in America—Orthodox, Conservative and Reform—instituted a draft procedure: rabbis were to be drafted compulsorily by their own rabbinic groups. For Orthodox rabbis, there was a significant halakhic problem. Could rabbis undertake to place any colleague in jeopardy? Furthermore, could they undertake to place a colleague in a position that might one day compel him to desecrate the Sabbath or another holy festival?

To this query Rabbi Soloveitchik gave an affirmative reply. In a magnificent unpublished responsum based on a keen analysis of talmudic sources, he upheld the action of Yeshiva University in calling for the drafting of its alumni for the military chaplaincy. He cited a medieval text permitting one to embark upon a voyage to fulfill a *mitzvah*, even though it was possible that in the course of the voyage it might be necessary to desecrate the Sabbath in order to save one's own life or the life of another. Rabbi Soloveitchik admitted that he had not approached the sources with complete objectivity; that he had certain intuitive feelings and held certain basic values that prejudiced him in favor of the decision rendered by Yeshiva University had guided him in his exploration of the various aspects and facets of the problem. But this lack of objectivity is merely a fundamental avowal of inevitable human limitation, and is not to be confused with arbitrariness. As anyone who has studied the Talmud knows, the Halakhah is too objective a discipline to permit an approach based on transient moods. Nevertheless, in the deepest strata of halakhic thinking, logical judgment is preceded by value judgment, and intuitive insight gives impetus to the logic of argument.

An important factor in his decision was the status of Orthodox Judaism in the eyes of the non-Orthodox and in the eyes of non-Jews—simply the matter of public relations. This consideration also played a part in his halakhic analysis of the question whether it was proper for Orthodox rabbis and synagogues to be associated with the non-Orthodox in the same organizations. What people would say about the separatism of the Orthodox was not to be ignored. What people will say is not a factor to be ignored in

Halakhah.

It is lamentable that today's "doctors of the Law" choose to remain oblivious of the negative impressions of the Halakhah they are conveying by their ultra-conservatism. While on the one hand, their rigidity may conserve the tradition, on the other hand it is alienating thousands of Jews from the Law.

The Use of History

The dates of Jewish history have always played a role in halakhic development; the Wissenschaft des Judentums of the nineteenth century is not to be credited with this discovery. Much of Jewish law has its unmistakable source in the events of the Jewish past and these events account for much biblical and rabbinic legislation. However, historical considerations also played a part in the revision of halakhic rules. Thus, for example, several rabbis held that a ruling promulgated by earlier authorities on the basis of conditions existing in their time was no longer applicable when the conditions changed; so there need be no formal nullification of the rule and it becomes obsolescent automatically. It was presumed that the original legislation was predicated on the continuance of the situation that existed at that time and that the rabbis who instituted it intended it to lapse automatically when the situation changed. R. Menahem ben Solomon Meiri (13th-14th century) was so bold as to suggest that there were only two rules that were impervious to this obsolescence: they involved the existence of the Temple in Jerusalem, and the promulgators of those rules could never have had in mind the destruction of the Temple and the exile of the Jews.[8]

On the basis of historical considerations, Menahem Elon has made a challenging suggestion for the liberalization of Jewish family law in our day. The question has been raised why rabbis today hesitate to liberalize the Halakhah so that they would be enabled to annul marriages as their forebears had done up until less than a thousand years ago. It is universally recognized that without renewed exercise of this power it will be almost impossible to accord women their due and to relieve them of many of the disadvantages and disabilities that the Halakhah imposes upon them. Moshe Silberg has been the most articulate exponent for such a move, and many Orthodox rabbis—especially those in the active rabbinate, as opposed to those who are the heads of

8. ET. 6 (1954), 703, and footnote 44.

yeshivot—agree with him. It is the rabbis who serve congregations who have to encounter day after day the inequalities of the Halakhah with respect to women, and it is they who clamor for the revival of an ancient rabbinic power. The resistance to Silberg's proposals is enormous, and despite the impressive arguments in support of him in unimpeachable scholarly works like the *Tenai bi-Nissu'in u-ve-Get* (1967) of Eliezer Berkovits there is no movement forward. The principal argument of the opposition is that for centuries rabbis have hesitated to do what Abraham H. Freimann demonstrated was done in the Middle Ages and earlier (*Seder Kiddushin ve-Nissuin Aharei Hatimat ha-Talmud* [1945]). On what basis can one resurrect a power that may have lapsed because of lack of usage—a species of legal atrophy?

Elon counters this challenge on the basis of history.[9] The power lapsed, he argued, because of the dispersion of Jews. It was unwise when Jews lived in hundreds of communities greatly distant from each other, and often without adequate communication, to exercise the power to annul marriages when one rabbinical court in one place would act on grounds or on the basis of takkanot not recognized by another court. One court would then hold the couple still wedded to each other while another court would regard them as divorced. Today, however, when the centrality in the Jewish world of the rabbinical courts of Israel is generally accepted, there is no reason that the power should not be revived and the enactments of Israel's supreme religious council recognized everywhere. This is an instance of the historical approach paving the way for real progress in halakhic development.

The Teleological Approach

This approach simply calls for recognition of the teleology of the Halakhah—the purpose which Jewish law is to fulfill. It is the boldest of all the controversial approaches, because halakhists were always reluctant to interpret the law with an eye to the achievement of its goal when the goal was not explicit in either biblical or talmudic literature. However, this has led to a tragic paradox. Louis I. Rabinowitz has made the telling point that in Israel today, were persons living in the same building to agree that occupancy was limited to "religious" people, a breach of that agreement would occur if a tenant drove his car into the parking area on the Sabbath,

9. M. Elon. in: *Petahim*, 4/5 (Sept. 1972), 24–25.

but not if he were found guilty of embezzlement.

A more tragic consequence of the refusal to reckon with the law's purpose is that many rabbis who resist changes in Jewish family law are committed to the idea that they want to preserve the integrity of Jewish family life and the unequivocal legitimacy of Jewish offspring when in fact their intransigence is only multiplying bastardy all over the world. Fortunately most of the tainted will never be identified, but the champions of no action prefer to play it safe rather than take the measures that would prevent increasing incidence of the stigma.

Indeed, one rabbi has argued that the annulment of marriages would mean that the offspring of such marriages will he deemed bastards by rabbinic standards, and quotes good authority for his view; however, he completely ignores the fact that the equally competent authority cited in the very same passage holds that this is a good way to legitimatize the status of many bastards and views this as a great gain for the Jewish people!

Perhaps it was because rabbis could not always agree on the purpose of the law that it was regarded as safe to rely on texts alone in judicial decision-making. Nevertheless, occasionally there were rabbis who did not hesitate to say that intuitively they felt what the correct decision was—on the basis of ethical or even political considerations—and they later supported their intuition with relevant texts. Indeed, were more rabbis to be this candid it would be discovered that a personal philosophy is a very important factor in the process. Needless to say, the conclusion must be based on the law, and its vast literature, and the reasoning must be objective and able to withstand criticism by peers. The subjective element cannot be the basis for decision, but honesty requires that its presence shall not be denied. If rabbis have no sympathy whatever with the demands of modern women for equal status in the Jewish law of marriage and divorce, they will find texts adequate to support their intransigence. If, however, they feel that the present situation is simply intolerable and an insult to God and God's law, they will be vociferous and militant in making use of the halakhic authorities and the texts available to propose revisions in the Halakhah. They are no less "Orthodox" than their colleagues, and indeed, they may even be more halakhically "authentic."

It is not only with regard to family law that the teleological approach is important. Another area involves the taking of interest or usury. The unrelenting erosion of the biblical and talmudic prohibitions against the taking and giving of interest has reached its climax in Israel, whose citizens are not only the most highly taxed people in the world but also the victims of the highest rates of interest. The moneylenders include banks and individuals identified with the strictest halakhic commitment. How will this travesty come to an end? One must ponder the rationale of the biblical and talmudic rules and then consider which needs of Jews in a Christian world prompted their relaxation, and finally ask whether in a Jewish state—among brothers and "a holy people and kingdom of priests"—some of the earlier prohibitions should not be restored.

In the matter of organ transplants, only the teleological approach can be productive. The Talmud tells us of that when people are in danger there is a list of priorities as to who is to be saved first. The criterion is the extent to which the person to be saved has the burden of *mitzvot*. The more halakhic obligations a person has, the greater is his worth for purposes of survival. A person with irreversible brain damage can perform no *mitzvot*. Perhaps, then, he should not be denied the choice to help another to perform many by his voluntary gift of parts of his body by means of a consent signed while he is still competent.

The leading halakhic authorities of our day differ among themselves as to how much of Israel's sacred soil may be returned to neighboring states in order to achieve peace and security. Some hold that none can be returned. It is a *mitzvah* to conquer the land—and the cost of war is immaterial. This one commandment transcends the commandment to save life. Others are not so sure. The analytical approach certainly justified the uncompromising position. However, by a teleological approach one must posit the survival of the Jewish people as a halakhic desideratum that is virtually an absolute. It might therefore not be a *mitzvah* to hold on to conquered territories and face the threat of annihilation. The mere fact that very distinguished halakhic authorities in Israel and in the Diaspora so hold is evidence of the fact that they are using the teleological approach even though they do not articulate it as such.

Perhaps the most dramatic use of this approach is to be found in the ruling of at least three of Israel's greatest halakhic authorities—Chief Rabbis Kook and Herzog and Rabbi Avraham Yeshayahu Karelitz, known as the "Hazon Ish"—that there is to be no religious coercion in the new state. There is no doubt that halakhic literature approved of religious coercion. The Jew who refused to perform any of the commandments could be subjected to lashes until he consented to conform. There was a single exception—the Jew who in his infancy had been taken captive by non-Jews and raised without the benefit of Jewish society and Jewish indoctrination. The refusal of such a Jew to accept the yoke of the Torah could be condoned. To preclude religious coercion in the modern state of Israel (although there are still extremists who hold to the more traditional view and deem every non-conformist as one unworthy of survival), it was held that every modern Jew is in the category of a Jew who was taken captive by non-Jews. Certainly this borders on legal fiction. Most Israelis for whose benefit the ruling was originally made were not only raised in a Jewish society but in a religiously committed one. They rejected that background and chose instead one of several other available philosophies of life and action. Why, then, should they be exempted from religious coercion, even were the state in the control of rabbinical authorities?

One must concede that considerations other than strict law prompted the relaxation of the talmudic rule. It is simply not feasible in the modern age to exercise religious coercion. Just as no proliferation of police can safeguard moral sexual behavior in any society, so no religious enforcement is possible. And the same applies to the entire galaxy of Jewish rituals. However, there is a more cogent reason for the change in the talmudic rule. That rule was designed to insure that in a closed Jewish society the deviationist would not place in jeopardy the very factors that made for the sentiment of social solidarity. Occasionally an individual could leave that society at his own risk, but discipline had to be maintained to consolidate its ranks internally. However, in a generally open society and with Jewish society equally open, religious coercion would be counter-productive. Instead of consolidating Jewish ranks it would decimate them. The rabbis were thus wise to recognize that the law's purpose would be served better by regarding every Jew—even those raised within the ghetto walls—as a child who had been taken captive. In the final analysis we are all captives in a world whose endless variety of doctrines fill the atmosphere and reach every one of us, even via the ether.

Conclusion

The very nature of the Halakhah as a legal system makes for a great diversity of opinions as to what rules are binding on Jews committed to it. However, the diversity itself is the result of many diverse approaches to the development of the Halakhah within the framework of its own methodology and the vast sea that are its sources. The sea feeds many rivers and tributaries, but somehow all the waters end up in the same sea—which is the glory of Judaism and the means by which the Jewish people forever remain afloat.

Theocentricity in Jewish Law

The study of ancient legal systems helps us to understand many biblical and talmudic texts. The Jews of antiquity had contact with other peoples and civilizations and inevitably there were reciprocal influences. Sometimes what was foreign they adopted, while at other times there was unmistakable rejection. However, from the point of view of the philosopher and theologian, the more important concern is what were the uniquely Jewish components and how they derived from the unique faith that the Jews embraced. This paper will suggest how the Covenant affected the rules of law. One has reason to doubt that the legal rules and principles could have been the same were it not for the theocentricity of the system.

I.

Professor Jacob I. Talmon wrote in his essay "Uniqueness and Universality of Jewish History" that when political theorists of the West spoke of Oriental despotism they meant that "the Orient did not know the problem of the legitimacy of power. Power to them was a datum, or fact of nature, an elemental amoral force to be taken for granted like sunshine and rain, storm and plague. It need not always be tyrannical and malign, it might be as benign as one could wish. But it is given, it is there, and we have to bow to it."[1]

It was the Jewish people who were obsessed with the notion of the legitimacy of power. And this obsession had its roots in the idea that they had but one sovereign—God alone. Because of this, Professor Talmon argues, mature Christian civilizations differed from other civilizations in that in Christendom there always was tension between Church and State. Elsewhere "there was no example of it in antiquity, and none . . . in Islam or the Eastern Asiatic civilizations. And this ingredient is substantially Jewish." Because Jews constituted a people committed to transcendental laws and aims with God alone as the ultimate source of law and values, all authority that is exercised by one person over another had to be legitimatized by resort to the Book. "It is not enough

---

1. See *The Unique and the Universal* (George Braziller, New York, 1966), pp. 64–90.

that the law is promulgated by the authority which is recognized to have power to legislate. King, Parliament, the sovereign people, even pope and council, must at all times exhibit their credentials in the face of divine or natural law. Natural law, is of course, of hellenistic and Roman provenance. Yet it is fair to say that without its being amalgamated with divine law, it would have failed to become the great formative influence that it did."

Josephus understood well this uniqueness of Judaism, and defined a "theocracy" as a state in which God and God alone is sovereign. It is not a state in which a pope or priests are sovereign. Nor is it a state in which spiritual and temporal authorities hold equal sway—as in the historic Gelasian conception of two swords. But it is a state in which all authority exercised by one human being over another is delegated by God and, therefore, when challenged, one must prove by resort to the Written or Oral Law that God did, in fact, delegate the power sought to be exercised. And it is because God alone is sovereign that Judaism is a "theocracy." As in the case of so many other attributes of God we cannot say positively what His sovereignty is. We know better what it negates. It means that no one else is sovereign. Only the ultimate Creator—He who is responsible for the "being" of everything—is sovereign. All created things have their place in that order which He ordained but none can exercise more power than He permitted. Indeed, it is precisely because Judaism was theocratic in the sense that it recognized only God's sovereignty that Judaism was able to inspire so much democratic thought.

II.

God—the only Sovereign—transmitted a Law, under which all derivative authority is exercised. No one—not kings, not priests, not rabbis, not majorities, not aristocracies—can exercise any authority which is inconsistent with the Law, and even the power to interpret the Law is as diffuse as all other forms of authority. This is the meaning of the sovereignty of God. And this was a revolutionary conception that Judaism brought to the world. It was revolutionary because kings in ancient times were god-kings. Either they themselves were deities or they descended directly from deities. It was, therefore, no accident, as Samson Raphael Hirsh once said, that when the Torah began to tell us about the life of Moses it started with a simple sentence telling us that our greatest prophet was a man, born of a man and a woman, and by implication not from the gods. This was a new note, a new approach. An unseen God was sovereign and no one else.

That no one other than God was sovereign, however, meant more than simply a limitation on man's pretentiousness. It meant that every man was subject to God's Law. No matter what a man's status, he was subject to what God had willed. Never before and never since was the sovereignty of law so placed above the sovereignty of man. Indeed, only in the light of this theocratic principle can one understand the biblical verses pertaining to kingship.

The Bible, in Deuteronomy, speaks of the appointment of a king in Israel.[2] Is such appointment mandatory or is it only permitted? Abarbanel—with justifiable hatred of the monarchy of Spain—held the latter view.[3] He regarded Nimrod as the progenitor of all that was despicable in a human sovereign. Moreover, he held that Samuel was justly critical of the people's desire to have a king. Maimonides, however, regarded the appointment of a king as mandatory.[4] Why did Samuel then deem the request for a king a flouting of God's will?

A careful reading of the text in Samuel[5] reveals that he was objecting to the fact that his people wanted a king who was the Lawgiver—as kings served in non-Jewish societies. They said "Give us a king to judge us as among all peoples." They completely misunderstood the unique role of a king in Judaism, for in Deuteronomy the verses dealing with a king are separate and distinct from the verses dealing with the judicial and legislative powers with regard to which the king enjoys no special prerogatives. The king, moreover, was to cause a copy of the Law to be written for his constant guidance—to such an extent was his office only a creature of the Law! However, in their gradual reversion to idolatry the Hebrews clamored for a king in pagan terms. That is why Samuel warned them about the consequences. They would have a king above the Law. Samuel deemed this a rejection of the prophet. God told him that it was not a rejection of the prophet but rather a rejection of God—the only Lawgiver. Nonetheless, they could have

2. Deut. 17:15.

3. For a brief summary of his view see R. Lerner, "Moses Maimonides," in *History of Political Philosophy*, ed. Strauss and Crofsey (Rand McNally: Chicago), 1963, p. 194.

4. Mishneh Torah, Hilkhot Melakhim, 1:1.

5. I Sam. 8:5–22.

what they wanted. Prophets, however, would do the anointing—prophets would make the selection, and the people's voice was expressed through the elders of the Sanhedrin.

It is important to bear in mind that the denial to the monarch of the role of lawgiver and the retention of that role for God alone, which is the essence of theocracy, had economic as well as political significance. The appointment of the king was not to take place until after the promised land had been conquered and divided among the Jews. No king could ever maintain—as was the case in all feudal societies—that land was acquired from the monarch. Land was acquired, according to the Torah, from God, and the entire system of land tenure, its alienation and its redemption, was ordained by God whose ultimate ownership Jews could never forget. And to corroborate this point, one might cite a coincidence Martin Buber noticed that only in two instances in Torah are the conquest and division of the land prerequisites for the performance of the *Mitzvot* described. These two instances are the appointment of a king and the law of *bikurim*—the law off the first fruits.[6] Each year, with the first fruit of his land, the Jew was to go to the city where the king ruled and then and there, thank God for the land which God—not the king—had given him. If any Jewish king should ever indulge himself the illusion that the land was his, and that it is he who dispensed it to his subjects, then the Torah ordained that once each year, in his own capital, the Jews would give their first fruits to the priest and recite a paragraph of Scripture which described exactly how and when God had made the gift of the land to them. Indeed, the language of that text seems to emphasize the fact that every Jew received his land directly from God—and not even via forbears. This also precluded the establishment of a feudal system—the land was not received from a king. Thus did Jewish theocracy deal a death blow to feudalism.

The institution of the Sabbatical year was to make both kings and subjects recognize "man's temporal tenancy of God's creation." One might also cite the ceremony of "Hakhel"[7] as another magnificent illustration of the Torah's intent that kings and subjects shall ever be aware of the ultimate sovereignty of the law. At the conclusion of the Sabbatical year—again in the king's capital—the text of the original covenant was read to all men, women and children. In the face of the verses of Deuteronomy what king could

6. Deut. 26:1.

7. Ibid., 31:12.

ever hold himself out as lawgiver?

III.

To all of this a functional or—realist—jurist would offer the rejoinder, "But even if the law is sovereign, it is man who must promulgate it, interpret it, or legislate with regard to it, and aren't these men in the final analysis, the lawgivers?" This challenge must be met, for otherwise the phrase "sovereignty of law" becomes only a pious mouthing of a meaningless concept. Judaism is almost congenitally practical, rather than theoretical. Philosophical principles are far less important than behavior patterns. Is the sovereignty of law, then, only a mirage since God's law, once given, is forever the responsibility of men who thereafter must decree what is lawful and unlawful?

Judaism meets this challenge in two ways. Both ways were far more highly developed in Judaism than in any other human society. First, the law-making power was so diffused among priests and elders, prophets and people, sages and scholars, rabbis and saints, that it was virtually impossible to pinpoint who had the ultimate authority in Jewish jurisprudence. Yet all the debates of these participants in the unfolding of God's will had to revolve around what it was that God had ordained. The many who shared the authority had to exercise it with erudition, but also with a prayer that they had discovered God's will and that those who were expected to obey would recognize it as such. Consequently, the second way emerged—all Jews themselves had to be expert in God's law. How else might they participate in the authority if they were not themselves students of Torah? Beginning with Moses, the command was given to teach the law. Nay, Abraham was chosen because God recognized that he would teach the law to his posterity. Thus authority was diffused among a numerous and learned people. Judaism became an exoteric religion instead of an esoteric one.

Indeed it was because man is created in the divine image, and Jews in particular had entered into a covenant with their Creator, that the law-making process even in a theocracy involves man, and many of them. Many different groups enjoyed what one might call jurisdiction in different areas. The priests, over whose election the people had minimum control, had a minimum voice in the legislative and judicial process. Even the prophet's role was minimal. The rabbis—the doctors of the law—had, by far, the more powerful voice, but their authority emanated from colleagues with the approval of the people who enjoyed some kind of unwritten veto over their ultimate selection. The community or the populace was thus very powerful. But that did not make Judaism a "democracy." The theocracy was democratic insofar as the people played so dominant a role in the preservation of the law. But the voice of the people was not the voice of God. What the people were expected to do was themselves to act as God had willed that they act. (Would that majorities and mobs would act today with this awareness of their responsibility to God in every political, social, and economic situation!)

IV.

However, it was not only by diffusing the lawmaking authority among many that Judaism safeguarded God's ultimate sovereignty as lawgiver. What was more important was the extent to which legal education made every Jew aware of his duties in that theocracy. Judge Moshe Silberg of the Supreme Court of Israel has pointed out that in Jewish law the emphasis was always on an individual's duties rather than on the rights of other persons against him.[8] This duty-orientation of Jewish law made Jews seek out how they should behave before committing sin rather than how they should right or mitigate wrongs already committed. This concern for righteousness makes of the sovereignty of law a truly potent force in the life of the community. Even a functional jurist must reckon with it. For especially among Jews, ideas had great force. A people that could martyr itself for a God no one ever saw is a people to whom the sovereignty of law could be a very real thing.

That universal legal education might make for the sovereignty of law rather than the sovereignty of men is an insight captured by Plato in his "Laws." In modern times, a Russian jurist, Petrashitsky, articulated it.[9] Indeed, it was not only fathomed by the Bible but articulated by it in a score of different texts beginning with the first commandments regarding the Passover and ending with Moses' final peroration to his people prior to his death.

Yet, even the fact that in Jewish law the focus of attention is on duties rather than rights is a consequence of its theocentricity. It is true that whenever there is a duty, someone has a right to expect

8. See his *Talmudic Law and the Modern State* (trans. Bokser) (Burning Bush Press: New York), 1973, pp. 66–70.

9. See E. N. Cahn, *The Sense of Injustice* (New York University Press: New York), 1949, p. 105.

the performance of that duty. One without the other is inconceivable. Right and duty are correlatives. But what counts is where one places the accent. In modern society the accent is on rights—rights against government, rights against teachers and parents, even the right to die. In classical Hebrew one rarely finds the word for "right"—*zechut*—but one encounters the word for duty—*mitzvah*—almost everywhere. What preoccupied the rabbis were duties of the body and of the heart, to man and God, to others and to the self—even duties to live and make live.

What must have prompted this concern for the duty rather than for right is the fact that the lawgiver was God and it was unthinkable that against Him a subject would have rights. To Him there are only duties, and even though He enters into covenants and obligates Himself to the performance of obligations, man is rarely presumptuous enough to make demands upon Him.

V.

Theocentricity not only accounts for the diffusion of authority but it also precipitates a separation between spiritual power and temporal power and this ultimately creates the permanent tension between Church and State—between the champions of what ought to be and the executors of what is. The former retain only moral force; the latter have virtually limitless power.

And this separation is of ancient origin. Moses himself, pursuant to God's command, divided even the succession to himself. Priestly power was given to his brother Aaron and the executive power was given to Joshua—of another tribe. Even Augustine recognized that the Bible did not approve of the merging of the spiritual and temporal authorities but diffused power.

The Rabbis before him were also aware of it when they frowned upon the Maccabees who arrogated unto themselves kingship and priesthood. Thus it appears that theocentric character of Jewish law made not only for the sovereignty of law but also for the separation of Church and State.

Milford Q. Sibley, in his *Political Ideas and Ideologies*, writes: "throughout most of their political experience and speculation, Hebrew thinkers repudiate the notion that the priestly and royal functions should be exercised by one man. No doubt this separation of functions is in part to be attributed to the very ambivalence with which Hebrews tended to look at kingship. It is also possibly rooted in a feeling that the priesthood must be independent of direct royal control if it is to be a critic of kingly government."[10]

Professor Sibley also cites the view that the early Jewish experience and theory of the independence of the religious community is the foundation for the very conception of "church" which played so important a role in western civilization and made possible its continuing juxtaposition to state in the democratization of the West. Who among the prophets and the priests, the saints and the sages, were the dominant factor in attaining the result is not our concern. What matters is that the theocentricity of Jewish law—the insistence that God is the one and only Sovereign—is responsible for the basic tenets that the legitimacy of the exercise of authority must always be questioned; that to prevent the unlawful seizure of power, sovereignty must be diffused; and that to insure the possibility of challenging authority the temporal and spiritual powers must be kept separate from each other.

VI.

Judicial review was the inevitable consequence of commitment to these tenets. The Bible itself did not instruct the courts to block the unlawful exercise of power by those to whom some of it was delegated. But they did have the power to protect slaves against masters, debtors against creditors, the weak against the strong; and they similarly undertook to prevent the abuse of power by kings. Precisely this happened in the United States. The federal Constitution failed to specify what might be done if the executive or legislative branches of the government did that which was unconstitutional. And Justice Marshall in the historic case of Marbury v. Madison made up for the deficiency.

One may call it a "usurper" by the Supreme Court but for many it does appear to come within the purview of the judicial function. The Sanhedrin did the same thousands of years earlier and as reported in the Talmud, and as subsequently codified by Maimonides, a person to whom a king gave a mandate which was in violation of the Torah might disobey the monarch with impunity.[11] He could defend himself against the charge of treason by charging that the king's command exceeded his authority.

More recently the problem appears in Jewish legal literature in reverse. If a king gives an unconstitutional command, and the subject obeys and commits the wrong, is he liable or can he defend

---

10. Harper & Row: New York, 1970, p. 20.

11. Mishneh Torah, ibid., 3:4.

himself by claiming that he did what he did in response to higher authority?[12]

The theocentricity of Jewish law was responsible for the principle that in the commission of a crime, only the person committing the crime pays the penalty and not the person who plotted it or even paid the criminal to execute it. The principal in such a case is not the criminal because the agent was not forced to heed him. He could have exercised his own free will and he should have obeyed the ultimate Principal—God Himself! Is the same rule applicable when the principal is the king or a commanding officer in war? Are commands from such powerful people coercive by their very nature? Whatever the answer, one realizes that the factor of theocentricity is still at work. Presently the problem is one of international law as evidenced by the Nurnberg trials.

The Talmud also records, in several different versions, how kings defied the Sanhedrin and refused to be accountable to the judiciary.[13] Pagan conceptions of kingship had been at work and that led to the conclusion that when such conceptions prevail—as happened in the case of the kings of Israel in antiquity as distinguished from the kings of Judah—then kings are ineligible to judge or be judged.[14] They are removed beyond the system of justice that has God's approval. Sad it is that offending monarchs should not be subject to law, but when this happens, they too shall be disqualified to be judges lest they corrupt the system altogether.

VII.

While theocentricity was, on the one hand, a liberalizing force insofar as it relieved man of subjection to excessive human authority, it also was a restricting force—it subjected man to more duties vis-a-vis his fellowman. The very fact that God created man in His image gave rise to many legal and ethical norms which are basic in Judaism.

Thus the Rabbis debated which was the more fundamental precept in Judaism—the requirement that man love his neighbor as himself

---

12. See A. Kirschenbaum, "A Cog In The Wheel," *Israel Yearbook on Human Rights* (Tel Aviv University: 1974), Vol. 4, 168–193; and A. Enker, שנתון המשפט העברי, רצח מתוך הכרח וצורך במשפט עברי (Hebrew University: 1975), Vol. 2, 154–174.

13. San. 19a.

14. Ibid.

or the dogma that God created man in His likeness.[15] The latter was deemed far more consequential. For, argued the Rabbis, there are persons who do not hesitate to demean themselves and if they subscribe only to the commandment that the love of oneself is the measure of one's love for one's neighbor, the neighbor may not fare so well. But if one must always bear in mind that one's fellow man is divine, then no matter how badly one treats one's own person, one may not do so to another—that other is to be respected as God is.

That man was endowed with the divine image meant also that every murder was deicide. Even suicide was deicide. The human body was God's and its spirit as well. To destroy either was an attack on Him. The famous talmudic rule that no human being may incriminate himself before a court of law—a rule much more extensive than that contained in American constitutions[16]—was understood by Maimonides to be a derivative of the law against self-destruction.[17] Alas, there are people who in their distress seek their own end and confessing to a crime may be a way of achieving the goal. Jewish law, therefore, would not tolerate it to happen.

Similarly, the manipulation or exploitation of another human being was immoral—it was like exploiting God. From this point of view, Martin Buber's important caveats regarding the exploitation of one's fellow-man have not only aggadic but also halakhic roots. Rabbinic attitudes toward human slavery are discussed in many places but one discussion is worthy of special mention here—the status of the person who is half-slave and half-free.

If one of two owners of a slave emancipates him, then thereafter the slave is bound to serve the other owner only half time. For that reason the school of Hillel said that he should work for the master Sundays, Tuesdays and Thursdays, and for himself on the remaining days. However, the school of Shammai objected. "You have provided for the master but you have not provided for the slave. A free woman he cannot marry because he is half slave and a slave woman he cannot marry because he is half free." The final solution which was unanimously accepted was that the court orders the master to emancipate him and as a free man he works and

---

15. Bereshit Rabba, 24:7.

16. See also below, p. 93f.

17. Mishneh Torah, Hilkhot Sanhedrin 18:6.

indemnifies the master for his financial loss.[18]

Jewish law would not tolerate a condition in which the slave could not fulfill himself as a human being and relate to a woman and establish a family with her. The rights of the owner had to yield to this humane consideration. Recognition must be given to the needs and drives with which God endowed man.

Similarly, the Torah explicitly prohibited a farmer to muzzle an ox at the time of the threshing of the wheat.[19] The Rabbis so interpreted another verse of the Torah that the same principle was applicable to a man working in the field.[20] As he harvested his employer's crop he could eat to his heart's content from all that he reaped. It would be the sheerest cruelty to muzzle the employee and make him feel doubly punished that he is not the field's owner and though he does the work he cannot partake of the fruit !

VIII.

The dogma that man is created by God in His image also proscribed man's rights vis-a-vis himself. If the body and its spirit are God's creation, then man is certainly not the sole arbiter as to what is to be done with them. That suicide was deicide has already been noted. But there were also restrictions on the abuse of one's person. Self-mutilation was prohibited.[21] Even in mourning one was to avoid excesses in the expression of one's grief.

The presently prevailing view that a woman's body is hers to do with as she pleases, and that, therefore, she alone may decide whether she wants an abortion, is not an authentic Jewish view. The notion that a foetus is like a limb of its mother's body was known and accepted in Jewish law, but not to justify its destruction. In Jewish law no person may inflict injury upon oneself. In the final analysis even our bodies belong to God, Who permits us to enjoy them only in accordance with His will, and He does not will our misuse of them. The practice of abortion was prohibited for both Jews and non-Jews. It is part of the Noahide laws.[22]

A notable exception to the general rule that self-mutilation is prohibited is the Covenantal rite of circumcision. Perhaps it was

---

18. Gittin 4–4.

19. Deut. 25:4.

20. BM 87a, ff.

21. BK 91b.

22. San. 57b.

appropriate that such a rite be chosen as the one evidencing religious commitment, because no other assault upon the body was countenanced and the one act permitted would always suggest its special meaning. Of course, if one's health or survival required surgery it was to be performed. God had given an overriding commandment that one was to live by the Law and not perish because of it. This would also apply to an abortion for reasons of health.

To such an extent was the body regarded as God's and its mutilation prohibited but for exceptional circumstances that even after one's death the Rabbis prohibited mutilation of the body by others. They ruled that no one may derive a benefit from the use or misuse of a cadaver.[23] This rule gave rise to the problem of post-mortem examinations in hospitals in Israel and elsewhere. Again in the interest of the health of humans the prohibition yields, but the principle is firmly established—the body of man and his spirit belong to God and only in accordance with His will are they to be treated. They are a bailment from Him and the bailees must ultimately render an account to the Bailor. This is not only a premise in the Aggadah; it is also basic in the Halakhah.

IX.

The impact of theocentricity on Jewish law is most easily discerned in the rules pertaining to charity. Like other legal systems Jewish law wrestled with the problem of promises—when they would be enforceable. Since courts do not compel promisors to keep their word under all circumstances, it was necessary to fashion criteria, and Anglo-American law developed the doctrine of consideration while continental systems searched for causa. The one type of promise that Anglo-American courts found especially difficult to enforce were promises to charity. In such cases the promisee gives nothing in return and in many situations the beneficiary never had a prior relationship to the benefactor. Thus the magic ingredient of either consideration or causa is not present. Yet in Jewish law promises to the poor or to the Temple were the easiest to enforce. Why?

All such promises were deemed executed and not executory. They required no fulfillment because they were fulfilled as soon as they were uttered. Since God was the trustee of the poor, the promise was in effect to Him, and since His is the earth and all

---

23. Arachin 7a and b.

that is therein, He was in possession of the promisor's assets as soon as the promise was expressed. Indeed, if only it could be proved, the mere thought of a gift to the poor would be enforceable because God also knows the thoughts of man.

The legal maxim which gave expression to this unusual rule was אמירתו לגבוה כמסירתו להדיוט the mere utterance of a gift to God is the equivalent of a delivery to an ordinary mortal.[24]

Less explicit but equally unique was the impact of theocentricity on the right to privacy and the protection of one's home against search and seizure. The right to privacy probably had its conception in the Jewish emphasis on privacy in sexual intercourse. The story of Adam and Eve in the Garden of Eden accounts for the sense of shame with regard to genital organs and a cherished Midrash makes it appear that the non-Jewish prophet Bilaam was impressed by the fact that already in his day Jews pitched their tents so that their entrances did not face each other. Families even in the wilderness of Sinai cherished privacy. Furthermore, the insistence in Jewish law that when men and women count days of uncleanness before qualifying for sundry privileges in temple service, it is they that do the counting on their honor—without the verification of disinterested witnesses—gave support to the notion that the condition of one's body is one's own inviolable area of concern.[25]

It comes as no surprise, therefore, that thousands of years before other legal systems became preoccupied with the right to privacy, Jewish law—in the Talmud and Codes—devoted hundreds of folios to the theme.[26] The right, which first applied to one's person and one's residence, was subsequently expanded to include one's court (where one stored assets) and one's garden—even to one's mail and trade secrets. The Bible also precluded creditors from entering the home of the debtor to seize property in payment of the debt, and the Rabbis extended the rule to preclude even the sheriff from doing it.[27]

From a philosophical point of view, the creation of man in God's image also makes for the right to privacy. In Neo-Platonic discourse God is the most lonely of all that is, and religion is the flight of one

---

24. Kiddushin 28b.

25. Ketubot 72a.

26. Baba Batra, beginning with 2a. See *Talmudic Encyclopedia*, Vol. VlII, pp 659–702.

27. Baba Mezia 113a.

who is lonely to the One Who is most alone. It would be unthinkable to invade the privacy of that flight. Indeed, Jewish mystics—unlike other mystics—rarely, if ever, described their mystical experiences. And they were thus secretive about them not only because such experiences are generally ineffable but also because they are so personal and private. Jewish ideas about God affected the development of Jewish legal ideals and rules. The secularization of Jewish law, however, may affect them adversely. The danger ought not be ignored.

Man's Partnership with God in Revelation

Fundamental in Judaism are God's attributes as Creator and Legislator. biblical passages are explicit on this point. Less explicit is the notion that man is God's partner in the exercise of both functions. However, Judaism does assign that role to man. As he joins God in Creation he has many questions involving the how and the why. But he is encouraged to explore the universe, conquer its resources, and search for purpose and meanings. In his role as God's partner in the development of God's law, he is encouraged to study it, to master its mandates and their corollaries, revealed and hidden, and to be preoccupied with their viability at all times, despite their presumed immutability because God had promulgated them. Man's imitation of God is thus fulfilled in two spheres—that of nature and that of human society.

If man had not been honored to share with God a creative function in nature, how would he dare to arrogate unto himself the privilege of frustrating God's will when God strikes with illness or other misfortunes? How would he focus on the emancipation of the enslaved and the enrichment of the impoverished? If he was meant to be inert with regard to all such evil simply because God had caused the sufferer to suffer and consequently no one should interfere, then the Bible would not have mandated the healing of the sick and support of the poor. True, not all religions adopted the authentic Jewish point of view. Indeed, neither did all Jews. However, the overwhelming majority did and they relied on verses, explicit and implicit, to justify their involvement in that which God had ordained—hopefully for the better, but, alas, ofttimes for the worse.

God had ordered man to "conquer" the earth (Gen. 1:28). Moreover, a verse in the second chapter describes all that God created as having been created "to continue functioning" (Ibid., 11:3). This implied that nature would be dynamic and man was authorized to respond to that dynamism. One verse specifically approves of attention to the ailing with an eye to curing them (Exod. 21:19) while another prohibits the wanton waste of natural resources which God had given (Deut. 20:19).

31

Less clear, however, is the authority to tamper with the Law. In this connection one asks first: Why did God reveal a Law which is less than perfect and inadequate for eternity without man's participation in its development? The Psalmist did sing that God's law was perfect. However, it was inevitable that as the conditions of man in nature and in society change—in great measure precisely because of man's partnership with God in contributing to the world's dynamism—the Law too would require innovation within the halakhic parameters. That man was endowed with free will and a penchant for evil played an important role in necessitating that creativity. And that creativity was the function of the "doctors of the Law," obedience to whom was mandated by the Law itself.

Consequently, one finds that as God made man His partner in a continuously changing universe, so He made man His partner in the continuous flowering of the Law which represents His abiding will. He presumably endowed that Law with the potential to cope with all that may come to pass but with unrelenting commitment to its values system and parameters.

Yet one question remains. In the absence of a specific grant of authority to modify the Law or innovate within limits, how did the rabbis justify their arrogance in making themselves God's partners in the sphere of law as in the sphere of nature? What were the verses on which they relied and what were the exegeses employed to make the Law cope with more than three thousand years of political, social, and economic change? It is to these questions that this paper purports to make reply. In connection with man's partnership with God in the flowering of the Law, the masters and custodians of the Oral Law were able to legitimatize what they were doing on the basis of at least two texts in the Pentateuch. These two texts were crucial for man's role in making the revealed Law viable forever.

The simplest one is the statement in Leviticus (17: 5) that the laws were given that the Jewish people shall "live by them." This statement ruled out any possibility of interpreting the Law as requiring martyrdom. Jews were to live by it and not die because of it. (Yoma 85b). It was for this reason, for example, that it was deemed permissible to wage a defensive war on the Sabbath.

The second text in Deuteronomy (17:8-12) assumes that there will be need to resolve questions that will arise in the future and authority was vested in the judges of every age to engage in their resolution. The Jews were ordered to respect and obey the authority of these judges. Despite the fact that their competence may vary from generation to generation, Jews owed obedience to the judges of their day.

A third text is found in the Psalms. The Psalms are not as authoritative a source of the Law as is the Pentateuch. But in Psalm 119: 126 the order is: "When the time comes to act for the Lord, violate the Law given you." In circumstances when a higher purpose for God's sake warrants ignoring the Law, do so. In at least two situations the Oral Law, because of this verse, based its permission to violate strict rules. First was the permission granted to commit the Oral Law to writing. And second was permission to Jews to use God's name as they greeted each other, which is in fact mentioning His name in vain.

Still other verses in the Bible supported resort to creativity and will be referred to hereafter in connection with specific areas of the law.

I.

One area in which there had to be greater accommodation to the realistic requirements of the social order in many periods of Jewish history was the arch of public law—the criminal law and the law of war. Both the Written and Oral Law contained many directives for each of these subjects. Indeed, much of the humanization of the laws of crimes and war is due to the influence of the Jewish tradition. Recently even the Supreme Court of the United States cited talmudic sources to support opposition to capital punishment. However, it appears that especially ancient and medieval society required a stronger hand for the authorities charged with the maintenance of public order and safety. For example, the biblical rules of evidence too often made possible the avoidance of prosecution and punishment. Consequently there was resort to what was virtually a parallel system of law.

Professor Arnold N. Enker developed this thesis in a brilliant essay[1] in whose summary he writes:

> Jewish criminal law for Jews functions on two tracks. One, which for want of a better term might be called the purely religious track, concerns man's relation with God. The religious courts have exclusive jurisdiction in this area. Special procedures and unusual rules of

1. A.N. Enker, "Aspects of Interaction between the Torah Law, the King's Law, and the Noahide Law in Jewish Criminal Law," *Cardozo Law Review*, 12 (1990), 1111–1130.

evidence and of substantive law apply in these cases and serve to limit punishment of offenders to the most serious and brazen acts of open defiance of God's will. The second track involves the day-to-day concerns of law enforcement and the protection of the social order. On this track, which is administered apparently primarily by the king's courts, although the religious courts also have such jurisdiction, the courts are mostly free to apply whatever rules of practice and evidence they see fit, to evaluate the evidence free of restraint by formal rules and to punish the defendant as seems to them appropriate to accomplish the protection and preservation of the social order.

There is biblical foundation for approaching the violation of God's law in these two ways. The earliest biblical chapters contain two stories describing man's sins. In the Garden of Eden story, Adam violates God's law by eating the fruit of the tree of life. In the second story, Cain murders his brother Abel. The law forbidding eating the fruit has no apparent social significance. Its behavioral content is not part of those norms of conduct essential to the social welfare. Note that God duly warned Adam that he may not eat the fruit of the tree and that the punishment for this offense will be death, but the Bible contains no record of God having warned Cain that he is forbidden to murder his brother. The essence of Adam's Sin is disobedience to God's command, rebellion against His will. In contrast, Cain's sin is murder, which is most destructive of civilized society.

There are several common themes running through both stories. Most strikingly, the punishment is the same in both—banishment and the cursing of the earth which will no longer give forth its fruit as readily as before. These two stories are essentially one, their object being to explore two aspects of sin. On the one level, the essence of sin is disobedience, rebellion against God's will. But·in its second aspect, sin is the violation of that order which is beneficial to society, the infliction of harm on others. In some cases one aspect is dominant, in others, the second aspect is more apparent, but both are present to some degree, and this division of criminal law into two tracks, one administered by the religious courts and concerned primarily with the aspect of rebellion against God, the other administered by the king, i.e. the civil authority, and concerned with protection of the Jewish law's primary sources.

This parallel system of law called "The King's Law" was based on a verse in the Book of Joshua (1:18). The verse states that the people invested Joshua with the power to give orders and to impose the death penalty on anyone who defied him. This blanket grant of power later became the basis for many a medieval monarch to claim that his right to rule derived from the people. In the same period Jewish communities in Europe hesitated to arrogate unto themselves the same power. They preferred another biblical source upon which to predicate their power to exercise control over the economy and in this way managed to maintain law and order. From a verse in the Book of Ezra (10:8) the Talmud derived the power of a rabbinical court to expropriate a person and by virtue of the property being ownerless it could then award it to whomsoever it deemed worthy of it. The power was to be exercised judiciously, but it was a very effective way both to legislate in matters involving property and also to exact from constituents obedience to new and old regulations.

The people had granted Ezra the power to issue an order disobedience to which would result in the forfeiture of all of the offender's property. This grant of power became the justification for the rule that a duly constituted rabbinical court can declare anyone's property ownerless and also transfer it to another. It was because of this power, one view in the Talmud holds, that Hillel was able to avoid the cancellation of all debts at the end of the sabbatical year. He provided a way for creditors to collect from debtors—in violation of biblical law—which in effect was an expropriation of debtors in favor of creditors. Circumstances warranted his innovation. It was not a capricious ruling. On the other hand, it was for the benefit of debtors—to make credit available in the years preceding the sabbatical year. But, nonetheless, it was revolutionary legislation. In the middle ages this power enabled the Jewish communities—and their councils and judiciary—to govern, to impose taxes and collect them, as well as to punish offenders against all the laws of the community. The combination of the two powers—that of the "King's Law" and that of declaring property encores—made it possible for communities to legislate in many areas pertaining to the economy, such as rent control, prohibiting resort by litigants to non-Jewish courts, punishment of informers, etc. In a general way, biblical law pertaining to virtually every area of commerce and industry could be updated to cope with general or local needs.

Another phrase in the Bible also made possible the amelioration of strict law to achieve equity, a higher standard of justice. For example, even in talmudic times, a debtor who mortgaged his property as security, and lost it to his creditor, could redeem it any time after the foreclosure. (BM 35b). There was no time limit on this right. Equity required it. And the biblical verse was clear. "One must do the righteous and the good." (Deut. 6:18).

Because of this verse, judges in Judaism were never as bound by precedent as they are in the Anglo-American system. They are to achieve justice as required in each case before them.

Nachmanides' commentary on this verse was also the source for one of the most insightful essays by Rabbi Professor Walter Wurzburger on what he called "Covenantal Imperatives."[2] While many have debated whether Jewish ethics are exclusively heteronymous Wurzburger clearly shows that Judaism permits a substantial measure of autonomy in resolving ethical issues. The precedents of the Halakhah are not always the ultimate source for the resolution of ethical questions. In many a case the Halakhah provides the guidelines or parameters within which decisions are made because of the Sinaitic covenant and the overriding mandate "to do the righteous and the good." Moreover, he correctly argues that no Jew should claim the right to be the sole decisor for another. Many may try to claim this right but the claim is usurper and not justified by the sources.

> Thus, true to its name, the Halakhah does not serve as the final goal of the Jew, but rather as the way, guiding him in his individuality towards authentic personal decisions in the domain of covenantal imperatives. After all, Jerusalem, so the Sages have told us, was destroyed because our forebears merely abided by the letter of the law. In the final analysis we can properly fulfill our covenantal obligations only when, reaching out beyond the minimum requirements of the law, we respond as free individuals to the summons to an all encompassing service which is issued to us as individuals in our existential subjectivity, uniqueness and particularity by a God who is One and Unique. (Ibid: p.12)

II.

It is in family law that we find the most extensive innovation or creativity despite the absence in the Written Law of any authority vested in the rabbis to do what they did. They simply posited an unrebuttable presumption that every man who betroths a woman intends that his act shall be subject to the approval of the rabbis. Though they do not mention that the bride's intention is similar, we must assume that she also approves of the same condition

---

2. *Samuel K. Mirsky Memorial Volume*, G. Appel, Ed., Sura Inst. and Yeshiva University, 1970, pp. 3–12.

because the betrothal would not be valid without her unequivocable agreement (Kiddushin 7a). Thus we have an implied condition in every halakhic marriage that its validity and continuance is based on rabbinic consent. Rabbis have differed as to how extensive the rabbis' power is, but there is adequate authority in support of the proposition that it is unlimited. The Jerusalem Talmud goes so far as to approve of the annulment of marriages, ex post facto, if they were consummated in a manner of which the rabbis disapproved. It does not rely on the presumption cited in the Babylonian Talmud.

There is a view that this power is given the rabbis because the groom in the marriage ceremony usually "consecrates" the bride, with her consent, "according to the law of Moses and Israel." But this is pure rationalization. The rabbinic power is exercised even if the bride and groom never mention those words.

It has also been suggested in the Talmud that this power of the rabbis is a corollary of the power the rabbis have to declare property ownerless, to divest one person of property and vest it in another. (Ket. 3a). With this power they can annul marriages by declaring that the gift given the bride by the groom was not his, which is enough to make the marriage a nullity. But as the Talmud asks, what do they do with a marriage consummated by sexual intercourse? The answer is that they can declare the coitus to have been between two unattached persons. In modern times distinguished halakhic authorities have held that a couple that does not arrange for a halakhic marriage under Orthodox auspices are not married ab initio. This might not apply to couples who live in countries where halakhic marriages are unavailable and, therefore, their failure to seek a halakhic marriage does not necessarily imply the rejection or the negation of intention to enter into one.

Despite the fact that the power is well established in both the Jerusalem and Babylonian Talmuds the source of the power is not indicated. The power may have been well established in the Oral Law from time immemorial but one finds no reference to it in the literature of the Tanaim. It is cited often in the literature of the Amoraim and later authorities.

A search of the literature on the subject does not yield very much with regard to the source or the basis for the exercise of the power. The Bible, however, does recognize the validity of conditional agreements (Numbers 32:20-24). And at least two medieval commentators suggested that the Talmud holds that if a man betroths a woman on the condition that her father approves and then the man cohabits with her, the marriage will be a nullity if the father does not consent. On the basis of this analogy the rabbis were given the status of the bride's father. If they withhold consent there is no marriage. The authority to legislate derived from the substitution of the rabbis for the father.

The Jerusalem Talmud appears to have assumed that the rabbis have the power to suspend and even to ignore a biblical command when circumstances require it. Interesting it is that this was done even in matters that are unequivocally of a religious nature, such as the laws pertaining to heave offerings to the priests. And instead of making the presumption that all who wed according to the Halakhah condition their deeds on the consent of the rabbinical authorities, the Jerusalem Talmud simply assumes that the rabbis have the authority to legislate even in variance with biblical rules. The instances in both Talmuds are legion. However, they have not yet been given adequate analysis so that one can form any conclusions as to when this can be done and when not.[3]
Perhaps the main source is the overriding mandate that the Law was given that Jews might live by it and not die because of it.

Some of the situations in family law in which biblical law was ignored are the following: a. The wife of a Kohen who claimed that she was raped and must be divorced by her husband, has credibility by biblical law, but is denied it by rabbinic law and continues to be the Kohen's wife in all respects—a flagrant suspension of biblical law which would terminate the relationship. b. Despite the firm requirement that in all matters of family law two competent witnesses are required, a woman whose husband is missing, can rewed upon the testimony of one witness and even on the basis of generally inadmissible hearsay evidence.

However, it was in the extensive use of conditions available to brides and grooms that the law was liberalized so that unhappy developments in the marital relationship were anticipated and provision made in advance to ease their impact.

Thus, for example, provision was made for the marriage to be automatically terminated if the husband died childless and the widow would have to obtain a release (Halitza) from a surviving brother of the husband who was a minor and could not grant the release—a situation causing untold grief in modem Israel especially in a period of war. When the rabbis put an end to conditional

---

3. See "A rabbinical court may decree the abrogation of a precept of the Torah," *Bar-Ilan Annual*, 7-8 (5732/1970), 117–132.

marriages this process of liberalization came to an end, not because of any lack of power but rather because the stability and permanence of marriages were adversely affected.

The ingenuity of the rabbis in solving problems that arose in Jewish family law because of established rules presumably originating in biblical sources is best reflected in an encapsulation of the entire corpus of Jewish family law in the well known formulation of Sir Henry Maine: "From status to contract." It is submitted that in Jewish family law we have a movement from status to contract, then from contract back to status, and most recently again from status to contract.

III.

One area insufficiently explored is that of human rights and how they were derived from biblical sources. One such right is the right to privacy. The area in which one would want maximum protection of the right to privacy is the area of religious thought and religious performance. Yet here one encounters a paradox. On the one hand, Judaism is a faith that prescribes in a most comprehensive fashion what one shall think and what one shall do. Yet, despite that, even in ancient Judaism no attempt was ever made to invade the privacy of Jews by ferreting out information as to what they believed or how they behaved. The Jew was generally on his honor. And God was the sole judge. If the Jew misbehaved in public then he might be punished for his offense against the prevailing norm. However, the Jewish state was never a police state. The faith may pertain to every aspect of life and action. It may also be in a measure authoritarian because it has many dogmas and doctrines, and the active propagation of heresy is proscribed. But there never was surveillance by the state as to what one did in private or what opinions one held.

The very important biblical source for this liberal approach, which is too often overlooked, is found in Leviticus. (15:13,28) Males and females become *temaaim* (ritually unclean) because of certain emissions from their genitals. To be relieved of such a state they must undergo immersion in water, but first they must count clean days. A man must count and a woman must count; there are separate commands for him and for her. And after each command to count there appears an added word meaning "for himself" and "for herself." No one else counts for them. There is no supervision to make sure that they do not cheat and thus accelerate the process of becoming *tahor* (ritually clean). They are on their honor. Thus

the Talmud interprets the verses. And in this way it expanded the
right to privacy some 2,000 years ago.

Unfortunately, there have been Jewish communities which did
not fathom this beautiful feature of the Jewish heritage, and in the
facilities which they established for the prescribed ritual immersion
they kept records that might reveal whether anyone cheated. This
is not consonant with the authentic tradition. One ought rather
associate the tradition with the decision of one of New York City's
Commissioners of Welfare to respect the mere statement of anyone
seeking help that he needed it. There was to be no investigation.
An investigation was only made when facts subsequently appeared
that created doubts as to the integrity of the claimant. Otherwise
the poor were on their honor, as are the rich with regard to their
income tax returns. I do not now pass judgment on New York's
policy but I do marvel that so long ago Jewish Law was very
sensitive with respect to the privacy of males and females in matters
of religious observance. Still the theme merits a more extensive
analysis.

Can it be perhaps that pragmatic considerations alone account
for the failure to monitor the private beliefs and behavior of
individuals? One might make a very good case for such a contention.
After all, how much could the Jewish state spend on spies or
informers? And without evidence how could the state prosecute?
The confessions of the accused were never admissible in criminal
proceedings conducted according to Jewish Law. Courts required
witnesses but there would be no witnesses unless the state provided
a cadre of spies. Therefore it might be thought that the state
reconciled itself to inaction because inaction was the only sensible,
realistic policy to adopt.

Yet this is not altogether correct. Jewish courts could have
encouraged informers by rewarding them as did the medieval
Church in Europe. What is more, it could have used decoys to
trap those who did not believe or behave as required. One must
note that Jewish Law recognized this tactic but tolerated it in only
one situation. That situation involved a person who sought actively
to propagate heresy by influencing others. Because he was a threat
to the ideological character of the state, it was permissible to trap
him. However, if he did not try to seduce others to share his point
of view, decoys could not be used simply to elicit from him what
his views were. Thus it appears that Jewish Law simply kept hands
off impious beliefs and behavior so long as they were not expressed
or performed in public. Only then could they be deemed subversive

of the society of the faithful.

That the right to privacy is based on verses related to human sexuality should not be surprising. In the Jewish tradition the value of privacy in sexual relationships between husband and wife became associated with the observation imputed to the non-Jewish prophet Balaam. He noted how goodly were Jewish tents because their openings did not face each other. Couples enjoyed privacy even in the wilderness. They did not cohabit in the presence of other couples. Indeed, this was deemed a hallmark of civilized human behavior as distinguished from that of some animals.

However, concern for privacy in sexual relationships was deemed worthy not only of the dignity of man, it also had a religious dimension. It is in their sexual conduct that men and women are called upon to act on their honor, out of their sense of duty to God and what He mandated. If in matters of sex there was to be no trust, then the authorities would have to give up, because constant supervision is impossible. Instead, self-control must be cultivated. The ability to exercise self-restraint must be induced; without it civilized life would be impossible. Human society itself would become worse than a jungle. Fathers and mothers, brothers and sisters had to learn to abstain from incest on their honor. And that applied to all illicit relationships.

One of the most specific mandates in the Pentateuch with regard to the right to privacy is the command that a creditor may not enter the home of the debtor to collect the debt due him (Deut. 23:11). The Talmud extended the prohibition to include the court's sheriff (BM 113a). However, it seems not to associate this commandment with the right to privacy. Perhaps the rabbis deemed it an extension of the right to property. But the United States Supreme Court (Griswold vs. Connecticut, 85 Supreme Court Report 1678) did base the right to privacy in part on the constitutional right to be protected against searches and seizures.

IV.

The talmudic term which comes closest to describing the notion of concern for the dignity and inviolability of the person is *kevod ha-b'riyot* (respect for persons). And the context in which it is most fully discussed in the Talmud involves the obligation of a Jew to undress in public when he discovers that he is wearing a garment made of a combination of materials that Jews are forbidden to wear. The obligation would be based on the general principle that God's will is primary and man must obey even at the sacrifice of his personal dignity. However, the Talmud's conclusions are impressive. First, there are times when God's will can be ignored by failure to act. This is passive disobedience. The Jerusalem Talmud also suggests in one version that if the disobedience would be only for a brief interval so as to allow the person wearing the prohibited garment to remove it privately, he may not need to suffer embarrassment. Second, by a very remote interpretation of a totally unrelated verse the High Priest is permitted to ignore the biblical mandate to avoid contact with a cadaver of a pauper who has no kin to bury him. The High Priest may perform the act of mercy although he thereby flouts an unambiguous biblical prohibition. (Berachot 20a).

One can cite many talmudic passages that protect the dignity and sanctity of human beings, but most of them do not involve any violation of biblical mandates. For the purpose of this study they represent no problem, because if the prohibition is rabbinic, and not biblical—and most of the prohibitions of Jewish law are of that kind—then consideration for the dignity of the person is the paramount consideration. This position is easily rationalized because it is assumed that all rabbinic prohibitions were made initially with the thought that they would not be applicable if the dignity of the human person was endangered.

For this reason many contemporary rabbis feel that this premise can become the basis for many innovations in Jewish life and practice in accordance with the Halakhah.

There is still another group of principles which in the past made possible what is in fact rabbinic legislation, and not only revision by judicial interpretation. These are the principles:

1. The requirements of a peaceful society must prevail.

2. The avoidance of evoking hate from Jews and non-Jews.

3. The need for "mending" the world—making life in it better than it was.

Many of the rules pertaining to the rights of persons to dignity, safety, and well-being, derived from these principles, and often property rights had to yield to them.

Moreover, without calling them natural rights, the rabbis recognized and enforced rights which were precisely that. For example, when the schools of Shammai and Hillel debated the status of a person who is half slave and half free—owned by one partner and emancipated by the other—the school of Shammai convinced the school of Hillel with an argument from natural law. The school of Hillel had thought that it would be possible for such a person to work for himself one day and for his half owner the next. The rejoinder of the school of Shammai is a classic. "You have taken good care of the master but have you taken care of the slave himself? He cannot marry a female slave because he is half free and he cannot marry a free woman because he is half slave. How will he fulfill God's will to populate the earth?" Needless to say, if his status does not allow him—because of God's law—to populate the earth, then he is under no obligation to do it. It is God's law that stops him. But the school of Shammai was concerned with the slave's natural right, though that term is not used. The slave is not to be denied his humanity.

This controversy clearly indicates that the rabbis are concerned with the existence of natural rights, in this instance, the right to have and raise a family equal in status to that enjoyed by others in that society. It is not simply because God gave the command to be fruitful and multiply to all humans, and the slave—half slave and half free—is entitled to fulfill that command given to him by God. The fact is that his right is broader. Even in his half slave and half free condition he could procreate. There are women with whom he may cohabit—at the very least women in the same status as he. But what he cannot do is to procreate and have completely free offspring. Yet it is this very right that the rabbis safeguarded for him, a natural right, to be equal to all in his society with regard to having and raising a family.

In a way the right to privacy is a right involving the protection of a person from intrusion by another, and the right of the person half slave and half free also required protection from a disability that would radically affect his personal life from limitation by others.

The same generous spirit inspired a very concerned commitment by the rabbis to the reduction, if not the total elimination, of the incidence of bastardy.

The rabbis were aware of the problematic character of the institution. They too queried, "Shall one enjoy the sin and another pay the penalty?" But they realized that the one sanction there was to deter immoral sexual behavior was the threat that the prohibited pleasure might yield a bastard. This threat might induce restraint. And they did not minimize the social stigma and the consequence of ostracism involved in illegitimacy. On the other hand, they magnified the horror of such a status. To such an extent did they magnify it that Jews were wont to prefer the death of such a child. One great rabbi, two centuries ago, sanctioned an abortion rather than permit the birth. And in a set of hypothetical cases the Talmud informs us by inference that the stigma attached to illegitimacy was so great that the mothers of illegitimate infants would rather murder than abandon them. If one came upon a foundling whose mother took precautions to ensure the child's survival, though she was then and there abandoning it, the foundling was presumed to be legitimate, for if the child were illegitimate the mother would rather have sought its death. So successfully did the Law induce the dread of illegitimacy!

At the same time, the Law was also very exacting. It made it very difficult to brand anyone a bastard. This was a typical instance of the Law's dialectic—balancing values, creating the threat of hardship, and then virtually eliminating its incidence.

First, it held that children born out of wedlock were legitimate, a radically different definition from that held by most peoples. Even some children born of unlawful marriages were legitimate. Only such were bastards as were the products of incestuous or adulterous relationships in which no lawful marriage could ever be consummated between the parties—for example, a child born because of the cohabitation of a brother and sister. Yet how can one ever prove an incestuous relationship to establish bastardy? One must never overlook the difficulty found in Jewish Law to prove any kind of guilt. And as for an adulterous relationship, that too was virtually impossible of proof in the face of the presumption that every husband is the father of all the children his wife bears—even if he was away from her for years. Perhaps he came on a magic carpet in the dead of night to cohabit with his wife and impregnate her! Perhaps the wife conceived artificially. The mother could not and would not testify against the child's interest. And the Law was quite clear: only those whose illegitimacy is certain are bastards. When there was doubt there was no bastardy.

V.

This paper does not deal with the diversity in the views of the rabbis with regard to problems that exclusively pertain to creed rather than practice. In that area too there was much bold creativity involving the literal meaning of biblical texts. However, it warrants a separate study beyond the scope of this paper, which concerns itself not with who God is and what He does, but rather with what man does with God's revealed will.

:

Legal Sanctions For Moral Obligations

In every society there is human behavior which is regarded as morally reprehensible but for which there is no legal redress. Yet creative judges, even in the absence of legislation, find ways to develop the law and provide either sanctions for, or deterrents against, the offensive acts. The legal order of the Jews and Judaism is no exception. Indeed, many writers on the Halakhah often overlook this and blithely convey the erroneous impression that much evil is left to God, for Him to punish on an ultimate day of judgment, while human tribunals can offer only censure to the offender and solace to his victim. This paper will present a number of illustrations to demonstrate how responsive Jewish judges were to the need for making strict law fulfill equitable or ethical desiderata.

I. Wrongs Which God Will Punish

We have noted elsewhere that the Talmud lists a number of wrongs for which Jewish tribunals can provide no remedy but for which a man is deemed liable "by the laws of Heaven."[1]

Rashi puts forward the suggestion that liabilty by the laws of heaven" is more punitive than compensatory. Hence when a tortfeasor is encouraged to pay damages the motive is to avoid punishment by divine agency. Rashi, it seems, felt that the obligation to pay should be classed as punitive rather than compensatory so that any failure to pay might not be regarded as failure to compensate since failure to compensate would be classed as theft (i.e. witholding from another his due). The Meiri takes the opposite view.[2] He believes that the court is required to inform a defendant that he should pay because failure to do so would lead him to be labelled a thief and hence he would make himself inable to testify in his own belf in other court cases, with the all the dangers described in the fourth section of this paper (see Hashlamah, BK 6:1, and Meiri, BK 56a).

---

1. BK 55b and 56a. See also below, p. 116.
2. See also *Ketzot ha-Hoshen*, 32a.

Furthermore, when one is liable by the laws of Heaven, the wronged party may in certain instances retain the property of the tortfeasor if he seized it forcibly. It may be that he may always do so (see Rashi, BM 9a). Others would limit the right to retain what was thus seized to cases where a biblical command was violated, as in the case of withholding testimony, or where there is liability which even a human tribunal could impose but for the fact that the defendant is liable to a greater punishment for the same act and the court cannot impose two punishments. (The authorities are collated and discussed in Shevut Yaakov 1:146.)

II. Interference with Another's Gain

If a poor man is examining a cake and another comes and takes it away from him . . . he is called a wicked man (Kiddushin 59a).

This rule became the basis in Halakhah for an extensive development with regard to precipitous grasping of economic opportunities that are still under consideration by another. Some authorities (see the Tosafists, ibid.) limit the condemnation to instances in which comparable opportunities are available to the offending party elsewhere. However, if what is involved is a trove, and this is a nonduplicable situation, then to act in self-interest is permissible and no moral turpitude attaches to the act. Other authorities are more demanding. (For a thorough analysis of the views, see Hasam Sofer, Hoshen Mishpat, 79.)

But for the purposes of this study, the key question is whether the rules are simply rules of morality or the basis for legal sanctions. The rules themselves make for some restraints on competition and unfair trading. They have even inspired a noblesse oblige in marketing and fishing.

Yet the talmudic ruling that the offender is a *rosho*, a wicked man, was regarded as requiring that a public pronouncement to that effect be made in the synagogue or other place of assembly. Thus the censure was formal and embarrassing. In a closed community the effect must have been devastating.[3]

Second, at least one authority held that the rule was sufficient warrant to coerce the offender to return the object he acquired immorally by purchase or otherwise. Another authority suggested that even this would not constitute atonement for the sin and further measures would be required.

---

3. See Pitchei Tshuvah, Hoshen Mishpat, 237.

And third, the *rosho* may in some instances be deemed a *masig gevul* (see *Perisha* and *Aruch ha-Shulhan*, Hoshen Mishpat, (237:1), and thus may be incompetent to testify as a witness, with the damaging consequences described in Section IV of this study.

III. Proximate Cause

Few areas of the Halakhah have evoked more frustrating analyses than the problem of proximate cause in torts. The general rule was stated that the Gerama creates no liability. This was taken to mean that a tortfeasor pays only for injuries or damages which result immediately—and without any intervening agent—from his acts. If there is but one additional intervening cause, he may in some instances pay only half-damages. However, if there are several intervening causes, he is totally exempt from liability.

As early as the tannaitic period, some torts were held to be actionable even though the damage was not immediately caused by the tortfeasor, and these were called cases of Garmi. What is the difference between Gerama and Garmi? To this question many authorities gave their attention. Some even felt that the terms were not meant to convey different types of acts. It was rather that when the rabbis relieved the defendant of liability they called it Gerama, and when they held the defendant accountable they called it Garmi.[4] This itself would mean that the rabbis created legal sanctions for such instances of indirect damage as they felt the circumstances warranted. They were not content with the basic rule and modified it by creating a new category—with liability. But they did more.

In those cases in which there was no liability, and for whose avoidance the tortfeasor had only a moral obligation, the rabbis also provided a legal sanction. They provided at least a mandatory injunction against the continuance of acts that might result in nonactionable damage.

Thus, for example, if a man should have a ladder on his premises and a weasel climbs it and jumps to his neighbor's fowl and devours them, the owner of the ladder is not liable for the damage done. However, the neighbor can enjoin the owner of the ladder from keeping it where it is likely to do the harm (BB 22b). The Talmud further illustrates the principle in connection with bloodletters who performed their work near a man's trees. The deposits of blood attracted birds who, after wallowing in the blood, flew to the trees

---

4. See Zevin, ed., *Talmudic Encyclopedia* 6, col. 461-97.

and spoiled the fruit. The blood letters had to discontinue using their own land for this purpose (ibid., 23a). The Meiri (on the aforementioned texts) sees no limitation on the rule unless there is an express agreement with the neighbors. Even long usage without protest may not create the presumption of an agreement or waiver in some cases. Thus neighbors can enjoin the use of property for purposes which create noxious odors or noises.

The rabbis enjoined when they could not award damages, and what might have been nonactionable unneighborly deportment acquired a legal sanction other than compensation.

IV. Incompetency to Testify Because of Dishonesty

According to the Halakhah, a man might be incompetent to testify in a lawsuit because he is related to one of the parties. In such a case no moral turpitude is involved. But a man might also be incompetent to testify because he is a thief or the beneficiary of illegal gains, such as a usurer or one who would eat tabooed foods to spare himself additional expenditures (San. 27a). There was a difference of opinion as to whether one who was honest but non-observant would be competent to testify—such as a man who ate pork not to economize but to defy the authority of Torah. The talmudic conclusion is that even he is incompetent to testify (ibid.).

Yet despite this conclusion there persisted in halakhic analysis a difference between the two situations, which difference influenced responsa in this century. The man who is dishonest is far more apt to lie than he who is simply not devout. The Hasam Sofer (Responsa, Hoshen Mishpat, 36) takes notes of the distinction and resolves what would appear to be contradictions in some of the authorities (especially in the Shach, Hoshen Mishpat, 34:33 and 35:7). He holds that the penitence of the person who is not observant is adequate to make him competent to testify even with respect to events that occurred prior to his penitence, while the penitence and restitution of the dishonest man is to no such avail.

The Hasam Sofer suggests several reasons for the distinction, but from the Talmud itself (see Strashoun, on Sanhedrin 27a) it would appear that he is correct. A non-observant man does not feel that he is sinning—he simply denies the authority of Torah and perhaps the existence of God. However, he is not apt to testify falsely, and his recollection of events in the past would be without bias or fraud. Consequently, while Jewish law denies him competency as a witness because of the strictness of the law, his penitence removes that disqualification and he is presumed completely trustworthy. However, a man who was presumed dishonest at the time the events occurred beheld the facts in his state of dishonesty. His subsequent penitence will not guarantee an accurate report of what took place at an earlier date. There are even authorities who hold that a witness is not competent to testify if he was an interested party at the time the events occurred even if he became detached at the time of testifying (see Hasam Sofer, ibid.).

Thus to enjoy a reputation for honesty and integrity all the time was most important. But our sages made this a value not only for social prestige or to insure competency as a witness. They added economic or legal sanctions.

V. The Rights of Redemption and Preemption

Many texts in the Talmud refer to equity, known as Lifnim mi-shurat ha-Din, and strict law, known as Din,. In most of these instances, the higher standard of performance is described as normative only for those who aspire to live by more righteous norms than are applicable to the common man. And while judges did urge all litigants before them to abide by the higher standard, they could not always coerce acceptance of their exhortations (Aruch ha-Shulhan, Hoshen Mishpat, 12 :2).

However, there is a general mandate in the Bible—"And thou shalt do what is right and good in the sight of the Lord" (Deut. 6:18)—and this mandate became the basis for rules of equity that were applicable to all men, irrespective of their status. On the basis of this text the rabbis legislated rights of redemption and preemption. By not treating the verse in Scripture as if it were only moral exhortation, they accorded their own, and the community's, sense of justice a creative role in the development of new legal rights and duties which were enforceable in court.

A creditor, for example, who collected his debt by execution against the real estate of the debtor was compelled to return the property whenever the debtor was in a position to pay (BM 35a). The right of the debtor to redeem his lost asset could only be cut off by the creditor's sale or gift of the property. The authorities are not unanimous as to whether the right might not also apply to movable property. Moreover, it was a right which the debtor's heirs could exercise.

Asheri—in opposition to the Toṣafists (ibid.) and Maimonides (Mishneh Torah, Hilkhot Loveh u-Malveh, 22:17)—held that though the applicable text in the Talmud might be interpreted as terminating the right with the death of the creditor, so that his heir would not have to return the realty, this was not the case. He interpreted the word Urta in the Talmud to mean "to give as a gift to one of one's heirs," either as a gift to take effect on death or as an increase in the intestate share of an heir. Thus it was only an irrevocable sale or gift by the creditor that could terminate the debtor's right of redemption or that of his heirs. But if title did not vest in the purchaser or donee before the right of redemption was exercised, it was not cut off. The ordinary automatic succession of heirs to the property did not destroy the right.[5]

In essence, what the law did was to say to the creditor: "So long as you are the owner of the realty, you are subject to the right of redemption. You can spite the debtor—and yourself at the same time by divesting yourself of title. You will thus lose the usufruct until the exercise of redemption, which you would have been permitted to retain." The law did not deem it necessary to subject the purchaser or donee to the debtor's claim. The protection afforded the debtor was considered adequate so long as the property was subject to the claim while it was in the creditor's hands, and it would be a rare creditor who would harm himself only to harm the debtor.

In the case of the right of preemption, the rabbis were even more thorough. The right of preemption, Bar Mizra, gave a neighbor the prior right to buy any property adjoining his. The owner could not sell it to a non-neighbor until the neighbor had declined to purchase on the same terms. This right was derived from the same verse in Deuteronomy. That verse was the only warrant for its creation. And it applied to everyone.   However, in connection with this right the rabbis held that it was not cut off by any sale or gift or bequest (see Shitah Mekubezet, BM 35a). A purchaser who violated the right of preemption of a neighbor could not cut off that right by a subsequent deal with another party. Why did the rabbis treat the right of preemption differently from the right of redemption, although both derive from the same biblical mandate? One difference is analytical; the other is functional.

In the case of the right of preemption, the first purchaser acquired title unethically—he subverted the right of the adjoining owner. Yet the law compels him to resell the property to the neighbor. It will do the same to those who succeed to his title. In the case of

5. See Asheri BM 45a, and the Tur, Hoshen Mishpat, 103; and the Beit Yosef, ibid.

the right of redemption, the creditor acquired title lawfully—as a result of a lawsuit against the debtor. And the law simply imposes upon him alone an obligation to permit redemption so long as he has the title. This was the extent of the burden placed upon him (Ravad, ibid.).

Yet functionally the difference between the two is even clearer. As already noted, in the case of the right of redemption, the protection afforded the debtor was deemed adequate. The right could only be subverted by the creditor's action against his own interest. In the case of the right of preemption, however, the right could be destroyed easily if subsequent purchasers were not obliged to respect it. Any vendor could nullify the right by selling first to a dummy who would in turn sell to the real purchaser. The intermediate transaction would cut off the right and the rabbis' creative equitable achievement would have been in vain. This is what emerges from two noteworthy illustrations of rabbinic action to translate moral obligation into legal duty. The rabbis did not leave to the heart alone the moral obligation of the creditor to help the debtor recover his land whenever he could repay his debt or the moral obligation of a neighbor to be neighborly. These moral obligations become enforceable legal duties.

VI. The Mi She-Pora

For title to pass from a vendor to a purchaser of movable goods, there must be, according to the Halakhah, something other than the payment of money. Reish Lakish held that it was a biblical requirement for the passing of title that the purchaser move the object, or perform some other physical act symbolizing his assumption of ownership. Rabbi Yohanan, on the other hand, held that from a biblical point of view payment would accomplish the same result, but the rabbis required the physical act, lest after payment for the goods, with the vendor still in possession of them, the goods might then be threatened by fire or otherwise, and the vendor would hardly extend himself to save them. By giving each party the right to rescind until final delivery, the safety of the goods is enhanced. Therefore, the rabbis legislated that only the purchaser's seizure of the property is effective to pass title. In any event, according to both views, either party can rescind the transaction prior to the seizure of the goods, even if payment had been made (BM 47b). However, the party so rescinding was punished with a curse.

Modern man may view such a curse as innocuous. In its time it was probably a most effective way to make it known that one was a bad credit risk. However, the rabbis went further and added legal sanctions to the religious ritual prescribed. They ruled that if it was the buyer who had the change of heart, he could not obtain the refund of his money until he subjected himself to the indignity that was his due, and in the interim the seller was not responsible for the money. And if it was the seller who had the change of heart, then he was to return the money and subject himself to the curse, and until the money was returned, he was an insurer of the coins delivered to him (Mishneh Torah, Hilkhot Mechira, 7:2, 3). Thus liability to the curse became a legal "power" in the hand of the offended party and created actionable duties. It was more than society's rebuke.

Furthermore, it would appear that until the money was returned the man subject to the curse was incompetent as a witness, with dire consequences to himself, as is described in Section IV of this paper (Nahlat Zevi, Hoshen Mishpat, 34 :5).

VII. Conclusion

That the judicial process is more than simply the logical extension of existing precedents and rules to new cases is now taken for granted by all students of law. This is also true of Jewish law. The rabbis were continuously creative in enriching the rules so that they would fulfill equity and satisfy the sense of justice of a community that was becoming more and more conscious of the need for law to sustain morality. This creative role must never be abdicated, especially in a legal system in which new legislation is rare.

Judaism has always relied less on preachment and more on law for the achievement of a just society—for brotherhood, neighborliness, and mutual responsibility for each other's welfare.

Therefore, the creative role of its judges must be proved to be historic and authentic even as Jewish judges are encouraged to continue this role in the present and future.

Yet one may ask why a revealed, God-given law should have need of such continuous upgrading. One would expect human law to be defective, requiring constant replenishment from ever-advancing conceptions of morality and justice. God's law one expects to be perfect ab initio. To this I make reply in chapter nine, "Secular Jurisprudence."

Concern For Others' Basic Human Needs And Judaism's Cardinal Tenet

We Jews generally enjoy a fine reputation in connection with philanthropy. Benevolence has always been a hallmark of our social and communal existence. We have a deep sense of responsibility for each other as well as for all mankind. And peace, not war, always lay at the heart of all our yearning. It behooves us, therefore, to consider some of the sources which broadened and deepened our commitment to the eternal value which our patriarch Abraham symbolizes in the Jewish tradition—Chesed—kindness, concern for others.

It behooves us to do this because this value, among others, was not spared attack by moderns who were influenced by the sciences of biology and psychology. From some biologists and geneticists came the view that in a struggle for survival, which may characterize all of life, it is inevitable that only the strong will endure.

These scientists, primarily concerned with improving the physical attributes of the human being, oppose charity for the weak, aged, disabled and disadvantaged, because these groups are a drain on available resources. These scientists urge that these weaker humans do not contribute to the survival of the species—they only endanger it. These Nazi-type scientists urge that compassion may be a sentiment we cherish but practical reason dictates that we overcome it.

Because it is intuitively repulsive, these scientists do not articulate their view that one day we may have to gas babies as they are born—or do it shortly thereafter, although they do not hesitate to articulate their view that for certain defectives this is an appropriate disposition.

"Kindness is self-centered"

From some psychologists came the view that kindness is simply another form of self-centeredness. They urge that we behave benevolently because it pleases our ego, our vanity. We like to patronize. We love to play God. Sometimes our children even tell us that what we do for them is for our pleasure, more than for theirs. Their contention is that altruism is just another form of egoism, and hardly worthy of celebration or special respect.

These attacks are of comparatively recent vintage. In the religious and philosophical traditions it was always assumed that the good was good. Scholars pondered the nature of good: how does one recognize it or define it and how does one attain it? That the good might be a mirage altogether, or a creature of the devil, of Satan, did not occur to many. Few, if any, challenged what was so fundamental a value to endow our lives and our actions with meaning. However, in the last 100 or more years the critics have gained in number and momentum. What does Judaism have to say about all this?

In Judaism, the role of benevolence is central. As we already noted, the founder of our faith, Abraham, is its principal exponent. Though he founded the faith, we know almost nothing about his doctrines, his creed. We know only of his great concern for justice and goodness. And in Judaism, God is the source for both these values.

Yet both of these are assumed by Judaism to be inherent in human nature. Before Revelation, Abraham challenged God not to do injustice when Abraham pleaded with Him not to destroy the righteous with the wicked in Sodom and Gomorrah. And as for goodness, Abraham needed no divine mandate to make him shun the spoils of war, or to redeem the captive, or to offer hospitality to strangers.

Part of human nature

In my view, sentiments—for the just and for the good—are part of human nature. Indeed, in the absence of goodness and altruism, there could be no human survival because, as Willard Gaylin points out, the human being is the only animal who at birth is not self-sufficient and requires "caring" by someone else if he is to live at all. Indeed, as Gaylin demonstrates in his book "Caring," the physical and emotional development of the human being is a reaction, in one way or another, to all that is done for him by those who care for him.

Therefore, it is difficult to argue that goodness is not a value if the survival of the human species is not possible without it. But Judaism comes in not to uphold the centrality of the value of goodness but to analyze its components, what it requires, what are its demands, when it is right and when it is wrong.

Once I wrote this of violence. Lorenz may argue that violence is also natural to humans. Judaism accepts this but tries to curb it, to regulate it, not to destroy it. Judaism explains when it is permitted and when not. With goodness too, Judaism is concerned with the parameters, and with depth and breadth of the value and its desired end, lest goodness overreach its proper limits.

And the first point Judaism makes with respect to it is that benevolence is a must, not only because the human infant cannot survive in its absence but also because goodness is the mortar out of which all relationships must be formed, both with God and man.

Total interdependence

The universe exists because God in his goodness stops the planets from crashing into each other and He created and preserves a world for man to enjoy. But He craves man's partnership in His creation and man's communication with Him. He wants us to care for Him as He cares for us.

It may sound absurd to a rationalist that an Infinite God needs puny man. But that belief of Judaism teaches us that if God can feel the need of man so keenly, how much more do we have need of each other! If God can be lonely, how much more so we! This is all simply a theological manner of expressing the utter and total dependency of each of us on the other. Only God could be independent. Yet He Himself doesn't cherish the loneliness that it spells.

Unfortunately most of us miss the main point contained in the verse "It is not good for man to be alone." This verse God uttered when He created Eve in order to dispel Adam's loneliness. But Jewish commentators did not take it to mean that Eve was created to provide man with companionship. Perhaps this is why the verse so irks feminists. As if woman were only an instrument for man's happiness!

Our sages saw in the verse the suggestion that it is not good for man to be like God—independent—self-sufficient, alone. Adam had to be reduced to size: he had to be made a dependent creature and a dependent creature he would always be. His ego required trimming. And so he was made dependent, as Eve was a dependent, as all are dependents, even as God craves dependency on us, despite His matchless independence.

Thus there is a religious dimension to the dependency of man. Man is made aware of his interdependence. And all his life he must seek goodness as a value. Thus point one: Judaism deems benevolence a cardinal value which must never be undermined.

Because of God's goodness the universe is intact. And because of His goodness and the goodness of men, humanity survives. Yet not all men have the capacity for input in the same measure. And not always are good intentions or good deeds promotive of the desired end.

Therefore, Judaism has much more to say about the subject, as I hope to demonstrate in the following two installments of this analysis of doing good.

Benevolence Means Giving of Oneself

Judaism distinguishes between acts of charity and acts of benevolence and deems the latter far more significant. Charity involves parting with money; acts of benevolence require the commitment of one's person as well as one's purse. Charity one can give only to the poor; acts of benevolence even the rich require. The Talmud adds that charity one can perform only for the living, whereas acts of benevolence are for all, including even the dead.

This simple but beautiful statement in the Talmud encapsulates the Jewish perspective on human interdependence. The rich too are in need. And also the dead. Indeed, in my life time I have known many lonely rich men. They craved genuine friendship but were obsessed with fears that anyone who tried to be friendly was only in quest of their wealth. They were like the rich princess who never wed because she suspected that all who wooed her sought only her station and treasures. Oft-times they who appear to be blessed with so much are to be pitied. They really require sympathy and understanding.

The dead may not be conscious of kindness toward them—our cherishing their memory. But the benevolent among us not only bury them, in the Jewish tradition as a labor of love, but also respect their wishes and regard it is a *mitzvah* to do their bidding. Even the living feel a glow in their hearts when they know that there are people whose regard for the dead is great; it not only makes it easier for one to die—it also makes one's striving in life more meaningful—one can hope for some voice in happenings after one is gone. In addition, sentiments of love and compassion are evoked by the dead and thus acts of benevolence toward them tenderize the human scene.

More than giving money

And acts of benevolence also involve more than the giving of money. Personal involvement is also required. Indeed, one can give money and yet forfeit the reward of the *mitzvah* because of the manner in which one gives. The Talmud teaches us that to humiliate the recipient is a cardinal sin. In fact, the highest form of giving, as Maimonides pointed out, is to help the recipient be independent of charity—to enable the needy to be self-sufficient. Help him that he may give charity himself.

The Talmud goes so far as to require the needy who receive charity to give charity themselves. From the public purse they are to receive their needs but their needs include the ability to do good unto others.

Many years ago I was asked by New York City's Welfare Commissioner, before the term "welfare" was interestingly discarded in favor of "social service" and "entitlements", how Jews would regard the giving of an allowance to welfare recipients that they may be able to make a contribution to their respective church or synagogue. I cited the talmudic passage, "Even he who is supported by charity, must perform acts of charity."

No great scholarship was required to resolve the issue. And the text makes good sense. The poor must not only eat—they must also be enabled to be human and to live with dignity and that means to be both charitable and benevolent.

Furthermore, the needy must be given not what we alone think is best for them. They are entitled to have a voice in the decision. A distinguished professor at Columbia asks, "Can we do good to others, but on their terms?" Judaism says, decidedly yes.

Our duty is to provide the poor man with his needs and that means that "even if it was his practice to ride on horseback with a servant as his herald, and he is now without means, we must buy him the horse and provide the servant because the Bible mandates that we provide his shortages. That which he lacks we are commanded to fulfill." (Maimonides, Mishneh Torah, Hilkhot Matnot Aniyim 7: 3).

Justice and charity

Judaism, however, does not simply exhort people to be considerate. Its greatest contribution to the concept of benevolence is that it grafted the notion of justice on the concept of charity. In the Bible one invariably finds the two words "charity and justice" as a compound phrase—both words almost always appear together.

The needy are deemed plaintiffs in a judicial setting. They are not clients of a social worker. They, so to speak, sue the community before a tribunal of three. The Talmud, Maimonides and all subsequent codifiers, call the distribution of charity "dinei mamonoth"—actions in civil law. One great saint, Rabbi Yonah, as if with a slip of the pen, wrote "dinei nefashot"—capital cases. He obviously erred because he required only a court of three judges while in a capital case twenty-three would have had to participate. But his slip of the pen was Freudian. To the poor person getting what he needs may indeed be a matter of life or death.

Professor Rothman of Columbia, whom I have already quoted, writes of social workers who were so "attached to a paternalistic model that they never concerned themselves with the potential of their programs to be as coercive as they were liberating." (Doing Good, The Limits of Benevolence, Pantheon, 1977.) And he quotes Lionel Trilling as having said, "Some paradox in our nature leads us, once we have made our fellow-men the objects of our enlightened interest, to go on to make them the objects of our pity, then of our wisdom, ultimately of our coercion."

This objectionable result could not happen if the needy were regarded as plaintiffs, in pursuit of their rights before a court of law, instead of the object of someone's bounty. This is what it means to graft the concept of justice on the concept of charity.

Even menial work preferred

I am not so sure that the court had the power to deny help to the poor when they refused to work. The rabbis did exhort the poor to seek the most menial employment rather than beg for alms. But we have no evidence that they could force an individual to do anything that would demean him. Yet more important than this unanswered question is the fact that unlike our situation today, the Jewish community would not have social workers who would be discharged because they were too generous to the client and not considerate enough of the state's budget. Under the Jewish system, such a social worker would also have his day in court, and not be the victim of zealous superiors to whom a reduced budget is more important than benevolence.

In one talmudic case the courts were hard on one class of needy. They refused to help any one who begged. This was a war on a very ugly phenomenon. And why should we beg if one had a better alternative course—recourse to the courts?

The Talmud tells a charming story about a beggar who would not give up his chosen "profession." One rabbi refused to give him anything. The students complained: "Rabbi, he had forfeited his right to court action because of the precedent to which we just referred. And if you give him nothing, he'll really starve!" The rabbi relented. It was permitted to give the beggar a pittance.

But the general talmudic practice ordained the preservation of the dignity of the needy and the avoidance of potential evils in the enterprise called "charity" or "benevolence."

Aged Should Be at Home

The two basic assumptions of Judaism—that the needy have a right to receive help in accordance with their needs as established by their own prior style of living and that the right is more than a moral right but one of which the judicial system takes cognizance lead to two additional principles sorely in need of fulfillment in our day. It may take generations before their importance is fathomed, but if modern society is to advance in benevolence as it has in technology, then these are two areas in which progress may be sought.

The first principle is that the needy should not be cared for in institutions but in surroundings that are natural—in family settings. Institutional care is not care in accordance with one's "prior style of living." Second, for the failure of public servants to do that which they should do for the needy—especially for wanton negligence—there ought be remedies in tort.

Benevolence in a frame of justice requires this result.

In comparatively modern times Jews did establish orphanages, homes for the aged, nursing homes, hospitals for the chronically ill, and many other kinds of institutions which cared for many persons similarly afflicted. Alas, what was once thought necessary only for lepers—the establishment of a separate community of those suffering similar privations—became the pattern for the parentless, the homeless, the incurable, the senile.

Many of these institutions were excellent; others were indescribably bad. But what the United States Supreme Court recently decided with regard to separate but equal facilities can be said of these institutions. The segregation of these people by itself is damaging. An orphan is entitled to a real home; so are the aged. Even when nothing but custodial care is called for, it may not be halakhically proper to accelerate death by placing the unaware person in a place where the attention is known in advance to be unequal to what loving children are biblically bound to render.

How far have we truly progressed from the African tribes whose weak and elderly were ceremonially placed upon a Death Rock to die? How can we condone the high mortality rate in the first six-month adjustment period in nursing homes? How do we explain the extraordinary growth of nursing homes in this generation?

Responsa on institutions

There is some discussion in the responsa literature of Judaism about these institutions. I am hopeful that one day a scholar will assemble and analyze the source material .However, even that which is readily accessible in the codes is of interest.

Maimonides wrote, "He whose father or mother becomes mentally incompetent must deal with them as their mental capacity requires until (the Lord) will have mercy upon them. And if it is impossible for him to endure it because of their excessive incompetence then he may leave them and order others to care for them as befits them."

What is of interest is that one of the glossators objects to Maimonides' suggestion that the responsibility can be delegated, although Maimonides relies upon a talmudic source for his view. One commentator suggests that that talmudic source can be interpreted to mean that one can only justify the child's leaving the parents when the child is prepared to make Aliyah to Israel.

A second commentator suggests that the son may place his parents in the custody of another because sometimes the parents will only be cured with a shock—a severe physical blow—and only a stranger, not a son, is permitted to administer that hurt. A third suggests, in a similar vein, that sometimes the senile parent must be physically restrained and incarcerated and a son could not bring himself to do something so heartbreaking.

De Facto care given

In any event, from even these few sources one can learn what according to Judaism is the requirement of benevolence vis-à-vis parents needing care. And when Jewish families were non-nuclear, non-conjugal, in character, all the needy in the family were cared for. There was a division of labor for the aged and the de facto adoption of orphans by members of the *mishpacha*.

Institutionalized benevolence is a comparatively new phenomenon in Jewish life, and while in many instances it was truly benevolent, in altogether too many instances it was more cruelty than kindness. Even the best institution cannot provide the family setting which is the right of the needy if they are to enjoy what was their standard prior to their indigence, or, if they were parentless almost from the moment of birth, what is standard for most people.

I know that altogether too few families make available foster home care for those who could benefit from such settings. Perhaps if the state appropriated as much for such care as it does for institutions, not only would more people respond to the call but even members of the family would be tempted to avoid the commitment of loved ones to nursing homes and hospitals.

In any event, the investigation of nursing homes in the United States produced little more than some candidates for political office. One wonders whether the states even retrieved as much money as they spent on the investigations. But a radical change for the better in the quality of lives of the patients is still an unfulfilled part of our dream world.

Public servants' accountability

However, benevolence in the frame of justice requires not only the care of the needy in the style to which they were accustomed but also accountability by public servants and public institutions for the damage they have done by the very process of removing the client from his or her natural setting.

Similar to common law, Jewish law makes a licensed physician liable for wanton negligence in the performance of his duty as a healer. If his patient dies, because of that negligence, he is punishable with exile as in the case of any person who kills by his negligence. The same rule even applies to a judge of the court or his surrogate who in the performance of his duty acts recklessly and injures or kills.

It is important to do good. It fulfils the Judaic principles of human interdependence and charity as justice. At this point in history we must strive to reverse the tide of increased institutional care. We must support community placement of those in need. We must deplore and oppose those who purport to favor community placement but who favor such placement in someone else's community.

We must apply our minds as well as our hearts in the cause of the good and follow basic Judaic principles if we are to do the best.

Modern Orthodoxy and the Status of the Jewish Woman

Before coming to grips with the status of Jewish women as seen by modern orthodoxy, I must define a few terms. I must clarify what modern Orthodoxy is. It is not a sect. It is not a movement. It is not even a seminar or a colloquium. There is no organized group. It has no publication of its own. The members are not members of any one organization. There is no such thing as a list of rabbis who call themselves "modern Orthodox". It is, at best, a group of rabbis who see each other from time to time, and share the same commitment: to wit, that the Torah does not have to be afraid of modernity. It can cope with modernity. There is no challenge that the Torah cannot cope with. We may be able to solve some problems which please moderns. Sometimes when we cannot solve a problem and please moderns, we have to help moderns acquire a new perspective. But the group as a whole does not fear to cope with any challenge and will not isolate itself because of challenges.

Rabbi Borowitz, a Reform Rabbi in the United States, has written a book in which he said that there were some six options available to Jews. One was the Soloveitchik approach, and he added that Rabbi Soloveitchik's approach collapses in the face of modernity. I took issue with him. He argues that Rabbi Soloveitchik's approach collapses in the face of modernity because it cannot solve the problems of modern women. And my debate with him was that it can solve the problems of modern women. Therefore I don't have to reject Soloveitchik, and I don't have to reject modernity. I reject some things in modernity that might be inconsistent with Orthodoxy, because I don't feel that all that is modern is sacred and inviolable. Therefore let us remember that the modern Orthodox are united on one proposition: that the Torah does not have to be afraid of challenges.

It has been said by several modern Orthodox rabbis that they prefer the term "centrist" rather than modern. The word "modern' has meanings that are associated with the vulgarity of the modern period, especially its permissiveness, and even its pornography. Therefore, they prefer the term "centrist" Orthodoxy. I still prefer the term modern Orthodoxy. Because, I don't know that I am in

the center on some issues. When ethics are involved I am an
extremist. So why should I call myself "centrist" when I am an
extremist from one point of view or another! Other Jews may
want to isolate themselves from the modern world. They don't
want any part of it. They insist upon different attire. They want to
avoid contact with other types of Jews. We feel differently .

In any event, the group to which I refer as modern Orthodox are
extremists with regard to the solution of the problems that confront
the Orthodox Jewish woman. That, all of us have in common. We
do not evade the problems. We don't always have a solution, but
we feel that one must be found. We must be intellectually honest,
and say that the problem is there. One day we may find the solution
and we are determined to do all we can to ameliorate suffering.
We goad, we irritate halakhic scholars to do more than they are
presently doing. And my argument with Professor Borowitz to
whom I referred earlier and who is a very articulate spokesman
for the Reform Movement, is that he and others are going too far
with their conception of modernity and what we must do to cope
with it. Professor Borowitz, for example, insists that any
differentiation between males and females is immoral because we
are all created equal before God, and the mere fact that we perpetuate
this differentiation lends itself to more and more unethical
consequences. To him I must say that we want to cope with
modernity, but my concept of modernity does not require that I
should say that there are no differences between men and women.
There are major differences, and these differences can be reflected
in any modern legal system as it is reflected in Judaism. I argue
that while I want equal treatment for women with men insofar as
equal pay is concerned I do not feel that it is unfair that only
women shall get pay on maternity leave, while men do not get
paid for paternity leave. I insist that there is a difference between
men and women and my modernity does not require that I shall
totally obliterate the difference between the sexes as Professor
Borowitz would have me do. As a result of the difference there
may emerge some halakhic consequences, but not necessarily
unalterable ones. A woman is not limited to a domestic career. In
the family's division of labor women generally assumed domestic
duties and the men communal affairs. However, this was not a
fixed pattern. It was subject to the will of the spouses. The books
on anthropology indicate that human society simply developed
that way. No one sat down thousands of years ago to work out
this division of labor between male and female. It developed

naturally, but changes were and are possible. Halakhah permits a woman to say to her husband that she prefers to keep her earnings and waive support by him. Separate property rights can also be a matter of agreement. This principle applies to almost every aspect of the marriage relationship excepting matters pertaining to conjugal rights. But the historic difference in major roles remains, at least in matters of ritual.

However, let us look at some of the simpler problems that disturb women and which modern Orthodox rabbis try to solve. What about a ceremony to name a girl at birth? The birth of a boy precipitates so much but it is not so with the birth of a girl. Some of the modern Orthodox rabbis have created such a ceremony in the Sabbath service.

In some of these synagogues women also have Hakafot on Simchat Torah. They do so in a separate area of the synagogue, but there has been a total rejection of the nonsense that a woman is not allowed to hold a Sefer Torah. There is a synagogue in Jerusalem where this point caused a major confrontation because a man who donated a Torah refused to have it used on Simchat Torah by the women during Hakafot.

The big issue in the United States today pertains to separate services for women. The first time I saw one was in a suburb of St. Louis, Missouri. The rabbi is a learned member of the Young Israel Council. Recently a number of rabbis in Yeshiva University ruled that separate women's services are halakhically improper. I do not know why these men took it upon themselves to say so. There is a Halakhah Committee in the Rabbinical Council that is official and it should have ruled. Moreover, there is at least an equal number of rabbis who permit it. Often this is the way Halakhah develops. Rabbis differ on an issue and in the course of time either both points of view become normative or one prevails over the other. This is probably what happened with regard to the blessings rendered by women when they perform *mitzvot* that they don't have to perform. Every time a woman takes a lulav and an ethrog on the holiday of Succot, and recites the appropriate blessing, she's really lying. She is saying: God, Blessed is He, Who commanded us to do this. But she was not commanded to do it. Women probably started to perform the *mitzvot* that they were exempt from performing, and after a period of time, they uttered the blessings too. And then came rabbis who rationalized approval.

There may come a day when rabbis will say with regard to women's separate services that as children have separate services and recite the Kaddish and the Kedusha, without anyone objecting, so women may do so too. I do not like such separate services. I prefer to have my entire family in the synagogue where I pray but I shall not prohibit them. On the other hand, a justification may be found in the principle of "chinuch"—the enrichment of their own lives and the lives of others in the performance of *mitzvot*.

That women are not counted in a "Minyan" may be unalterable but I shed no tears because of it. The exclusion is an affirmation of the halakhic pattern that the family shall be the wife's concern and the community the husband's concern. Many a psychoanalyst tells us that the pattern avoids emasculation of the head of the family in the household. In Jewish tradition he had been the symbol of authority, as the mother had been the symbol of love. However, these are not fixed patterns, and they may be changed. In many cases, women are expressing more authority in the home than some of the men. And the Halakhah does not fault them for it. The pattern which has developed, historically and anthropologically, is accepted by Judaism. And Judaism retained it. However, the range for choice by spouses is enormous in virtually every area.

Rabbi Meir Berlin, for example, wrote in "Hatorah Ve-Hamdina" that the day must come in a democratic society when the Halakhah, in accordance with a constitution adopted by the majority, approves women as judges. A few limitations would remain. They would not be able to participate in a capital case. Another limitation would be in serving as a witness to a marriage. They could be witnesses in other matters but a witness to a marriage is not simply testifying to something that happened. He is creating the marriage. It is not the rabbi who creates the marriage, according to Halakhah; it is the witnesses who create the legal relationship. And that role is a role for men, because it is essentially a communal matter. It is the male who in performing one of his communal duties creates the status of marriage, which has legal implications in the present and for the future. And that brings us to the issue of women rabbis. Here is a controversy which rocked the Jewish Theological Seminary. There is nothing wrong with a woman learning as much Torah as a man, and "smicha" now is not the traditional "smicha" anyway, so that being a rabbi means no more than that one has a law degree in Jewish law. It is to be hoped that many women will learn as much Torah as men or more. And no Orthodox Jew should object. Yeshiva University was the first school to establish a college for women. Ignored was the tradition that women are not to be taught the "Torah Shebe'al Peh." Bar-Ilan University also ignores the prohibition. A woman can get a doctorate there in Talmud, if she wants it. And that may help to achieve a solution to the problems of women in marriage and divorce. So "Smicha" is not the problem. Especially when you have such authorities as Rav Meir Berlin, for whom the University is named, saying that in a democracy women may be witnesses and judges with but few exceptions. Then they may one day propose halakhic ways to ameliorate some of the hardships they presently suffer under Jewish law. I noticed only recently that women have two additional complaints of which I was unaware. One magnificent woman who knows Torah well wrote in a symposium that it bothers her that women do not get the same "sekhar"—reward—that men do for the performance of the same *mitzvot*. In other words, men—who are obligated, will get "sekhar"—will be rewarded. But since women are doing it voluntarily, there will be no reward. To which I must retort that women should appreciate how lucky they are! My reaction is based on a tale told of the Gaon of Vilna. Once it was difficult for him to find an ethrog for the Succot holiday. One Jew was more successful and the Gaon of Vilna asked him to sell it. The man said, "On one condition."

"What is the condition?" asked the Gaon.

"The condition is that the reward that you will get in 'Olam Habah' for using the ethrog you will give to me."

Whereupon the Gaon of Vilna said. "I agree. Thank God! I finally have one *mitzvah* for which I will never get a reward, and I am so grateful for the opportunity to perform the *mitzvah* totally *leshmah*!"

It seems to me that this problem ought not disturb Jewish women. We have only remote allusions as to how God keeps the records, what rewards He gives and what rewards He does not give. And I am sure that in His good judgment, He will take care of the women as well as the men. I can't as a Halakhist decide for God. And the same answer applies to another halakhic statement to which Jewish women take exception. One blind rabbi complained: "I was wont to think that since I am blind and I am relieved of the obligation to perform *mitzvot*, and nevertheless I perform them, then God will give me a greater reward. However, I was taught that this is not true. A greater reward awaits him who is commanded and performs than one who is not commanded and performs." It is difficult to rationalize why. The most charming answer is that if one is commanded to perform, then human nature is such that one may "dafka" not obey. Therefore, one gets more of a reward for being commanded and doing because one has to overcome one's "yetzer hara" to disobey. If one is not commanded, one does not have to fight the "yetzer hara." It does not take much will power to cope, if the "yetzer hara" is inert. Yet, the entire statement by the rabbi shows that he himself did not think the case was so. He felt that he who is not commanded and performs, should get more "sekhar" than a person who is commanded and performs. And he may be right. So I must ask Jewish women not to give heed to this problem. Let us trust God to do the proper thing and let us cease from guessing as to what He will do. It is presumptuousness on our part to decide for God how He shall act.

These are problems that involve other worldly considerations and some feminists may be sensitive about them. But Halakhah is law and law deals with worldly rights and duties. In economic affairs, equal rights for men and women is the rule. The Torah spoke of "Mishpat Ehad." A tort committed against a woman is as actionable as one committed against a man. The Talmud even suggests that if a husband should injure his wife during the course of cohabitation, she may have a right to damages against her husband. In torts and in criminal law, they have the same rights and responsibility as men. As for equal pay, there is no foundation whatever in Halakhah that would entitle an employer to say that he will pay a woman less than a man. Halakhah protects the woman's property during the marriage and thereafter if she is widowed or divorced. Even the "nedunya" (the dowry) that her father invested in the marriage is protected.

The one area in which we have our major problems is the area of marriage and divorce. That is the "sore-spot" for the status of the Jewish woman—and her justifiable complaints. It is in this area that modern Orthodoxy has been most vocal. And this is an area in which I, too, have been militant and impatient. There is an impressive literature on the subject. Professor Eliezer Berkovits wrote an entire book suggesting a solution to virtually all the problems of the Agunah. Professor Menachem Elon, who is now a judge of the Supreme Court of Israel, has also made a most valuable proposal. I, too, have written on the subject. I want to describe briefly the nature of the several approaches. The solution will come and will develop along one of the several lines that I shall indicate in this lecture. All have merit if only the rabbinate will conclude once and for all that a solution must be found and that one does not have to wait for the Messiah's coming to give the final answer. In Jewish history there always was concern that a woman might have a husband who died before they had children. She would be subject to "yibum," the levirate law. She'd have to marry a brother of her deceased husband or obtain his release. Sometimes he was under-age and she remained an Agunah during the best years of her life. It happened during Israel's wars a number of times. And the widow had to wait as many as thirteen years until she could obtain "halitzah" (the ceremonial release).

To avoid such tragedies and others, the fathers of the brides would often make the marriage conditional. In Professor Freimann's great work on the subject, he discusses the customs that developed and the "takanot" (legislation) of different communities. Thus one approach to solving the problem is to have an agreement before marriage. By means of the prenuptual agreement almost all the problems are solved. This approach has been fully developed by Professor Eliezer Berkovitz. His plan had the approval of one of the halakhic giants of this century, the late Rabbi Weinberg of Montreux. A great controversy ensued, the details of which are irrelevant at the moment. But Rabbi Berkovitz' approach, even if not exactly in the language or terms he outlined, is an approach that will not die.

It suffers from two weaknesses, one political and the other psychological. But, in my humble opinion, neither is worthy of respect. The political problem is that his idea too closely resembles the proposals of the Conservative Rabbi Louis Epstein of Brookline, Mass., and the proposal of the Rabbinical Assembly, the organization of the Conservative rabbis. Maimonides taught us that we can learn good things—and true ideas—from non-Jews. But too often Orthodox rabbis dismiss any proposal—even good ones—if they come from non-orthodox Jews.

The psychological objection is that it is indelicate, at a wedding, to have an agreement signed which spells out in detail so many tragic events that may come to pass. Yet the "Ketuba" itself already relates to death and divorce. Why should it not have its scope widened? Moreover, modern couples are too sophisticated not to be sensitive to the realities of birth, marriage and death. They are less superstitious than their forebears.

Another solution helps tremendously and was used by the late Chief Rabbi Isaac Halevi Herzog. It was an approach that was developed by a Sephardi rabbi centuries earlier. In the event that a woman married, was then abandoned by her husband, and then she married someone else without getting a "get," her children by the second husband are *mamzerim*. They bear the stigma of illegitimacy. (Parenthetically we must always remember that illegitimacy, under Jewish Law, attaches only to a child who is born of an incestuous or an adulterous relationship. Let us never confuse Judaism with Christianity. A child is illegitimate in Christianity if it is born out of wedlock. That is not Jewish Law. A Jewish child is only illegitimate if it is born of an incestuous or adulterous intercourse.) What does one do for the children born of a woman's second marriage if she married before receiving the religious divorce?

The technique that was developed was to convince the first husband to give the "get" in such a way that the divorce would not be a divorce with regard to the first marriage but rather an annulment. The first marriage simply vanished. The Talmud gives at least two ways in which one can give a "get," and the result would be, not a divorce, but the status of never having been married. That means the children of the so called second marriage are not *mamzerim* at all, because there was no first marriage. This technique, used by Rabbi Herzog, was based on the afore-mentioned Sephardi responsum.

Chief Rabbi Goren even improved on that which Rabbi Herzog did and used a double-edged route to the annulment. In this way many children were saved from illegitimacy.

Why is that solution not enough? The difficulty is that if the husband is not alive, he cannot give the "get." Or if he's incompetent. Or if he is obstinate and refuses to give the "get."

The third approach is that of the late Rabbi Moshe Feinstein in the States. He is not modern Orthodox, but on this issue, he has been one of the most liberal in solving problems. He had a heart as big as he was and he knew the anguish of the Agunah.

Rabbi Moshe Feinstein suggested ways to annul almost all marriages that are performed by non-Orthodox rabbis. Many rabbis, and very Orthodox ones, refuse to go to such an extreme. And I, too, don't like it. I cannot say that all the marriages that are performed by the majority of rabbis in the world are null and void. It certainly does not contribute to "Ahavat Yisrael", to mutual respect. If there is no better way to help the woman, one may resort to it. But there must be better ways.

The most serious objection to the proposal is that it does not help precisely the woman who went to an Orthodox rabbi to get married. She is penalized because she is Orthodox.

The best way, of course, is to find ways of annulling marriages whereby the woman is regarded as one who never had a husband. One course is to annul marriages because of fraud or mistake, just as one rescinds a business transaction if one of the parties lies. Or if there was a mistake. For fraud or mistake, a marriage should be annulled. In an annulment one does not care whether the husband is dead or insane or simply disappeared. He becomes irrelevant. But a Beth Din would have to decide whether there were adequate grounds.

Permit me to give you a talmudic source. It is well known that a woman must consent to the marriage. That is why marriages are so much like contracts. Now, if her husband should die childless and she must now marry a surviving brother-in-law whom she cannot tolerate because of his repulsive condition, why can she not argue that she never married with the expectation that she would have to marry a brother-in law whom she cannot tolerate? The Talmud accepts the argument but adds that there is a presumption that even if she knew the future she would have married because a woman prefers any kind of marriage to none. Whether that presumption is still true is debatable. In talmudic times it was true. The woman who was alone was lost in the society of the times. In our day it is no longer true. If that presumption is the only thing standing in the way, then it should be possible to annul marriages whenever circumstances develop which she did not anticipate and never would have accepted had she known of them in advance. She ought to be able to say that she married the man, but did not know that he was a sadist; that he was irresponsible; that he would be incompetent; that he would refuse a "get" even for cause. This approach was used by Rabbi Moshe Feinstein in an historic case, where the man simply concealed from his wife that he had spent time in the hospital but was discharged, cured, served in the army, and was released with an honorable discharge, before he married her. He was certainly normal when he married. Why then did he have to disclose the fact? Yet, the fact that he failed to disclose this fact before the marriage justified Rabbi Feinstein in saying that there was no need for a "get." Concealing an important fact in selling a piece of property can justify the annulment of the sale. The same argument can be applied with regard to a marriage.

This approach actually used by Rabbi Feinstein can be very productive for a solution of most problems. Some authorities say that one can do this only if there has been no cohabitation. However, if the couple has cohabited then it must be assumed that there was unequivocal consent to stay married under any and all circumstances. This is the view of the Tosaphists but other authorities disagree and today certainly the rationale for the difference is not justified, but to prove this would involve me in a major detour from my subject.

The Maharam of Rothenburg, centuries ago, approved of the annulment of the marriage of a woman whose husband had died childless simply because the brother-in-law who would have to perform the "Yibum" or "Chalitza" had been baptized a Christian. The Rabbi said that she did not consent to marry and be bound to one who was a Christian.

But what of the presumption of the Talmud that a woman would prefer any kind of marriage to no marriage? The answer is that that presumption was never absolute. It was always rebuttable and my revered teacher Rabbi Joseph B. Soloveitchik should not have deemed the presumption a meta-historical value, as he once did.

The enormous power that the Beth Din has with regard to marriage, divorce, and annulment is based on the talmudic maxim that all marriages are subject to the consent of the Beth Din. Sometimes they simply declare the marriage void and sometimes because of the ugly behavior of one party or another, declare it voidable. This power must be studied carefully in our day to revive both forms of action—בטול הקידושין—(the nullification of the act of betrothal at the time of the action) and הפקעת הקידושין (the exorcising of the betrothal retroactively). And here is where Professor Elon's point must be made.

Rabbis in the past may have hesitated to exercise the power too readily. Jews were scattered all over the earth and there was no one rabbinic authority recognized by all or most of world Jewry. Therefore, what one Beth Din might decide would be rejected by another and there would be chaos in family law. Now, however, there is a central authority in Jerusalem and there can be developed a universal Jewish family law and decisions which most of world Jewry would accept.

What of the future? I, for one, accept the notion that Israel will, from the point of view of religious practices, be a pluralistic society. However, I would mourn a multiplicity of halakhic systems and the resulting exacerbation of the divisiveness in our ranks that has already reached dangerous proportions. Jewish women should pressure the rabbinate for action, for solutions, and perhaps even finance with a hundred thousand dollars or more a special commission of scholars to find the solutions. Women themselves ought to become experts in the field, study the sources, and propose solutions. It did not happen often, but in the past a woman who was a "Tana" debated her point in the Sanhedrin and won her point.

This does not mean that the rabbis who are males are insensitive to the plight of many Jewish women. They shed plenty of tears because they cannot find the way in one case or another but today they hesitate to be creative in Halakhah simply because it may give comfort to Reform rabbis. But I would rather give them comfort than multiply *mamzerim* or punish the observant Jewish woman who accepts the yoke of the Law.

May the Lord provide us with the light we seek and the courage to use it!

Violence and the Value of Life:
The Halakhic View

Let me begin by saying that I approach our subject as a political scientist and not as a professional historian. As a political scientist I begin as Plato and Aristotle did, with a discussion of human nature. Moreover, I plan to deal with the subject conceptually and analytically rather than chronologically.

Perhaps by way of introduction I might also add a point about myself, and the best way to explain this would be with a story. A man had been prevailed upon by his wife, after much importuning, to clean their attic. After he had cleared everything out of the attic, he realized that among the things he had burned was an old family Bible, and he began to have misgivings about having destroyed this family treasure. He turned to a friend of his and said, "I'm beginning to worry; perhaps it wasn't a nice thing to do, to burn the old family Bible. What's more, I seem to recall that on the frontispiece of that Bible there were large letters, G U T E N." Whereupon the friend said, "You idiot, you probably burned a Gutenberg Bible. The last copy sold for about $40,000." "Oh, no," said the husband. "Mine wouldn't have brought a cent. Some nincompoop by the name of Martin Luther wrote all over the margins."

My prejudice, I might say, is that I am loath to discard any part of the Bible or any of the glosses that the rabbis have written on the Bible through the millennia. While I do not always agree with rabbis and have on many occasions expressed considerable dissent, by the same token I have altogether too much respect for the integrity and sincerity of my forebears not to try to understand, empathetically at least, that which they tried to create and contribute to Jewish thought and survival.

That is a prejudice of mine and I must record it in advance. However, starting with human nature, as I promised, I think we must posit in advance that to act violently, to act with aggression, is human. This is recognized, for example, by Konrad Lorenz, who discusses aggression and violence in the animal kingdom and in the human kingdom. Jewish law, or Halakhah, recognized this. There is a tendency to violence in human nature, but as with all instincts, whether the instinct is for food, for sex, or for recognition,

Jewish law seeks never to repress totally, only to control, to regulate, to make constructive, to dignify, even to sanctify, every instinct that human beings have, including the instinct for violence and aggression. For this reason generally it must be conceded that Judaism is not committed to pacifism. It may be, as Reuven Kimmelman suggests, that there were rabbis in the third or fourth century who opposed violence as a means of ensuring Jewish survival, but theirs was decidedly a minority point of view.[1] On the other hand, Maurice Lamm, in his essay "Red or Dead," shows that the sources would well establish that pacifism is not a Jewish ideal.[2] If pacifism is the pursuit of peace at any and all costs, then it was never an authoritative Jewish teaching. Tolstoy rejected all violent resistance to evil in the social order, regardless of cause and circumstance, because an active revolution must fight evil with another evil, namely violence. He believed in passive, individual resistance and derived it from the New Testament, from Matthew: "Resist not evil." Gandhi also made it a strategy of politics and later attempted to make it a policy of state. Gandhi's proposal for Jews during the Holocaust was also passive resistance. It was counsel given after the tragedy and thus untenable. Gandhi's passive resistance might have been effective against an England which had a conscience, but it would not have accomplished anything vis-à-vis Hitler. Quite the contrary, it was precisely what Hitler would have wanted.

But even in situations in which humans less beastly than Hitler are the enemy, passive resistance often has serious limitations. It either cannot be consistently maintained, or it results in the loss of the best manpower that a cause can possibly mobilize. One such situation in modern times is that of the Student Non-Violent Coordinating Committee, which played an important role in the black revolution in the United States during the sixties. Howard Zinn's *The New Abolitionists* questions how nonviolent nonviolent direct action can be, and he proves, for example, that in 1964 the group had to concede that it would not stop a Negro farmer in Mississippi from arming himself to defend his home against attack.

Judaism, therefore, is more concerned with regulating the circumstances which would permit the exercise of violence—by

1. Reuven Kimmelman, "Non-Violence in the Talmud," *Judaism* 17, no. 3 (Summer 1968), 316–34.

2. Maurice Lamm, "Red or Dead," *Tradition* 4, no. 2 (Spring 1962), 165–97.

individuals, by groups, and by states—than it is with the elimination of violence at all costs. Violence is at one and the same time an important way both to destroy and to conserve one of the most important values in the value system of Judaism—human life. Violent action usually endangers the life of the aggressor as well as the lives of those against whom the violence is directed. Generally one's own life is regarded as having the highest priority, but if one is to engage in violence it must be in accord with Jewish law and in behalf of the value of life or a value even higher than the value of life. Never is one to lose sight of the ultimate value to be achieved. Thus, war for war's sake, which in Judaism is represented by Amalek, is the essence of evil. There can be no compromise in the opposition to such a policy. Duels to vindicate one's honor are heinously sinful. Sadism and masochism are not to be tolerated. Even asceticism is frowned upon in that it is held to be a form of violence against the self, except in the very special cases where nothing less will help one to overcome physically or spiritually self-destructive behavior.

Violence Against the Self

It is in the light of this brief statement on the approach of Judaism to violence that we can proceed to analyze many different kinds of violence. Some I shall discuss briefly, others at greater length. My first category is violence against oneself. The first instance of that is suicide, which is prohibited. If the Halakhah had a prohibition against self-incrimination and the confession of a criminal was of no value in a criminal prosecution, then this form of violence against one's self was regarded by Maimonides as unacceptable because there are people who want to destroy themselves and may seek to do so by confessing to the commission of crimes.[3]

It is remarkable that in the thirteenth century Maimonides should have been concerned with the death impulse emphasized by Sigmund Freud centuries later, and this is the very reason that Maimonides gives for outlawing confessions in a criminal prosecution. Still another form of violence against the self is heroism, risking one's life to save another. This, too, is a form of violence against one's self, entering upon what in Halakhah is called *safek sakanah*. I enter upon a course of conduct which might lead to my end, but I am hoping to save someone who is in a *vadai sakanah*. definitely in danger of losing his life. This problem is discussed in

3. Mishneh Torah, XIV, Judges, Hilkhot Sanhedrin 28.6.

commentaries on the Rambam, especially the *Kesef Mishneh* and the *Shulhan Arukh*.

During the months immediately following the Yom Kippur War, a case arose in the Israeli army with regard to this legal issue. Israeli soldiers had been given an order not to bathe in the Suez Canal because of the danger; yet, because of the heat, many soldiers did violate the command and bathed in the Canal. Certain Orthodox soldiers raised the question whether soldiers who obeyed the command might lawfully risk their lives to save those who seemed ready to forfeit their lives by violating the command and bathing in the waters of the Suez in order to refresh themselves. The Israeli rabbinate resolved the question in the affirmative. The soldiers were permitted to enter a *safek sakanah*, a possibility of danger, in order to save those soldiers who were in a *vadai sakanah*, a certainty of danger. What is especially interesting is the rationale set forth in a responsum by Rabbi Yehuda Gershuni, the great talmudic scholar.[4] Gershuni's rationale was simply that the mere fact that someone recklessly endangers his own life does not mean that he has forfeited God's interest in him. His body does not belong to him. It is God's. Therefore, it is the duty of bystanders not to suppose that it "serves him right" if he were killed.

The same principle, that one's body is not his to forfeit, applies also to organ transplants. Halakhah does not accept the notion that irreversible brain damage constitutes death. May a man leave a will to the effect that should he suffer irreversible brain damage his heart should be donated to another? Unfortunately, according to Halakhah, he is not the proprietor of his organs and therefore cannot make a decision with regard to their disposition. The Jewish principle is that the body does not belong to the individual, and if the body does not belong to the individual, then the mere fact that one risks it does not relieve a bystander from entering into *safek sakanah* in order to save the person.[5]

This principle also relates to the problem of abortion, which may be regarded as violence against the person. Generally speaking, abortion is prohibited according to Jewish law unless there is danger to the mother. At that time the foetus is in the category of a *rodef*: it is threatening the life of the mother and therefore can be removed. However, in this connection too there is a tremendous literature

4. Yehuda Gershuni, "Or ha-Mizrach," *World Zionist Organization*, 21, no. I (Tishre 5732, 1972), 3–8.

5. J. Emden, *She'elat Yavetz* (Altona, c. 1740), Responsum 43.

debating this subject, and as far back as two centuries ago, one of the great talmudic scholars wrote that an abortion should be permitted where the child would be a *mamzer* (a bastard) and consequently would suffer immeasurably.[6] The criterion here is not physical suffering. This opinion is not concerned with abortions to save children who would have been diseased or physically handicapped, but abortions to spare a child the emotional hurt of being treated as an outcast in a society which frowns upon bastards and does not give them the right to marry as they chose. In a case such as this, violence against life was permitted because life without a certain quality was not regarded as sufficiently sacred to warrant the avoidance of violence.

This brings us to the most problematic of all situations involving violence against self-martyrdom. While the concept of martyrdom may have been a psychological means for Jews to confront their situation, from the point of view of the halakhic value system of Judaism, it is not a *mitzvah* of the first order. It is a much greater *mitzvah* to save one's life, and we are placing things in the wrong perspective when we put the emphasis on martyrdom instead of on self-help and self-preservation. Zionist activism is therefore not a new position, for this was the position of Judaism throughout the ages. It was possible in the nineteenth and twentieth centuries to do more about self-preservation than one was able to do before, but at no time in Jewish history was martyrdom thought of as preferable to self-preservation. This is an important point in understanding the Jewish situation.

Thus, to begin with, martyrdom is to be avoided if at all possible. No place in the Torah, no place in the written law, is it a *mitzvah* to sacrifice one's life for God. However, you will find in the Torah the command to preserve one's life. When we seek sources concerning martyrdom in talmudic literature, we find only three situations in which one is expected to submit to being killed: if one is asked to murder another, to commit illicit intercourse, or to commit idolatry. Therefore, when we think of the martyrs who heroically declared that they would rather die than be captured at Masada, it would be very difficult in halakhic terms to say that they performed the *mitzvah* of dying *al kiddush ha-Shem*, for the

---

6. *Mamzerut* (technical bastardy), according to Jewish law, applies only to the offspring of adulterous or incestuous sexual relationships, not to children born out of wedlock, and proof of *mamzerut* is most difficult. See my *One Man's Judaism* (New York, 1970), pp 212-16.

sanctity of God's name. It is a misreading of Jewish law to give primacy to martyrdom.

The term *kiddush ha-Shem* is used in talmudic literature not only in connection with death but also in connection with life.[7] In talmudic discourse *kiddush ha-Shem* means the following: so deport yourself that anyone seeing your behavior will say, "Blessed is that man's God." When I return a trove to a non-Jew, or when a non-Jew gives me change in excess of that to which I am entitled and I return the change and he says, "That is an honest man; blessed is the God that inspires that man to perform good deeds"—that is *kiddush ha-Shem*. This is the only talmudic definition we have of *kiddush ha-Shem*: to prompt someone to acknowledge that the Jewish God must be great to inspire the kind of behavior that is observed in the Jew.

It has been suggested that Jews at one period substituted martyrdom for actual resistance, and in the modern age we have reverted again to active resistance. This thesis is difficult to accept, however, since Jews have always engaged in every type of defense that was possible. There were four types of response behavior that were possible when Jews were subject to violence: they could engage in self-defense and always did; they could submit to martyrdom; they could engage in flight; or they could accommodate, as the Marranos did.

Halakhah prefers self-defense, but many of us, under the influence of modern theorists such as Hannah Arendt, unfortunately think that *kiddush ha-Shem* was preferable to the preservation of life. But Jews, we must remember, during the Holocaust and prior to it as well, were under an enormous disadvantage when self-help or self-preservation was involved. At least four or five points must be considered by us. First, there were many instances of self-defense in Jewish history, but Jews too often found themselves defenseless in the face of superior numbers, training, and weaponry of their attackers. As early as 1096 at Bishop Square, Mainz, the Jews fought valiantly against the Crusaders. Salo Baron has written that although in 1648 Polish Jews defended many cities against besieging Cossacks, they never had sufficient arms and hardly ever had any military training. Furthermore, Jews were always widely scattered and easily exposed to the wrath of their neighbors. The Jews were not notorious cowards—this is an unfortunate canard. As Israel Abraham writes:

---

7. Louis Jacobs, *Jewish Values* (London, 1960), chap. 5, pp. 74–85.

The Spanish armies contained a large number of Jewish soldiers who fought both under the Cross and the Crescent in the great wars that raged between the Christians and the Moors. The martial spirit of the Jews of Spain showed itself in their constant claim of the right to wear arms and engage in knightly pastimes. Spanish mobs did not attack the Jewish quarters with impunity, but elsewhere in Europe and in the East, the Jews occasionally displayed a courage and a proficiency in self-help which, had it been more frequently exercised, would have put an entirely different complexion on the relations between the governments of many states and their Jewish subjects in later centuries.[8]

A curious sidelight on the courage of Jews is cast by the fact that the royal lion-tamers in Spain were Jews. One Jew was also a famous pirate who prepared a strong fleet to meet the Spanish galleys, as the English state papers of the year 1521 bear witness. Yet, and this is my second point, as always, the Jewish situation was unique. It was not only that Jews were defenseless. A Muslim minority in a Christian country could always threaten the assailants with reprisals against the Christian minorities in other lands, but Jews, even when they were in a position to deal a strong blow, found that they had to subordinate the destiny of their particular community to the welfare of the whole people. They had a strong sense of solidarity with their coreligionists everywhere, and thus, for example, the Jews of Tulczyn in 1648 refrained from attacking treacherous fellow combatants among the noblemen. They chose to die instead when their leaders exhorted them: "We are in exile among the nations. If you lay hands upon the nobles, then all the kings of Christianity will hear of it and take revenge on all our brethren in the dispersion, God forbid."

In our own century we have a tragic but eloquent example of what the Jews always dreaded. I refer to the bullet fired in 1938 by Herschel Grynzpan, whose story is beautifully told by Abram Sachar in *Sufferance is the Badge*.[9] At that time Poland was calling back all of her citizens, and Herschel Grynzpan's parents were caught in a vise. After receiving a letter from his parents describing their distress, he decided to take revenge by destroying some great Nazi officials, made his way into an embassy in Paris, and killed a

---

8. Israel Abrahams, *Jewish Life in the Middle Ages*, ed. by C. Roth (London, 1932), p 253.

9. A. L. Sachar, *Sufferance is the Badge* (New York, 1939), pp. 60–68.

third-rate bureaucrat of Nazidom. That shot was the pretext for the dreadful pogrom of November 1938, which precipitated a reprisal against all the Jews in Germany.

Is the situation so different today? Self-defense may sometimes be helpful to one Jewish community, but Jews must always be terribly concerned about how it will affect Jewish communities elsewhere. Thus Jews in South Africa are concerned when the State of Israel exercises its sovereign right to vote in the United Nations in accordance with the dictates of its conscience against South Africa. And the Jews of the Soviet Union are hostages in order to force Jews in the United States not to be too militant in support of the Jackson Amendment. Thus, the uniqueness of the Jewish situation has a very important impact on the use of self-defense by Jews in any part of the world, whether in 1648 or 1938 or 1974. The problem of our dispersion and our sense of responsibility for each other prompts us to be more circumspect before we resort to tactics that may avail in one place but can cause irreparable damage in another.

Thus, when Jews were able to engage in self-defense they did, but not always was this, the halakhic desideratum, available to them. Not always was it possible; sometimes for logistical reasons it was impossible. After Germany's defeat in World War 1, havoc broke loose in Germany. Rosa Luxemburg was done to death as she was being carried to prison, and there was fear in Berlin that the Jewish quarter would be attacked. Jewish front-line veterans formed a unit for self-defense and the catastrophe was averted. In Germany this was possible, but in Poland there was a different situation to confront. Poles sought to expel the Ukrainians from eastern Galicia. They stormed Lemberg on November 22, 1918, and promised their troops, in good Cossack manner, that as a reward they would receive permission to plunder the Jews for forty-eight hours. The Jewish self-defense was disarmed; bars and bolts were removed from the Jewish quarter by squads of engineers with their equipment; and a pogrom ensued in which seventy-three were killed on the spot, while many died later of their wounds.

In addition to these two external problems, the might of the enemy and the dispersion of the Jews, there were also internal problems. Jews were always a thinking people and were always plagued by ideology. Even when they agreed among themselves on self-defense they could not always agree on methods because of ideological differences. Thus, for example, the horrors of Kishinev in 1903 prompted Hayyim Nahman Bialik and Simon Dubnow to complain that Jews permit themselves to go to slaughter. And when the pogroms of 1905 came around the Jews prepared themselves. They were going to resist and fight for self-preservation. But alas, by the time the pogrom epidemic of 1905 broke out, every tiny faction among the Jews was stuck fast in an ideological web and the attainment of unity proved impossible. Israel Zangwill derided the numerous factions within Jewish self-defense organizations in his "Ghetto Comedies," and Milton Konvitz, in his essay "From Jewish Rights to Human Rights," bears out this analysis. Konvitz gives the details of the events of 1905 and shows how the effectiveness of these groups was sapped by class and party divisions. In Zhitomir, for instance, there were three separate defense groups: a Bund defense unit, a Poalei Zion self-defense unit, and a non-labor Zionist defense unit. The result was that coordinated self-defense proved impossible. Similar was the experience of the Jewish Defense League. It started off simply as a self-defense organization, but soon it became political with the result that its effectiveness was virtually destroyed. This involvement in ideology is one of the problems we constantly face, for war requires regimentation, the galvanization of a force.

A further point is prompted by the kabbalists in the Middle Ages, who tried to rush the advent of the Messiah. There were speculative kabbalists who were interested in theory, but there were also operative kabbalists who sought to accomplish practical results—to twist God's arm, so to speak, and hasten the coming of the Messiah. The whole concept of the making of a Golem indicates the extent to which Jews were always interested in self help rather than in martyrdom. They did not rely on God alone. They wanted to push God, to force Him to act. As in many other instances in the past, they did not have the right formula; they did not have atomic weapons, but they never preferred slaughter to survival.

This brings me to the last point, a point which is developed very fully in the Holocaust literature, particularly by a young writer named Michael Shazar, who points to the fact that even during the Holocaust, in addition to self-defense, there was a manner of resistance which is a form of survival. Jews who did not survive physically at least tried to show the Nazis that they could not crush them spiritually. Out of the Holocaust came a responsum about one Jew in the concentration camps who insisted on putting his phylacteries on his head no matter what the Nazis did to him. Work started very early in the morning, so he could not do this secretly; it was done openly, as an act of defiance. Shazar talks extensively about the act of defiance as a way of saying, "You can break my back, but you are not going to crush my spirit; I shall continue to live, and even if I don't live physically, I am going to live, my people are going to live, my traditions are going to continue to live." Finally the Nazis decided to brand a swastika into the forehead of this Jew who put his *tefillin* on his forehead every day. The Jew then felt that he could not put the *tefillin* over a swastika since by Jewish law nothing can intervene between the skin and the *tefillin*. But he wanted to know whether under those circumstances he would be permitted to put a bandage on the swastika so the *tefillin* would not rest on an unholy symbol. This was a unique kind of resistance, and the emphasis was not on dying for the sake of getting some share of the world to come. It was not martyrdom to be assured of immortal life, as in Islam, or to atone for the sins of others, as in Christianity. It was a way of struggling to ensure the survival of the Jewish people and their tradition in whatever way possible.

In Germany in 1946, immediately after the Holocaust, I saw a *siddur* that had been handwritten from memory by a Jew who was afraid that the Jewish prayer book would disappear from the face of the earth. This point can perhaps best be summed up with a beautiful insight by Yitzhak Nissenbaum, one of the martyrs of the Holocaust. Nissenbaum, in an unenviable position, had to preach to the inmates of the concentration camp on the Day of Atonement. *Kiddush ha-Shem* may be a *mitzvah*, he told them, it may be a *mitzvah* to sanctify God's name, but the circumstances vary from time to time and from place to place. In the Middle Ages, he said, Jews may have felt that they were performing the commandment of *kiddush ha-Shem* by committing suicide because at that time the Christians wanted to conquer the souls of Jews and convert them to Christianity. Therefore, the only way to frustrate Christians was by making it impossible for them to win Jewish souls; if a Jew died, then Christianity lost a target for baptism. Today, Nissenbaum told the other inmates, what the Nazi wants is not the soul but the body of the Jew. He wants Jews to perish. Therefore, the greatest *mitzvah* is to survive, to frustrate the Nazis by preserving Jewish lives. Therefore, he urged them, escape, hide in the forest, join the underground, do whatever you must to live. Nissenbaum was being consistent with the Jewish tradition when he placed the greatest emphasis on self-preservation.

Violence Against Others

Now I come to the second category, violence against other human beings, and the best I can do as a political scientist is to classify the material and offer several illustrations of each type. There are many forms of this type of violence. First, there is violence against one's attacker, which is permitted. Halakhah allows one to engage in self-defense against the attacker, who is called a *rodef*: It is licit for me to kill anyone who wants to murder me or sexually abuse me, but this is the only justification that the Talmud gives for the exercise of violence other than by constituted authority, as in war or by sentence of a court. (Sol Roth's article on the "Morality of Revolution" discusses this in great detail.[10]) The concept of *rodef* was extended to include informers. Jews were allowed to kill an informer, even try him and execute him, because he was attacking the Jewish community. If he could no longer perform his nefarious deeds—if, for example, there was a way to make certain that he would never inform against the Jews again—then the death penalty was not allowed. Thus, execution was permitted as a preventive measure, not a punitive one.[11]

In our day it has been suggested by Aharon Lichtenstein that when a person threatens the Jewish community not only by informing but also by adversely affecting the entire social, economic, or health structure of a community, he is in the category of a rodef; and violence against such a person would be permitted. A threat to poison the water or sabotage the communications or power systems of a country would come under this classification.

Third, one may engage in violence to redeem captives because captives are in danger of losing their lives, and thus one would be acting to save other people. Jews always have assumed that anyone taken into captivity might suffer the fate of those Israeli prisoners who were taken by Syria in the Yom Kippur War. This may help us to understand why the patriarch Jacob did not object to the plan of his sons Simeon and Levi to weaken the inhabitants of Shechem by making them undergo circumcision. The Bible clearly indicates that their sister Dinah, after her rape, was still in captivity. Simeon and Levi wanted to save her from the house of her captor, and for that purpose the use of violence is permitted. This, however, did involve approval of the massacre of the weakened Shechemites,

10. Sol Roth, "The Morality of Revolution," *Judaism* 20, no. 4 (Fall 1971), 431–42

11. I. A. Agus, *Rabbi Meir of Rothenburg* (Philadelphia, 1947), II, p. 665–66.

for which Jacob bitterly censured his sons prior to his death.[12]

Fourth, one is allowed to engage in violence in defense of property, but that is a limited license; for even then, in the final analysis, one may engage in violence only to preserve life. If I may kill to defend my property it is, says the Talmud, because there is a presumption that the burglar knows that it is human nature for a proprietor or the owner of a house to do everything to defend his family. Therefore, the burglar knows that he may be killed, and when he comes to burglarize the property he is assuming that he himself may have to kill in self-defense. Consequently, the proprietor may kill on the presumption that the attacker is going to kill. Again, resort to violence from a halakhic point of view revolves around the central value of the sanctity of life, and these are the only circumstances under which I can defend my property at the risk of someone else's life.

Fifth, one may sometimes resort to force in defense of one's religious convictions, but not to the point of killing. Thus, I have a right to expel from my house a slave who has been emancipated and now may no longer cohabit with a non-Jewish slave. If I injure him in the process of expelling him, I might not have to pay, but I may not kill him except in self-defense (Baba Kama 28a).

Outside my home do I have a right to engage in violence in order to uphold God's honor, to champion God's law? May I kill one who desecrates the Sabbath, or a man and woman engaged in illicit intercourse? In the Bible we are told that Aaron's grandson Phinehas did precisely that. But God's response to him, says Rabbi Naftali Zevi Judah Berlin, was that he was given "a covenant of peace," to calm him and restore his peace of mind. God does not want vindictiveness in His behalf, although the zealous saints sometimes forget this. Vindictiveness brings guilt and guilt feelings in its train.

A distinguished commentator on the Talmud, known as the Makne, provides us with an interesting insight with regard to one of the best known laws of the Bible. In the Book of Deuteronomy we have the laws of war, which direct that if in the course of a war a soldier should fall in love with one of his captives she will enjoy a great measure of humanitarian consideration (Deut. 21:10). If he seeks to marry her he must take a number of steps designed to prevent hasty action and, should marriage follow, to assure the

---

12. See N. Levovitz, *Iyunim be-Seder Bereshit* (Jerusalem, 1967), pp. 264–65 Haamek Davar on Numbers 25:12.

dignity of her person. Many have asked why the Bible is so indulgent as to grant the right to cohabit with a captive and ultimately marry her. However, HaMakne tells us that in time of war it is to be expected that moral standards will be lowered. This might prompt a zealot to try to defend God's honor as Phinehas did. He might kill the soldier and his beloved. Therefore, by being permissive, the Torah protected the soldier and the "beautiful woman" with whom he was infatuated and made any interference by the zealot a capital offense if the zealot should become so exercised over the breach of the moral law that he kills in consequence thereof. In time of war Jewish law does not expect superhuman conduct from those engaged in it.

Another category is violence to avenge wrongs. Under no circumstances are Jews permitted to engage in violence for the sake of vengeance. Such acts of revenge are prohibited by the Bible. Samuel Belkin makes a beautiful point on this subject in his book *In His Image*.[13] Belkin tells us that even though in the ethical literature of Judaism one finds the doctrine of *imitatio Dei*—just as God is merciful we must be merciful, and just as God is kind we must be kind, and just as God is compassionate we must be compassionate—nonetheless one will never find in Jewish literature, either halakhic or aggadic, a statement to the effect that just as God is zealous so must we be zealous, or just as God is vengeful so must we be vengeful.

One exception regarding vengeance begs for explanation, the case of the *goel ha-dam*. If a man commits an accidental murder he is not subject to the death penalty but has the privilege of fleeing to seek asylum in a "city of refuge." A relative of the victim is allowed to pursue him and kill him; the assassin is at the mercy of the blood avenger, the *goel ha-dam*, until he reaches the city of refuge. This would indicate that we do have one situation in which it is permitted to commit violence in order to avenge a wrong. However, this must be understood properly. There is a difference of opinion in the Talmud as to whether this is permissive or mandatory. The prevailing view is that it is permissive—pursuit by the *goel ha-dam* is allowed but is not a *mitzvah*. It is a greater *mitzvah* not to engage in violence. Yet the *goel ha-dam* serves an important purpose within the context of Jewish law in primitive or semiprimitive times.

How, then, in a society with no investigative agencies, did one

---

13. S. Belkin, *In His Image* (New York, 1960), pp. 29–30.

apprehend a killer? There simply was not the law enforcement machinery that is available in modern societies, and what the Torah conceived of was a method of making the law self-operative. When a man killed accidentally the first thing he did was to flee. Instead of trying to hide, he fled immediately to a city of refuge, where he declared himself and received protection from any avenger. In that way it was possible to determine who committed the crime. He was then told that if he had committed the crime intentionally he would be tried for a capital offense. He was brought back in safe custody to the city where the crime was committed and tried there. If he committed the crime with malice or forethought he was executed. If, on the other hand, he committed the crime unintentionally he was brought back to the city of refuge, where he stayed until the high priest died. There he was to atone for his sin.

In other words, according to most authorities, the institution of the *goel ha-dam* was certainly not a *mitzvah*; it was a way of setting the law enforcement machinery in motion by having criminals present themselves for trial. This form of violence was indulged so that society could apprehend those who committed homicides, and from that point on the judicial machinery took its course through trials to determine whether the killing was intentional or unintentional.

Thus we conclude our discussion of the instances of violence by individuals against individuals and move on to violence by the state against individuals, individuals against the state, and violence between states.

Violence Against Constituted Authority

Let us first consider violence against constituted authority. There is a dearth of materials with regard to violence against the Jewish state because Jews have not had a state for such a long time. Yet it would be a mistake to assume that because there was no Jewish state there was no kind of constituted authority with virtual sovereignty in the Jewish community. Jews in their own communities have enjoyed legal autonomy over the centuries; they wanted it and even paid for the right to enjoy it. They taxed themselves in order to have control of their own courts, and very often the king, or feudal lord, entered into an agreement with a Jewish community for a quid pro quo to grant them legal autonomy.

This was the situation in Muslim countries, where all religious minorities enjoyed legal autonomy. Thus, one can visualize violence against constituted authority in a Jewish community which had legal autonomy; but, generally speaking, the commission of such acts was not permitted. The legal term was *mored be-malkhut*, rebellion against the king or against kingship, punishable by death.

The source for this doctrine is not in the Pentateuch but in the Book of Joshua. The Jews, so to speak, delegated the power of enforcement to Joshua and his successors. Very similar to the covenant of Hobbes and Locke was the covenant between the Jews and their king, and one of the provisions of that covenant was that they would give the king obedience. Anyone who did *not* do so could be punished for committing a crime mentioned in the Bible. There is nothing in the Bible about treason, but a man who challenged God's authority or any authority delegated by Him was considered a *rodef*, a pursuer. He was undermining the fabric that kept the community together. Thus Jews developed through the years this notion of a contract between the constituted authority and themselves. There were obligations on both sides, and for the breach of these obligations there were sanctions. This does not mean that because Jews were not permitted to rebel or practice violence against constituted authority they had to be submissive. There is a respectable body of literature sanctioning nonviolent protest and an enormous amount of writing about the ethics of protest against constituted authority. Jews had an obligation to make even kings do the right thing, and certainly those who were responsible for the welfare of the Jewish community. Making them aware of their duties and penitent with regard to their evil was in the best prophetic tradition. The prophets were rebels against constituted authority; but even Elijah, who was the greatest rebel of all and so often in flight from the wrath of Queen Jezebel and King Ahab, paid deference to the king he denounced because it was necessary to respect the king and maintain his authority. Violence was not sanctioned, but there was an ethic of protest.

There is also a Jewish tradition of civil disobedience, and a classic example is to be found in the Talmud itself. The rabbis legislated against the use of wine made by non-Jews and tried to do the same with respect to oil. The Jews accepted the former but not the latter, and the rabbis had to abolish the prohibition. As a result, there is a classic maxim of Jewish law that no court with legislative power can ever legislate anything that the majority of people cannot or will not accept. This is one of the great democratic aspects of Jewish law.

Just as in the United States one can challenge the constitutionality of the President, of Congress, or even of a judge if their actions appear to violate the basic law of the country, so in antiquity Jews were able to challenge the mandate of a king. One was not allowed to rebel, but if one disobeyed on the basis that the command given was in violation of the law of the Torah, one was not punished. A Sanhedrin would hear the case, and there was no punishment if it was found that the king had given an unconstitutional command. This kind of judicial review was also a form of resistance.

In Jewish law there is one additional form of resistance to constituted authority often overlooked—the law of *zaken mamreh*. In this case a high court ruled that an elder or judge had been in error, reversed him, and sent the case back to him. It then became his duty to apply the law as it had been decided by a majority in the high court. If he refused to do so, if he defied the Sanhedrin, he committed an unpardonable offense and a capital crime. However, said the Talmud, while he could be deemed a criminal for breaking the very fabric of the social order and the judicial system, that did not preclude him from going up and down the countryside to preach that the court in Jerusalem had erred. He was guaranteed the right to continue his dissent, not in action but in speech. There would of course be anarchy and bedlam if lower courts did not obey higher courts, but in the talmudic system anyone could proclaim his dissent. Thus the right of protest against constituted authority is deeply rooted in the Jewish tradition.

Generally, one ought to take note of the importance of dissent in Jewish law and in Jewish communal life. The Talmud recorded all dissenting opinions, and there was always the possibility that what was the dissenting view in one century might become the majority view in another, precisely as has happened in the history of the United States. Child labor laws, for example, were held unconstitutional by two courts in succession until a third court finally held them to be constitutional.

However, the major problem in revolts against constituted authority involves not the courts but the underprivileged, those who are disadvantaged by the constituted authority. George Sorel, in *Reflections on Violence* (1961), says that nothing good was ever accomplished except through violence. However, Jewish law holds that violence is not permitted unless life is at stake. Was there, then, any way in which the poor could unshackle the yoke of those who were oppressing them? First, there was the right to strike, which is as ancient as the Talmud itself. Second, the right of the poor was a right against the community, a legal right: the poor did not have to rebel because they could sue the community for subsistence. They did not sue for compassion or empathy but sought enforcement of what was their legal right to live.

The poor could also benefit from the fact that the community had the right to fix wages and prices. The fixing of the price of wheat, for example, was in the hands of the seven elders of the city, who were democratically elected and had the power to adjust the economy in order to cope with crises, with drought, or with agreements in restraint of trade.

In effect, then, what the community had were means to make unnecessary what Herbert Marcuse has called the "counterviolence of the poor." There were built-in techniques to prevent exploitation by the affluent, which, according to Marcuse, constitutes violence against the poor. One such means that deserves special consideration is the closest equivalent that Jewish law has to the modern ombudsman. The Talmud tells us that a group of butchers made an agreement among themselves to control the supply of meat and thus perhaps increase the price. For breach of the agreement the offending party would suffer the destruction of the hides of the cattle he had slaughtered. One butcher committed this offense, and his colleagues destroyed his hides; he sued for damages and won his case. The agreement was nullified because it did not have the approval of the "important man" in town who, so to speak, was the defender of the public interest. Indeed, in labor disputes in the United States it would be advantageous for the public if settlement agreements required not only the approval of employers and employees but also of someone who was designated to see to it that the interest of consumers and the public at large is not placed in jeopardy.

What about violence by Jews not against constituted Jewish authority but against the state in which they live? This has been a basic problem for Jews who live in a country that is not their own. To what extent must they avoid rebellion? First, there is doubt as to whether Judaism would permit a revolution for political freedom, or what we call political sovereignty. This question goes back to the time of the Maccabees, when there was a controversy as to whether the war against the Greeks would have been justified for any goal other than the right to worship God in accordance with their beliefs. Political sovereignty in itself was not deemed very consequential.

Even today, Joseph Schultz takes the position that fighting for political sovereignty may be the undoing of the Jewish people,[14] a view that is certainly consistent with that of the Hasidim in the time of the Maccabees. He maintains that Jews, because of their messianic complex, frequently box themselves in at the risk of their survival, as they did in the years 70-71. He is critical of Chief Rabbi Shlomo Goren and others for encouraging the Jewish people in that complex, for he believes that Jews may not be able to retreat if they become obsessed with the idea that this is the messianic era and that therefore we must not relinquish one inch of Israeli soil. This was the controversy of Rabbi Johanan ben Zakkai, and it may adversely affect present chances for survival as it did in the years 70-71. With regard to rebelling against non-Jewish states, Jews must be cautious, and there are fewer legal ways available to them than when they challenge authority within the Jewish community.

The opposite point of view is represented by Albert Memmi, who holds that what really counts is political sovereignty. According to Memmi, all of Jewish history up until now has been a mistake; the whole Jewish tradition is simply evidence of Jews having been colonialized, developing in the process a rationale and a philosophy of Judaism that made it possible to live as colonials. Now, Memmi says, Jews must determine their own destiny, but the revolution is not yet complete because Jews have not yet substituted a new tradition to provide the ideology appropriate for the new era. What matters, he believes, is for Jews to be completely free and independent.

On the question of whether Jews may engage in violence for the state in which they live, one also finds a difference of opinion The Hofetz Hayyim, who lived only a generation ago and was one of the most respected of all halakhic authorities in the twentieth century, takes the position that Jews should fight for the country in which they live because, according to Halakhah, all rules pertaining to kingship, all laws applicable to Jewish kings, are applicable to non-Jewish kings. Jewish kings are responsible for the maintenance of law and order, and so are non-Jewish kings. We owe them our obedience. Therefore, whatever privileges a Jewish king would have to mobilize, to conscript, and to tax, non-Jewish kings also have; Jews must obey, even to fight in the army of the country in which they live. Others have taken the opposite position. One nineteenth-century authority, for example, felt that

---

14. J. Schultz, "Jewish Militarism and Jewish Survival," *Judaism* 22, no. 4 (Fall 1973), 468–74.

one may not risk one's life in the wars of non-Jews. Certainly a Jew may not be a mercenary.

State Violence Against Individuals

What does the Halakhah have to say about violence by states against individuals? The first form, of course, is punishment and corporal punishment, which in Jewish law meant either capital punishment or lashes. We have very little proof of punishment by imprisonment until the Middle Ages. Certainly one of the greatest achievements of Jewish law is the fact that imprisonment for debt was not authorized either by the Bible or the Talmud. We derive this from a verse in the Bible which speaks of a Hebrew being sold into bondage for theft but not for having borrowed money and being unable to repay. Thus there was no imprisonment for debt and ancient Jewish society was spared the scourge of sixteenth, seventeenth, and eighteenth-century England until the days of Charles Dickens and his protests against imprisonment for debt. The Talmud expanded upon this and it protected the debtor not only against slavery or imprisonment but also against search and seizure. According to biblical and talmudic law, one could not enter his house to see what he had.

Unfortunately, both of these rules for the protection of the debtor were relaxed in the Middle Ages. It is a rather sad chapter in Jewish history that imprisonment for debt was then introduced.[15] Apparently there were too many Jews who owed money while living in luxury, and Rabbenu Tam held that it was necessary to enter their homes and make searches and seizures.

When Jews in the Middle Ages got into the moneylending business some biblical and talmudic prohibitions were relaxed and some rights were expanded. For example, the right to privacy which dates back to the earliest days of Jews in the desert, was expanded in the Talmud in a magnificent way. Jews had the right to privacy some three to four thousand years before Justice Louis D. Brandeis recognized that it was emerging in American constitutional law. In the Middle Ages the right to privacy was expanded. The French talmudist Menahem ben Solomon of Perpignan, known as the Meiri, even talked about "bugging"; although electronic eavesdropping was then unknown, he wrote about the right to privacy with regard to speech. This is another example of the ways in which Jewish

---

15. M. Elon, "Le-Ma'asar be-Mishpat ha-Ivri," *Jubilee Volume for Pinhas Rosen* (Jerusalem, 1962), pp. 171–201.

law was very protective of the accused.

With regard to self-incrimination, I already indicated that the prohibition against it was based upon the fact that Jews did not want to give any scope to the death impulse. However, what is generally not well known is that the Jewish right against self-incrimination is still broader than any such right elsewhere. In the United States one has a right not to confess, and if a confession is coerced one can plead so. This is a constitutional privilege rather than a right. Moreover, if one refuses to take the stand in one's own defense, the judge will tell the jury to remember that the mere fact that the defendant did not take the stand in his defense is not to be held against him. His failure to testify is not to be regarded as consequential, even though it is often difficult for the jury to ignore his refusal. During the 1950s, for example, many individuals lost their jobs not because they were proved to be Communists but because they failed to indicate whether or not they were. In effect, they had no protection whatever from the self-incrimination clauses of the Constitution of the United States or the Constitution of the State of New York. In Jewish law, however, it is not a privilege against self-incrimination—it is an absolute immunity. I can come into court and say I killed so-and-so, but by Jewish law such a statement must be held of no consequence. This is the extent to which Halakhah protects the individual against one form of violence by the state, forced confessions.

What is Judaism's position on religious coercion? One cannot gainsay that according to Judaism the state can coerce individuals to perform God's commandments. There are many rationalizations in the apologetic literature for this point of view—none very satisfying. Karl Lewellyn used to say that in every society there are individuals who resist while most people are "drifters," conformists who go along with the stream. Maimonides seemed to feel that only some kind of emotional block would prompt an individual to exercise his will against God's will and that coercion, or the threat of it, would make him identify once again with the majority. It restores his sanity, so to speak, his emotional balance, his real free will. In modern times the problem is a very serious one—especially for the leaders of religious Zionism in the State of Israel. Would they exercise coercion against the minority if they were in the majority? Replies have been made in this century by Chief Rabbis Abraham Kook and Yitzhak Herzog, who were deeply committed to the establishment of a Jewish state, and by the distinguished halakhic authority known as the Hazon Ish, who was opposed to the establishment of the State of Israel: they all agreed that there should be no coercion whatever.

There is one exception in the halakhic tradition to the rule that dissenters can be coerced. If a Jewish child has been taken captive in infancy, has been raised among non-Jews and then restored to the Jewish community, there is no right to coerce him. He cannot be accused of disobeying God's will because of some emotional or intellectual failure. Rabbis Kook and Herzog, as well as the Hazon Ish, argue that everyone today is in the category of such a captive Jewish infant. Because of the environment in which we live and the winds of doctrine blowing everywhere, most of us are the captives of mores and outlooks to which we succumb unwittingly. In this sense, all are comparable to the infants against whom no religious coercion is to be exercised. Indeed, this is a legal fiction. The early pioneers of Israel, and even its most distinguished leaders, were raised in environments in which there was total commitment to all of Judaism. Their rebellion came much after their infancy, and it is nonsense to regard them as Jews who in infancy were taken captive by non-Jews. But legal fictions are a very much respected manner of updating legal systems, including the Halakhah.

Violence Among States

With regard to violence by states against other states, there is a rich halakhic literature distinguishing between obligatory wars and permissive wars. Much has been written about this subject, notably Maurice Lamm's essay "Red or Dead" and Solomon Zevin's essay in *L'Or ha-Halakhah*. Let me also make but a few points here.

In the halakhic view an obligatory war—to conquer the Land of Israel and to defend it—was mandated by God. A permissive war—to expand one's territory or to improve the economy—required the combined consent of the king and the Sanhedrin of seventy-one, the group which had supreme legislative and judicial authority. Thus the executive, legislative, and judicial authorities of the Jewish state had to agree. In the United States the pattern is very similar, except that the Supreme Court has no share in the decision.

When the Sanhedrin and the king agreed, however, could their declaration of war ever be regarded as unjust? Maimonides would not so hold. Yet centuries later Samuel David Luzzatto took the position that there is no biblical or talmudic justification for a war against anyone who is not an enemy and offers no threat to your safety. The fact that the Bible speaks of war against *oyveikhem*—your foe—means that wars may be waged only against those who present a danger. In any other circumstance the waging of war is not permitted.

As for serving in the armies of states in which Jews lived, we have already seen that this was permitted by most halakhic authorities. When Jews began to enjoy the blessings of democratic countries they even fought for the right so to serve. Asser Levy in New Amsterdam insisted on the privilege and refused to pay a tax in lieu of military duty. Dubnow cites many other such instances. We ought to remember, moreover, that Asser Levy was no assimilationist Jew: he also fought for the right to have a kosher abbatoir in New Amsterdam.

The final point one might make with regard to the exercise of violence is that it is unlikely that it will accomplish its objective. I have already indicated that one may exercise violence for the loftiest value, which is the sanctity of life itself. But if there is little likelihood that this value will be conserved, and if, on the other hand, it will be placed in greater jeopardy, then one must be very hesitant about exercising violence.

This point is especially relevant to Israel's present problem of the return of the conquered territories. On the one hand, you have in Israel a very respectable group of halakhic authorities who argue that Jews may not give back an inch of sacred soil on obvious halakhic grounds. This land is ours, they say, given to us by God. God ordered us to take it and to hold it by risking our lives for it. We were told to engage in war—in violence—for that purpose, and war ipso facto means the loss of life. Therefore, Chief Rabbi Yitzhak Nissim, and Rabbi Zevi Yehuda Kook, the son of the former chief rabbi, are unequivocally opposed to the return of any part of the land.

The "doves," on the other side, include Rabbi Joseph B. Soloveitchik, whose public statements and essays on the subject have received attention all over the world. To him the issue is whether the sanctity of life is not so great that if Jews can buy peace with the return of some of the soil it is not more important to save life. Yet how do these authorities answer the question of Rabbi Nissim, which on its face is such a logical one. The answer is simple: Jews were told to go to war only when victory was something that was likely. It is a halakhic requirement that one does not engage in violence or war unless victory is probable. When God told the Jews to conquer the Holy Land He was on their side. Today victory is not necessarily something of which Israel can be assured and thus the problem is whether on the basis of the present situation Halakhah would dictate the return of the territories.

In this connection Rabbi Yehuda Gershuni makes a fine point. Gershuni cites the story of Johanan ben Zakkai, who in the year 70 C.E. held that Judea could not win against the Romans. Victory was impossible. The Zealots had said they could win, and this was the issue of their day When Johanan ben Zakkai was about to die he was agitated, and when his students asked him why he trembled he said, "Why should I not tremble! If I were about to face a human sovereign, I would tremble. Now, when I am about to face the King of Kings, should I not tremble?" Perhaps, said Rabbi Gershuni, his speech revealed his feeling of guilt. Perhaps he had done wrong. Perhaps he capitulated to the Romans when he should have stood by the side of his own kin who wanted to resist. Rabbi Gershuni based his insight on the fact that Ben Zakkai committed a "Freudian slip" when he told his students, "Prepare a chair for King Hezekiah." Why did Hezekiah come to his mind? Simply because that king had had the same challenge in his day. Sennacherib was outside the gates of Jerusalem. King Hezekiah did not know whether to fight the head of the great empire of Assyria. Could little Judea stand up against that lion? He decided to fight and a miracle occurred: the enemy was stricken with a plague and Jerusalem was liberated from siege. On his deathbed Rabbi Johanan ben Zakkai thought of him and wondered whether perhaps he too could have relied on a miracle. Or perhaps the situation was then different and one should not have relied on miracles thereafter.

Israel's present situation raises still other problems. Even if one were to disagree with the Hasidim of the Maccabean period and hold that political sovereignty is a cause for which war and violence are justified according to Halakhah, one must ponder whether in the modern age any small state can ever achieve it—at any sacrifice. Israel is now totally dependent for survival upon the United States, and to wage suicidal warfare in defiance of the will of the United States may be to engage in a war in which victory is virtually impossible. Could this be a just war?

The Talmud, in connection with a slave who is only half-slave but half-free—as in the case of a slave who had been owned by partners, one of whom emancipated him while the other retained his ownership—suggests that no one is free unless he has but one master, God. Even the Exilarch in Babylon was not a free agent; he had a human and foreign master other than God. Can Israel delude itself into believing that it is free, autonomous, and sovereign?

Perhaps Israel's destiny now—even as a state—is to play its historic role, which, in the view of Jacob Talmon, is ever to question the legitimacy of human authority over other humans. Those imposing authority resort to violence; so do those resisting authority. The question always is not whether there shall be violence but when and how. This is the authentic halakhic approach, and it will still bear further analysis and development.

In a statement made after the Yom Kippur War, Andre Schwarz-Bart said: "We [Jews] are human beings like everyone else. We have hardly any illusions on the subject and any time we had a national history it was as bloody as any other. Nevertheless, it seems to me that it is not because of our injustices, but because of our insistence upon absolute justice, even when we were unfaithful to it, that we have come to experience our particular fate among the nations."

The truth is that we Jews have had a tremendous amount of violence in our history. Yet we never lost sight of what was absolute justice, and we tried at least to curb, to regulate, and in someway to make a contribution to human dignity and sanctity in the unique way that was ours.

The Underground: An Halakhic View

Violent acts were committed recently in Israel by presumably religious persons for allegedly religious goals. It behooves us, therefore, to ask when, according to the Halakhah, one may engage in violence even to accomplish a halakhic purpose.

Needless to say, a state must resort to violence which the Halakhah sanctions, but the Halakhah dictates when and how. The punishment of criminals is one such instance. The waging of war—offensive, defensive, and preemptive—is another. Less known examples are forced medical treatment and preventive detention. These acts of violence by the state can be deemed fulfillment of religious obligations, but even states founded on the principle of separation between church and state commit them. Such states also punish people who are guilty of crimes whose criminal character derives from the religious tradition, such as adultery, incest, sodomy and blasphemy. Individuals, however, are more restricted than states in the pursuit of violence, even if the goal is religious.

Not all who planned and executed the acts of terror against Arabs in Israel were motivated by halakhic considerations. For many the acts of terror were simply designed to remove an enemy—a measure in self-defense sanctioned by the Halakhah.

For others, however, a greater purpose was being served—the reclamation of sacred soil from non-Jews and thus allegedly a step to hasten the coming of the Messiah.

Overwhelmingly, the rabbinate in Israel and abroad denounced what the terrorists did. They rejected the terrorists' conception of what their religious obligation was, and held that the Written and Oral Law give no sanction to what they did. Yet there are times when an individual may engage in violent self-help when he is motivated by what he deems his duty to God and himself, and intellectual honesty requires that one consider these situations.

The thrust of this paper is to establish, first, the fact that Judaism does not outlaw all violence either by the state or even by individuals; second, that Judaism sometimes permits a Jew to resist even the authority of government and not only by passive disobedience; and third, that in given circumstances one individual may act violently against another without seeking the involvement of the state. Lastly, it will deal with the issue most relevant to the recent happenings in Israel which involve the priority of values for which there can be resort to violence—and more specifically, when does God wish one to use violence to fulfill His commands and when does He prefer only verbal action—persuasion and not force.

I.

It must be obvious that when one practices violence against an aggressor to save one's own life, one is committed to a value—the value of one's own life. One has a right to prefer one's own life to the life of the attacker. However, may one use an innocent bystander to protect oneself?

Or may one kill another, complying with the request of a villain, in order to save one's own life? Jewish law in such cases says that it is morally wrong to do this, although one may not be punished for so doing except by God Himself.

Jewish law also held that if an enemy should demand that a city surrender to it one person—male or female—or face total destruction, it is better that all should die rather than save themselves by betraying an innocent human being. In Jewish history, communities may have been saved by volunteers who martyred themselves. But to use the life of an innocent person for any purpose was absolutely forbidden, even if the purpose was to save many lives.

Are modern terrorists guided by such an ethic? I refer especially to terrorists who are killing their own people, not even enemies. They have no regard whatever for human life. And when they are the trainees of a foreign state who infiltrate another country to destroy it, they certainly are not guided by any regard for the value of human life.

What was so remarkable about the underground activity of Jews in Palestine before the establishment of the State of Israel was that they attacked principally military objectives, never civilians, and only rarely the military personnel of Britain. They were mindful of the sanctity of human life. How can one equate them with most terrorists of today!

During the Holocaust many Jews suffered martyrdom because they would not substitute someone else for themselves on the lists for the gas chambers. It also happened at other times in Jewish history that many a community refused to resist and kill Christian attackers because of the disastrous effect their resistance would have on Jews elsewhere.

From all of this it appears that even in self-defense one must be mindful of values. Even in self-defense there is no absolute right to engage in violence. Thus, while Jewish law does not absolutely outlaw the right to rebel or resort to violence, it is preoccupied with the when, where and how.

II.

Individuals may commit acts of violence against the state but such acts are so dangerous to the self that only in the most unusual of circumstances should one resort to them.

The Bible provides for the appointment of a king, but the king is not an absolute monarch. He is subject to the Law. He is not the legislator. Only God and those who are the custodians of the Law are. Cursing God was a capital offense, but not cursing the king. Indeed the Torah provides no punishment for disobedience to the ruler. One is punished only for disobedience to God. The ruler too must function within the parameters of the Torah as must everyone else, and the ruler can be punished for a breach of the Law.

One might call this a constitutional limitation on the executive authority. However, when Joshua succeeded Moses as the Jewish leader, the Jewish people—not God—extended Joshua's powers. They promised obedience to his commands and authorized him to give the death penalty to anyone who would disobey him. It is only because of this that revolution against constituted authority—treason—became a capital offense. The people made this decision. However, they could not possibly have meant to give the monarch the right to do what the Torah binds him not to do. Thus, even after the so-called grant of power to Joshua by the people, the ruler could not order anyone to do what was in violation of the Law, nor could he violate the Law himself.

The Talmud has a very impressive discussion of this limitation, but I will cite one clear biblical illustration. King Ahab coveted the vineyard of Naboth. Naboth refused to part with his patrimony. Queen Jezebel goaded her husband to charge Naboth with cursing God and the king, whereupon Naboth was executed and his property was confiscated.

Mind you, no death penalty would have ensued for cursing the king alone. Ahab had to add the charge that God too was cursed. However, Elijah denounced the king with the immortal words: "Did you commit murder and then become your victim's heir?" This story encapsulates two fundamental views of Judaism—no monarch is above the Law, and no human being may profit by his own wrong.

The notion that there are limitations on all who exercise authority is so all-pervasive in Jewish thought that in the Middle Ages the Torah was the basis for denying even a majority of the community the power to deprive the minority of its rights—even the right not to be forced to bear an unreasonable share of the community's tax burden.

And when the ruler orders what is wrongful, one can disobey. A Jewish court will uphold the disobedience. This is a just rebellion. The right to rebel is thus safeguarded by the Jewish legal order when the ruler, so to speak, breaks the Law or orders others to do so.

From sources such as exist in Jewish literature one would have expected Christian theologians of the first millennium to have been less tolerant of the tyrants of their day. Why they preached unswerving obedience instead may have been due to many factors. In the later Middle Ages and on the threshold of the modern period, the Bible became the inspiration for all who sought to end tyranny and injustice. Before the 12th century, however, this was not generally accepted.

During that same period Christian theologians were also too willing to reconcile themselves to the institution of slavery, which Jewish law frowned upon. Christian theologians preferred the Aristotelian notion that slavery was natural, or the Stoic perspective that slavery of the soul could not be achieved and therefore slavery of the body did not matter, or the Augustinian view that slavery was punishment for sin.

In any event, one cannot fault people who have the courage to defy constituted authority when that authority acts or gives orders which offend the constitution, or a higher law, or what is generally accepted to be right and proper. This is the Jewish view, and most revolutions prior to those of this century were of that kind.

The revolt of the Maccabees, and the approval given to the desecration of the Sabbath to further that revolt, attest to the right to resort to violence against constituted authority. And I doubt that the fact that the authority was non-Jewish made a difference.

III.

According to Jewish law, one may resort to violence in defense of one's self and one may also act with violence to protect another from murder or rape. In such cases one is morally bound to come to the rescue of the victim and one may even kill the offender. However, may one resort to violence to stop a fellow Jew from committing the sin of idolatry—as heinous an offense as there is—or the desecration of the Sabbath? It was argued a fortiori. If one may use force to stop an individual from hurting another human being all the more that it should be possible to use the same force—even to kill—against one who flouts God's will. God is, after all, more important than individuals! As sound as the argument is, it was not accepted, and the Law is clearly established that God will take care of His enemies and wants man to take care only of his.

This is a remarkable conclusion[1] and should deter zealots from acting as surrogates to enforce God's law. When human life requires protection, or human chastity and dignity, the situation is quite different. That Aaron's grandson, Phinehas, resorted to violence in Moses' day required God's forgiveness, but his behavior must never be a model for Jews. No Jew may arrogate to himself the compliment that his motives are as pure as those of Phinehas and, therefore, he can emulate Phinehas in zealotry.

There is a biblical command that a Jew must chastise another who is committing a sin. And the rabbis permit the use of violence. One may strike a fellow Jew to obtain compliance with God's mandates. As far back as talmudic times the rabbis questioned whether this rule is still applicable. They doubted that even in their generation there was anyone "saintly" enough to perform the commandment without malice. Consequently, the use of coercion to force a Jew to obey a religious commandment is no longer lawful. And Maimonides' explanation as to why it was ever lawful is worthy of study. He makes it abundantly clear why in our day religious coercion cannot be deemed a desideratum of the Halakhah.

IV.

From all of the foregoing it would appear that there is no halakhic justification whatever for the recent terrorist activity of some well-meaning but misguided Israeli Jews. Certainly, one cannot justify violence against innocent passengers on buses. Violence even against the Arab mayors was wrong unless they were deemed *rodfim*—criminals about to commit murder, which they were not. And violence against the duly constituted State of Israel was

---

1. See also above, p. 85.

unwarranted—the State had done nothing unlawful. If it was failing in its duty to protect some of its citizens, the remedy was to pressure for more protection but not to strike out at other human beings recklessly and wantonly with no regard for the consequences of such behavior to the State and the Jewish people all over the world.

This brings one to the only defense still not considered. May one resort to violence to rid the Land of Arabs and thus make all the Land available for Jews—the Kahane platform or obsession?

The claim is that the Bible approves. If one rejects the Oral Law, one may thus hold. But the Rabbis have ruled that the biblical commands cited apply exclusively to idolaters who no longer live in Israel. Furthermore, only a person obsessed could fail to realize what effect this position would have on millions of Jews living in lands other than Israel.

Interestingly enough, there is one case in the Talmud which is relevant but not applicable.

In one's own home one has the right to use force against that person who enters with permission but overstays the visit and flouts God's will in the private domain of the host. Perhaps this is one of the rights that flow from private ownership.

The Babylonian Talmud (Baba Kama 27b and 28a) discusses the right to engage in self-help in order to protect one's rights. The accepted rule is quite liberal. A person may take the law into his own hands if failure to do so might result in a loss of time or money. He need not always look to the courts for the enforcement of his rights. In connection with the discussion of this theme, the Talmud permits a master whose erstwhile slave is now emancipated to be moved bodily from the master's home if he refuses to go. As an emancipated slave he may no longer cohabit with female slaves and the master may even inflict bodily harm on him if he refuses to leave peaceably. One may resort to violence to protect one's home from becoming the site of sinful behavior.

Can one rely on this precedent to exclude Arabs from Israeli territory? That Israel is the homeland of the Jewish people does not negate the ownership of land therein by non-Jews. It would require a great stretch of the imagination to apply a rule which refers to one's residence to a territory which may be a homeland, but also the place where so many live lawfully and for whom it may not be a homeland.

The conclusion is inescapable. The recent activity of the Jewish terrorists in Israel has no support in Jewish law as it has no support in the moral law or the law of nations.

Secular Jurisprudence and Halakhah[1]

In halakhic literature one can find support for virtually every theory of legal philosophy known to secular jurisprudence. No one theory by itself dominates the scene. This is true of many other legal systems. Indeed, in many a jurisdiction, members of the same judicial tribunal can agree on a specific decision but arrive at it from diverse stances in legal philosophy. One judge may be a positivist; another may favor natural law theories; and a third may be partial to social needs; but all might arrive at the same conclusion. However, many are surprised that this can happen in a legal system whose basic norm is that God is the ultimate source of authority. They ask: How can a God-given law yield to social needs? Did He not anticipate them in His divine commands? Or how can His mandates be reviewed and interpreted in the light of natural law? Is He limited by that law? And if positivism is the proper approach, what can Jews do to get legislative relief when the Legislator is so inaccessible? Is rejection of the Covenant the only way out?

These challenges are not really as serious as they sound. It is conceivable that the Jewish people will reject their Covenant with God. The legal order based upon that Covenant will then be no more, precisely as in the case of Hobbes' social contract when the people reject the sovereign because he no longer affords them with the protection for which they committed themselves to him without reserving any rights to themselves. Hobbes' system is positivistic but eternal until rejected. And some halakhic authorities deal with Jewish law the same way. The Jews who reject the Covenant are outside the pale while those who are loyal to it are bound by the Law without regard to any considerations other than the Law itself and that which logically can be deduced from it. Tradition has furnished the exegesis by which there can be some development from existing rules and texts but without reference to ideal ends or social facts. For these Jews there can be

1. With only a few changes, this essay was the inaugural lecture of the Jack D. Weiler Chair in the Philosophy of Halakhah at Bar-Ilan University.

no legislation, for there is but one Legislator—God himself. Yet, there are many halakhic authorities who differ and reckon very often both with demands of justice and human needs, individual and social.

Furthermore, there is biblical authority for the proposition that God respects natural law. It is, therefore, part of the Covenant. It was the patriarch Abraham himself who challenged God on the basis of an assumption of natural lawyers—that the Judge of all the earth must do justice and not punish the righteous with the wicked.[2] If Abraham could do it, why should Jewish judges of a later date be precluded from pondering mandates that appear to offend against natural law and why should they not arrive at interpretations that do not offend? In this connection the American experience is relevant. The power to declare legislative or executive action in the United States unconstitutional—very often because of natural law—resides in the judiciary, but not because the federal constitution so states. It was assumed that this power is, of necessity, a judicial function.[3] Historians have complained about this usurper of power but others have regarded it as a blessing. At least for the judiciary to exercise this power in Judaism there are explicit verses in Deuteronomy.[4] Pursuant to them, the Supreme Covenantor approved that human judges shall resolve questions which arise in the future. He anticipated that such questions would arise and He vested authority in those who in fact have been exercising it. And they may reckon with natural law as indeed they have.

One must also reckon with the fact that Moses himself appealed to the people of Israel to appreciate the law given unto them because of its justice content by comparison with other legal systems.[5] Apparently human beings have the capacity to evaluate and pass judgment on God's prescriptions. On what do they rely if not on standards which are very much a part of natural law?

There are scholars who hold that Maimonides recognized only divine commandments as the basis for morality and justice.[6] It is their view that Maimonides did not believe that moral principles

2. Gen. 18:23–25.

3. Marbury v. Madison 1 Cranch 137.

4. 17:8–11.

5. Deut. 4:7.

6. M. Fox, "Maimonides and Aquinas on Natural Law", *Dine Israel* 3 (1972), V–XXXV.

could be derived autonomously.

Crucial to their argument is the manner of reading one paragraph in Maimonides' Mishneh Torah.[7]

> A heathen who accepts the seven commandments and observes them scrupulously is a 'righteous heathen', and will have a position in the world to come, provided that he accepts them and performs them because the Holy One, blessed be He, commanded them in the Law and made known through Moses our Teacher that the observance thereof had been enjoined on the descendants of Noah even before the Law was given. But if his observance thereof is based upon a reasoned conclusion he is not deemed a resident alien, or one of the pious of the Gentiles, but one of their wise men.

These scholars substitute for the word "but" in the very last phrase the words "and not" and in that way justify their conclusion that Maimonides was not committed to any principles of natural law.

However, Maimonides in a passage dealing with a revealed law—the banning of witchcraft—says the following:

> These practices are false and deceptive . . . It is not proper for Israelites who are highly intelligent to suffer themselves to be deluded by such inanities . . . Whoever believes in these and similar things and, in his heart, holds them to be true and scientific and only forbidden by the Torah, is nothing but a fool, deficient in understanding . . . Sensible people, however, who possess sound mental faculties, know by clear proof that all these practices which the Torah prohibited have no scientific basis but are chimerical and inane . . .[8]

Now, if Maimonides holds that with respect to witchcraft no divine commandment was necessary, and by virtue of the exercise of reason alone one must abhor it, then is it conceivable that he would say that with respect to murder one must desist from homicide only because God revealed that it was wrong? Perhaps Maimonides did not conceive of, or define, natural law as Aristotle did before, and Aquinas after him. But no Jewish philosopher could justify God's punishment of Cain for his fratricide unless there are moral imperatives which require no divine revelation

---

7. Hilkhot Melakhim 8:11.

8. Hilkhot Avodat Kokhavim 11:16. See also N. Lamm and A. Kirschenbaum, "Freedom and Constraint in The Jewish Judicial Process", *Cardozo Law Review* 1:1 (1979), 99, 109–120.

but are derived either a priori from man's nature or reason, or a posteriori from the nature of society.

Yet, one may ask, even if the authorities reckoned with what we now call natural law, how did they dare consider social ends? Is God's legislation not for eternity and is it subject to change because of change in human circumstance? One may expect human law to be defective, requiring constant replenishment from ever advancing conceptions of morality and justice, but God's law one expects to be perfect ab initio.

To all of this, a religiously committed sociologist might reply that since God endowed man with free will, it is inevitable that there will always be changes in man's political, social, and economic institutions. The unexpected is to be expected. And to cope with such changes the revealed law provides for the exercise of equity and other rules for autonomous action by executives, legislators, and judges. Jewish theology affords an even simpler reply. God made man His partner in continuous creation. He also made the Jew His partner in the continuous process called Torah. In the process, the Jew is more than God's obedient servant. He participates in the discovery of God's word for every situation and, therefore, his own needs must enter into the dialogue. One of those needs is the fulfillment of justice in society for man's own self-fulfillment.

Yet, does the Torah provide for rabbinic regulation of society through judicial action which reckons with social needs? Again an affirmative answer is available. The Torah contains not only specific rules of law but also general rules by whose terms one may properly consider social needs. Such a general rule is the rule not to oppress strangers, widows, and orphans.[9] Oppression is not defined. Therefore, it is by no means unreasonable for halakhic authorities to deal with social and economic conditions that are oppressive. They may also follow Moses' pattern and in an emergency break the Law as he broke the tablets. Sometimes they justified action which ran counter to biblical prescriptions by reference to a verse in the Psalms,[10] but Moses' precedent is at least as good.

One impressive but little known argument for reckoning with individual needs (in addition to all the specific commands that stress the Torah's concern for human happiness) is the manner in which Moses handled four cases for which he did not have God's

---

9. Ex. 22:20–21.

10. Ps. 119:126.

mandate. Two cases involved sinners—a man who cursed God[11] and one who desecrated the Sabbath.[12] The other two involved persons who felt disadvantaged, one group that could not observe the Passover because they were ritually unclean[13] and the other group, the daughters of Zelafhad who feared that they might be denied the right to inherit their father.[14] Moses dealt quite differently with the two sinners than he did with the groups who complained that they were being disadvantaged. It appears that he was in no hurry to ascertain the penalty that was to be meted out to the former, while he countenanced no delay whatever in obtaining relief for the latter. The Targum Yerushalmi explains why. It is to teach us how alert one must be when persons' rights are in jeopardy or when they suffer feelings of deprivation but how slow one may be when one has to punish the wicked.

Thus, not only rabbinic literature but even the Bible sensitizes us to be mindful of individual and social needs in the judicial process and thus the so-called sociological jurisprudence also has its place in the development of Jewish law with biblical warrant and support.

There is diversity among halakhic authorities not only in legal philosophical positions but also with regard to the rules. Two factors contribute to the inordinate diversity with regard to rules.

First, there is the fact that the law was given not only to specified authorities but to all who joined in the Covenant. The inevitable consequence of such an agreement with God is that all who are covenanted have a voice in the development of the Law and will decide many issues for themselves. There would be anarchy if in all matters such autonomy prevailed. As a general rule, therefore, in most matters affecting others, or the group as a whole, the duly chosen authorities have the last word, but in matters affecting one's self the individual has considerable freedom of interpretation and action.

Second, although the term Halakhah is generally used to describe the literature of Jewish law, in contradistinction to the aggadah, which comprises the non-legal literature of Judaism, Jewish law in fact comprises much more than is generally deemed law by modern states. It is important to bear this in mind when trying to understand

---

11. Num. 24:10–16.

12. Num. 5:32–36.

13. Num. 9:6–12.

14. Num. 27:1–18

why there is so much diversity and why there are so many different approaches to its development, even among those fervently committed to it.

In modern states one of the most important characteristics of law is its enforceability. A law without sanctions is not regarded as law at all, but as mere exhortation. Yet a very substantial portion of the Halakhah is only exhortation, directed only to the conscience of individuals. No action by courts was ever contemplated in such matters. Disobedience often entails no punishment by human tribunals. Moreover, the Halakhah does not hesitate to prohibit action of which no one other than the actor is aware. It enjoins the mind with regard to beliefs and attitudes. Thus Halakhah is much more than law, insofar as it encompasses almost all the behavior and thought of those who live by it.

Recently, one halakhic authority dealt with the problem whether a prisoner of war may commit suicide to spare himself the torture that was likely to be inflicted upon him to compel him to reveal military secrets, and also whether one may give him the wherewithal to commit suicide. As for the prisoner himself, the conclusion was that he may kill himself but as for the accessory before the fact—the person providing the means for suicide—there was a difference of opinion. According to Jewish law it is clear that he would not be punished as a murderer though he made possible the death of a human being. Therefore, no court would ever be involved and the question involved only the action of individuals who may opt to obey the Halakhah or ignore it. Nonetheless, the issue is debated as a very serious halakhic one.[15]

In a system in which the scope of law is limited in that it deals only with matters that can be brought to court for final resolution, there must be an ultimate authority that hands down decisions binding on all the courts within that judicial system. No judicial system could tolerate for long a situation wherein different courts in the same jurisdiction apply the law differently. That would in effect mean that all citizens are not subject to the same law, a denial of the basic ideal of equality before the law. In the United States, for example, the United States Supreme Court is frequently called upon to make the final decision when lower courts in different regions arrive at contradictory rulings. The Supreme Court makes the decision which then binds all the judges in the land. However, since the Halakhah—even when ideally there is a Sanhedrin and a

---

15. Y. Gershuni, *Kol Tsofayikh* (Jerusalem: Gershuni, 1980), 216–220.

system of lower and appellate courts—pertains so overwhelmingly to matters that never come before courts for resolution—matters pertaining principally to personal behavior, with no sanctions attached—there is no way to impose the will of an ultimate authority on the diversity of opinions that are advanced. It is virtually impossible to create regimentation. There are differences with regard to almost every new issue that arises. In addition, in matters of religious observance there is a plethora of local custom. In matters of creed there is hardly ever a precise formulation. And with respect to almost all matters that do not evoke the resistance of another, an applicant is practically always autonomous both with regard to the choice of an authority as well as whether to obey or not.

Thus, for example, in connection with medical ethics, one finds that a distinguished halakhic authority in Israel allows abortion when it is likely that the foetus will be afflicted with Tay-Sachs disease.[16] Another authority, in the United States, disapproves.[17] The pregnant woman may consult a rabbi who will recommend one view or the other.

With respect to a very pressing public issue, one finds similarly polar positions. On the one hand there is the view represented both within the state of Israel and outside it by a highly respected number of halakhic experts who argue on equally respectable halakhic grounds that not one square inch of holy soil should be given up. They argue, of course, that the Land is God's gift to the people of Israel. Jews were ordered to accept it and to maintain possession of it even at the risk of their own lives. We Jews were instructed by God to go to war—to resort to violence—to defend that territory and war, by its very nature, implies the loss of life. It is for this reason that Chief Rabbi Yitshak Nissim, and Rabbi Zevi Yehuda Kook, the son of the former chief rabbi, are adamantly opposed to returning any part of the Land.

On the other hand there are the so-called "doves," represented by amongst others, Rabbi Joseph B. Soloveitchik, whose views have been very widely disseminated. For Rabbi Soloveitchik the point at issue is the sanctity of life. He would argue that peace if can be bought by giving up some of the land then perhaps lives

16. E.J. Waldenberg, cited in J.D. Bleich and F. Rosner, *Jewish Bioethics* (London and New York: Sanhedrin Press, 1978), 186.

17. J.D. Bleich, "Sexuality and Procreation," *Biomedical Ethics in Perspective of Jewish Teaching and Tradition.* ed. I. Franck (Washington, D.C.: College of Jewish Studies of Greater Washington, 1980). 1, 9–10.

can be saved by so doing. Naturally one is likely to ask how the "doves" would respond to Rabbi Nissim's question, which in the surface, at least, is a very logical one to pose. The answer is straightforward. There is a rider to the commandment to go to war, viz. only when victory is likely. Jews have the option of not going to war unless victory is likely. When Israel was first given possession of the Land, God declared to them that He would support them and hence victory was assured. Today, of course, victory is not necessarily likely and hence the question is whether in this situation Halakhah would not require the return of land. Which view the people of Israel will adopt remains to be seen.

Yet, in many matters it is necessary for the rabbinical courts to make a decision in the face of a diversity of rulings. It was long held by some halakhic authorities that a corporation has no legal personality independent of the persons who create it and own its shares.[18] They are partners and no more. The rabbinical courts, however, now subscribe to the view that a corporation has legal personality on its own.[19] That ruling is now binding on all rabbinical courts in Israel.

It thus appears that the presumably totalitarian character of the Halakhah contains a paradox. Because the Halakhah affects almost everything that a person thinks, says, or does, his personal freedom is radically proscribed. Yet, precisely because its scope is so extensive and most of it is beyond the possibility of enforcement, the diversity in rules and opinions that it contains defies description and makes it the least monolithic system of law known to legal scholars in the West.

It has been suggested that the existence of so much diversity of opinion in the halakhic system is not intrinsic, nor ideal, but rather one of the unfortunate consequences of the Jewish dispersion. "Ideally," it is said, the Halakhah "envisages some ultimate authority in which there is vested the final responsibility for the determination of all questions which fall within the purview of problems to be settled by reference to halakhic standards."[20] This is simply not true unless the ultimate authority meant is God Himself. So long as it is only men who exercise the authority, not

18. S. Miron, "Ma'amad ha-Hevrah, B.E.M. bemishpat Ivri", *Sinai* 59 (1966), 228–245.

19. *Piske Din Rabbaniyim* Vol.10, p. 278, at 285–291.

20. W.S. Wurzburger, "Plural Modes and the Authority of the Halakhah," *Judaism* 20:4 (1971), 391.

even a unanimous Sanhedrin relieves the Jew of his obligation to ignore its decision when he knows it has erred.[21] He must obey the Sanhedrin if he is acting as a judge in a lower court; without such a rule, there would be anarchy in the judicial system. Moreover, if the Sanhedrin is trying to establish its authority in a period when there is the threat of chaos, it is the moral obligation of the dissenter to make his contribution to the establishment of order. In addition, when the decision affects persons other than himself, he cannot, of course, use his dissent as an excuse for disobedience. However, when the mandate pertains to his religious observance, and he is certain that he is right and the Sanhedrin is wrong, he must express himself and act accordingly. Thus even ideally neither a majority nor a unanimous Sanhedrin becomes a surrogate for personal commitment to the Covenant and the will of God that must be fulfilled because of it.

Furthermore, the halakhic system prescribes much that can never fall within the purview of problems that enter the jurisdiction of the Sanhedrin. For example there is a wide range of prohibitions the flouting of which draws neither divine nor human punishment. Of these prohibitions the individual Jew can, if he so wishes, be critical, and he can disobey them with impunity. Insofar as such matters are concerned, even the Halakhah's highest tribunal engages in nothing more than exhortation. And surely if, in the exercise of personal autonomy, the will of the Sanhedrin can be flouted in matters involving biblical mandates, all the more can this pertain when the prohibitions are only rabbinic ordinances!

What, then, unites all who are committed to the Halakhah, those presently called "Orthodox"? It is simply the belief that from the Covenant between God and Israel there emerged the obligation to obey His Law, which is subject to change and development only as that Law—Written and Oral—made such change and development possible. The dissenter, or the champion of a new rule, must base his dissent or his effort at legislation on these fundamental norms and the methodology they prescribe.

It might appear, at first glance, that the difference between enforceable and non-enforceable Halakhah resembles Kant's differentiation between law and ethics and Hart's differentiation between law and morality. However, in the Halakhah the two are totally integrated and one cannot study or understand the one without the other.

---

21. Hor. 2a and 3b.

For example, the halakhic source material pertaining to usury is voluminous and covers almost every type of loan transaction imaginable even in modern times. Yet the instances in which the transactions are voidable or in which a borrower may retrieve the money he paid as interest on the loan are notably few. But that does not mean that all the other forms of loan which are prohibited but not voidable are to be relegated to the domains of ethics and morality. The fact is that a lender who lends money in any manner disapproved by the Halakhah may never be required to make restitution but he may forfeit his competency as a witness before a court because he engaged in transactions upon which the Halakhah frowns.[22] Thus, for the law of evidence one requires knowledge of all the halakhic rules on usury, because one who offends against any of the rules may lose his credibility. Indeed, he may suffer other disabilities as well.

A man who was presumed dishonest could not take an oath. This was a disability of major consequence. According to Jewish law, most oaths were taken by parties to relieve themselves of liability.[23]

Thus, for example, if the creditor claimed money from the alleged debtor and had but one witness instead of two, the alleged debtor could take an oath that he owed nothing and that was the end of the case. Or if the creditor claimed more money than the debtor admitted owing, then the debtor took an oath that his obligation was less than that alleged. However, if the debtor was disqualified from taking the oath, his adversary could take it and collect his full claim.[24] Dishonest men were, therefore, at the mercy of claimants, and thus the Halakhah created a very meaningful legal sanction for men to seek to retain their reputations as presumptively honest.

Furthermore, a man who was known to the judge to be dishonest or even suspect in the matter of oaths might be denied the right to take an oath to clear himself, and his adversary could take the oath as plaintiff and recover. It was simply dangerous for any man to forfeit his claim to a good name.[25]

Another example involves the legal personality of a corporation,

---

22. Sanh. 3:3.

23. Shebu 7:1

24. Ibid; and 7:4.

25. Mishneh Torah, Hilkhot Sanhedrin 24: 1.

to which reference has already been made. One important source to support this conclusion is a text involving religious vows. One man can adjure another and prohibit him from deriving any benefit from property owned by the person making the declaration (which is regarded as a vow). The prohibition also applies to property in which the person making the declaration has an undivided partnership interest. And this includes property which belongs to all the inhabitants of the city since they are deemed partners in the assets of their municipality. However, the vow does not apply to the assets of the Jewish people as a whole. Of no individual Jew can it be said that he has property in those assets.[26] They belong to the Jewish people as such, independently of the individuals who constitute the Jewish people. And this entity with an independent existence is comparable to a corporation.

Presently this problem is under discussion with regard to the property of a Kibbutz.[27] Are its members partners or is the Kibbutz like a corporation? Rabbi Joseph B. Soloveitchik in a volume on "Penitence"[28] derives the corporate character of the Jewish people from texts dealing with animal offerings and liturgy. He holds that in addition to the sins of individual Jews, and the sins of the group for collective conduct that is sinful, there are sins of the eternal House of Israel—unconnected with any individual or group of individuals. It is the guilt of the entity which has an independent existence and comprises the dead, the living, and the still unborn, and makes of them a metaphysical reality for which there must be atonement. To such an extent are religious and legal thought interwoven in halakhic thought and enterprise!

The Halakhah also describes many situations in which one person harms another but no liability attaches. The conduct is immoral but punishable only by God—"by the laws of Heaven."[29] Thus a

---

26. Ned. 5:4 and 5.

27. N. Bar-Ilan, "Hakibuts Keshutafut vekekehilah beHalakhah," *Tehumin* I (1980), 414–422: Y. Cohen, "The Kibbutz as a Legal Entity," in N. Rakover, ed., *Jewish Law and Current Legal Problems* (Jerusalem: The Library of Jewish Law, 1984), 55–65.

28. *Al Hateshuvah* (Jewish Agency: Jerusalem, 1974), 78.

29. BK 55b and 56a. On this *sugya*, see further B.S. Jackson, *Essays in Jewish and Comparative Legal History* (Leiden: EJ. Brill, 1975), ch.10; L Jacobs, *The Talmudic Argument* (Cambridge: Cambridge University Press 1984), ch. 20.

man who places fire in the hands of a child or an incompetent in order to burn his neighbor's property is not liable by the Jewish law of tort because it was the act of the intervening agent, the child or the incompetent, that caused the damage (Gerama). Similarly, he who places poison near his neighbor's animal is not liable because it was the animal's own act that killed it. Even a man whose testimony could have availed another in a lawsuit is not liable for his failure to testify though he violated a biblical injunction. These are only a few of the instances of malfeasance and misfeasance in which a human tribunal awards no damages. In the eyes of Heaven, however, there is liability. From the point of view of morality, a wrong has been committed. Could the rabbis leave it at that? No, they provided legal sanctions for what they deemed morally reprehensible behavior.

Rashi suggests that liability by "the laws of Heaven" is of a punitive character rather than compensatory, and the tortfeasor is only encouraged to pay to avoid punishment by God.[30] Rashi apparently does not regard the liability as liability to compensate so that failure to compensate might be deemed theft—withholding from another man what is his due. The Meiri holds differently.[31] For him, it becomes the duty of the court to tell the defendant that he ought to pay, and for failure to pay he is presumed a thief and, therefore, incompetent to testify in other litigation or to take oaths in lawsuits against him, with all the dangers described above in connection with usurious transactions.[32] Again, what "Heaven" forbade has practical legal consequences.

In modern times no one has done more to articulate the total unity of the Halakhah and the interdependence of all its parts than Dr. Soloveitchik.

Given the premise that all the Law is God's revealed will, it follows logically that all of it will have theological significance. The totality of the Law is taken by Soloveitchik as a realm of ideas in the Platonic sense, given by God for application to the realm. Just as the mathematician creates an internally logical and coherent fabric of formulas with which he interprets and integrates the appearance of the visible world, so the Jew, the "Man of Halakhah," has the Torah as the divine idea that vests all of human life with direction and sanctity. Legislative change is irreconcilable with

---

30. On BK 104a.

31. Meiri on BK 56a. (See also Ketsot ha-Hoshen, 32a)

32. Ibid., and Rabbenu Meshulam, ha-Hashlamah, BK 6:1.

Halakhah, yet creativity is of its very essence. "The Halakhah is a multi-dimensional ever-expanding continuum which cuts through all levels of human existence from the most primitive and intimate to the most complex relationships" (from an unpublished lecture by Dr. Soloveitchik). Thus, though Halakhah refers to the ideal, its creativity must be affected by the real.

Halakhic creativity is not an ingenious academic exercise. The man who would bridge the distance between the ideal and the real, who would discover what is the intent of divine will in a new and unprecedented situation, must employ the dialectic of reason in "fear and trembling;" his thinking must be part of a religious agony. God willed that man obey his Law. God also willed man's welfare. Sometimes the Law and man's welfare come into seeming conflict. The pious jurist must then probe the sources and the commentaries of the saints, and descend into that same crucible of pain out of which the right way was originally revealed.

Two other responsa by Rabbi Soloveitchik reveal the vitality of the Halakhah for the resolution of uniquely modern problems. For many years it was the practice in New York City for all foundlings to be turned over to Catholic and Protestant adoption agencies. Recently the city's Jewish adoption agency made a request for its share, since a third of New York's inhabitants are Jewish. Was the request halakhically proper, since there was no way of identifying the faith of the foundlings' parents and the greater mathematical probability in the ease of each child was that it was non-Jewish? Could foundlings be reared as Jews and converted to Judaism by foster parents?

Dr. Soloveitchik sustained the propriety of the agency's request, in a responsum that cited halakhic sources but also referred to mathematical formulas of probability. The Jewish Law frowns upon the use of mathematical probabilities in capital cases. On complex philosophical grounds,[33] Dr. Soloveitchik placed cases involving

---

33. The following may serve as a sample: "One school sees, in a naturalistic fashion, life and death on a biological level exclusively and identifies Pikuah Nefesh (the obligation to conserve life) with the saving of a carnal existence from extinction. The other school introduces an idealistic motif. It maintains that the law of Pikuah Nefesh which is based upon a value judgment–the appraisal of life as the highest good—transcends the bounds of biological fact and extends into the domain of spiritual activity. Life is not only a factum but also an actus, not only a tangible reality but also an abstract ethical value to be attained. Death is both a biological

religious identity in the same category. Hence the fact that the majority of foundlings may be non Jewish becomes inconsequential; if only one foundling may be Jewish, the Jewish community must assert its claim.

On another occasion he was asked about the use of anthropomorphic symbols in the stained-glass windows of an interfaith chapel on a college campus. He opposed their use, and his responsum revealed how the historical method may be used in solving halakhic problems. Since talmudic law, which was developed principally in Babylon, did not support him, he relied upon later medieval Jewish law, which had been developed in Christian Europe. His responsum explains why, in a Christian society, it was more imperative to expand, rather than restrict, the prohibition against icons that suggest the Christological idea of God-man. "To what our sages in a non-Christian Babylonia did not object, our forefathers in Christian countries were very sensitive."

In these decisions one can see how laws pertaining to the Sabbath have a bearing on the right to draft personnel for war and the right of a Jewish community to demand a share of the foundlings for adoption. Furthermore, one can see that Soloveitchik also reckons with history and sociology in the case of anthropomorphic symbols in a chapel and with teleology in his analysis of what one means when one says that the saving of a life includes saving a person from being raised in a faith different from the one in which he was born.

Thus, halakhic development involves much more than logic. It also involves man's sense of justice and all his needs as an animal and a creature with a unique relationship to God.

If the Halakhah, whose basic norm is the Covenant or Revelation, can be developed not only by the exercise of logic but also in response to man's sense of justice and man's social and personal

---

and ethical-spiritual phenomenon. The failure of an individual to realize his own personality in a manner decreed by his creator at birth is as tragic as his physical disintegration. One may save a life not only through medical skill but also by extending moral help. Hence, whenever man's inner life, his unique relationship to God, and the mode of his existence as an individual and social being are to be determined, we encounter the problem of Pikuah Nefesh, which means here the preservation of a spiritual identity. Hence (the concept of) majority finds no application in this case."

needs, what is the measure of God's input and man's input?

The late Justice Benjamin Cardozo once essayed to describe what it is that a judge does when he engages in the judicial process creatively. The conclusion is inescapable that one can acquire the art only after years of preoccupation with the law, its history, its ideals, its methodology, its philosophy. So it is with Torah. Until one has studied long and much from earlier masters, one does not learn how to balance one's commitment to authority with one's obligation to be master instead of the obedient servant. Both imitation and originality play their part in the process. Modesty coupled with respect for forebears commingles with self-reliance.

Thus, the halakhic authority faces on the one hand the authorities: revealed texts, revealed norms, and the dicta of sages whose prescriptions are almost as sacred as the revealed data (because what the sages of each generation ordain becomes part of the tradition which the revealed texts enjoin us to obey). On the other hand, the Law's doctors are themselves partners in the development of the Law. Indeed God abdicated in their favor when He bequeathed the Law to them. He thereby restrained Himself from any further revelations.[34] The Talmud tells us that Rabbis are not to rely upon heavenly voices or miracles. They are to act as sovereigns in the sphere of halakhic creativity allocated to them. Can one conceive a more difficult equilibrium than this—subservience to mountains of authority coupled with a well-nigh arrogant usurpation of legislative and judicial power over the divine legacy? Yet both poles play their necessary roles in halakhic development.

If not for Halakhah's theocentric character, it would be no different from other legal systems that are rooted only in history and economics. Because its students are committed to the divine origin of the Law, their creative achievement in the law is ever oriented to the fulfillment of God's Will. In order that we never lose sight of this commitment, the Law includes mandates that are also supra-rational—inexplicable in terms of human values and interests. Thus Dr. Samuel Belkin, the late President of Yeshiva University, maintains that even the supra-rational commandments of the Torah have a purpose, although we may not fathom their reason.[35] These mandates are to be obeyed solely because God decreed them. Such

---

34. BM 59b.

35. S. Belkin, "Philosophy of Purpose", in *Studies in Torah Judaism*, ed. L. D. Stitskin (New York: Yeshiva University Press & Ktav Publishing House Inc., 1969), 1–29.

mandates are to be found in every branch of the Law. Obedience to them is of the essence of one's religious experience—one obeys not because one understands but rather because one believes. As children sometimes obey parents not because they comprehend but because they trust, so are we to obey God. It was to conserve this attitude that our Sages hesitated to make too explicit their own analysis of the Law in terms of human values and interests. Such analyses might prompt students to embrace a completely humanistic approach to the Law which would thus lose its theocentric character altogether. In a general way they did explore the rationale of most of the mitzvot, but in the articulation of specific rules they did not presume that they completely fathomed the teleology of all the revealed texts.

Yet God gave the Law to the Jewish people who alone were responsible for its development. As humans they crave to understand what they are commanded to perform. Moreover, their needs are not the same in every age or clime. The Torah itself takes note of these factors. It appeals to man to comprehend the justice-content of the law. It also bids him to live by the law, and not perish because of it. Moses' successors were vested with authority not only to interpret the law but to constitute themselves as authorities in every generation. The Rabbis often undertook not only to rationalize the presumptively suprarational, but also to suspend, even overrule, the revealed words of God.

Furthermore, the halakhic authority must not only steer between what God mandated and what man requires, but he must also veer frequently between antithetical values found in the basic norm, the Covenant itself, such as universalism and particularism, freedom and self-control, the needs of society and the needs of the self, this-worldliness and other-worldliness.

It is in this connection that the principle of polarity of Morris Raphael Cohen can be so helpful. In virtually all of life he saw "necessary opposition in determinate effects" as a "heuristic principle directing inquiry in the search for adequate explanations."[36] Professor Cohen mentions as an excellent example of polarity Professor Felix Adler's use of the opposing action of the blades of scissors "to denote the fact the mind never operates effectively except by using both unity and plurality."[37] It would appear that Dr. Soloveitchik uses a similar approach. He rejects

---

36. *Studies in Philosophy and Science* (New York: H. Holt & Co, 1949), 12.

37. *Reason and Nature* (2nd ed., Glencoe: Free Press, 1949), 165, n. 4.

Hegel's idea of thesis, antithesis and synthesis as suitable for the dialectic of the Halakhah, simply because the revealed antinomies never lose their validity. Forever they remain poles. However, the halakhic authority veers between them in making decisions.

One example to illustrate this approach is the attitude of most halakhic authorities to the status of women in modern times. The status of women in Jewish law unmistakably involves some deeply entrenched ideas which are in conflict with each other, and veering between them is not an easy task for the creative halakhic expert. One finds, on the one hand, a biblical command with regard to the equality of males and females. All have the divine image. All are equally responsible to the civil and criminal code and are equally protected by it. Yet, one finds on the other hand that in Rabbinic literature there is a deep-seated distrust of males in the matter of sex. They are easily stimulated—even a woman's voice can be the cause. And the only safeguard against sexual immorality is separation, as total as it can be. Between husbands and wives many a rabbi so encouraged the practice of the art of love that even the passion of the most virile of men is gratified. But, as between men and forbidden women, no one is to be trusted. It was not easy even to permit fathers and their daughters to be together unchaperoned. When the taboo of incest became well established, parents and their offspring were not expected to abide by the strict rules forbidding a male and a female to be together alone. However, it is because of this pole—call it a "fixation" if you will—pertaining to the weakness of the male and his uncontrollable sexual drive (it is difficult to deny that they knew whereof they spoke; they, themselves, were male!) that halakhic authorities insisted on separation of the sexes in the synagogue and domestic careers for women. From this there derive separate seating in the synagogue, the exclusion of women from most civic, communal, and religious functioning, and much else that makes the tradition offensive to many modern women.

Now, a Jewish legislator today, confronted by the two poles, somehow finds it easier to decide, as did several halakhic giants in Israel, that women can be involved in the political process as voters,[38] and in the judicial process as witnesses and judges,[39] but not in synagogue procedures and leadership. So to interpret the

---

38. B.Z.M. Uziel, *Piske Uziel* (Mossad Rav Kook: Jerusalem, 1977), 228–234.

39. M. Bar-Ilan, "Tazkir", *Yavneh* 3 (Nisan, 5709, April 1949), 32.

law that the disability of women to be judges and witnesses is removed is a fulfillment of the biblical pole of equality, and if it impinges upon the purity of thought of males, at least the sanctity of a synagogue is not thereby affected, nor is the meditation of any worshipper. Quite different is the situation where the synagogue is concerned. In that connection the other pole comes into play. And the reluctance to change the rules is great.

Yet, the debates among halakhic authorities may involve not only the measure of the "veering between antinomies" when the poles are well defined, but also the very existence of the pole and its definition. As an example, in one instance Dr. Soloveitchik reacted quite strongly to this writer's suggestion that an important presumption in Jewish family law no longer be valid and if this could be proved, it might be possible to annul many marriages and dispense with the need for a Get (divorce). The Talmud asks[40] why a woman betrothed to a man who died before consummation of the marriage—and thus in need of a release from a surviving brother-in-law (halitsah) before being permitted to remarry—cannot obtain annulment of the betrothal on the ground that her husband's untimely death was a circumstance that would have deterred her from entering upon the marital relationship. The answer is that there is a presumption that every woman prefers any kind of a marriage, even a bad one, to living alone, and therefore when she married she was prepared to do so unconditionally and without regard to any future developments. But this presumption cannot be said to reflect modern conditions. In today's society, which has witnessed the "Woman's Liberation" movement, it can be said unequivocally that the overwhelming majority of women would prefer to be single and cope very well as such, rather than be bound in any way to dead men or their kin. One might readily object that the challenge to the presumption may not help in cases where the marriage was fully consummated, for all conditions are presumed waived once the spouses cohabit. There may be ways to overcome this objection but that was not the basis of Dr. Soloveitchik's demurrer. He argued that the talmudic statement to the effect that every woman prefers any kind of marriage, even a bad one, to living alone is a metaphysical pronouncement and not subject to rebuttal. Perhaps the biblical statement that in God's view it is not good for man to be alone is the basis for it.[41] Thus one would

---

40. BK 110b and 111a.

41. Gen. 2:18.

here find a "pole" whose existence this writer would challenge, especially since God's pronouncement that man should not be alone was interpreted by the Rabbis[42] to have no reference to the misery of loneliness but rather to the fact that if, unlike other animals, males had no mates they might think they are equal of God—He is alone and they too are alone. (Echoes of Plotinus!).

The Talmud is regarded by its lovers as a sea. Perhaps the metaphor is meant to suggest not only the matter of size but also the image of waves. And perhaps even the phenomenon of winds and storms. These storms will also rage with regard to the philosophy of law that a study of the folios can and ought generate.

---

42. See Rashi's commentary.

Jewish Law in the State of Israel: Reflections from History

A cherished Jewish aphorism assures us that even a Scroll of the Law in the ark requires *mazal*, good fortune. All the more, a new book on Judaism: Professor Menachem Elon's monumental three volumes, *Jewish Law*[1] were published at a time when worldwide Jewry was in depressed mood—comparable only to that of holocaust days. That may account for the failure of many to hail the publication as an event of major significance. Yet it is precisely that, and what, in its time, may have been an inadequately celebrated occurrence will, in years to come, receive more and more recognition and win for its author the crown of a this-worldly immortality.

In this review I shall essay to describe what the author set out to do, and how well he executed his design. I shall try to evaluate the significance of his achievement for the future study of Jewish law as well as the reception of Jewish law as the basis for the legal system of the new Jewish state. Lastly, I shall try to point out areas for future exploration and analysis with which the volumes deal minimally but which require the attention of scholars, who, like himself, hold that the cultural renaissance of the Jewish people requires the renaissance of Jewish law.

I.

Law is not essentially a body of rules at all. Rules are an important part of the tools which law uses. But it is foolish to approach law in the first instance through one of the devices which it employs. The student of society, above all, should study law as a social institution.[2]

Professor Elon chose not to write about the rules of Jewish law. He deemed that task well fulfilled by Professor Gulok several decades ago. He undertook rather to write a history of the role of Jewish

---

1. Menachem Elon, *Jewish Law: History, Sources, Principles* (Hebrew; Jerusalem The Magnes Press/The Hebrew University, 1973), 3 vols., 1594 pp.

2. H.J. Berman and W.R. Greiner, *The Nature and Functions of Law* (2nd Ed.; Brooklyn: Foundation Press; 1966), p. 6.

law in Jewish society from the patriarchal period to the present. And the impact of his tale is powerful. The secret of the survival of the Jewish people is to be found in their conscious or subconscious commitment to the notion that their legal tradition is the essence of their social order. For this reason it may be most accurate to regard Judaism as a legal order rather than a religion or faith. It is the legal order of the Jewish people throughout their generations and in all their habitats. Even when they had no political sovereignty—and this they rarely had—they always sought legal autonomy. Ofttimes they paid for it. And it was legal autonomy with sanctions that ranged from fines and excommunication to imprisonment and even the death penalty. Curiously enough, while the State of Israel after its establishment could find no executioners for those sentenced to death by the mandatory power, there were instances in Jewish history when as part of their obligation to the non-Jewish sovereign state, the Jewish community had to provide hangmen even for non-Jewish criminals sentenced by the courts of the host country (p. 11, fn. 26).

To preserve this legal autonomy and to provide continuity to the legal tradition, it was necessary to cope with many challenges. First, it was necessary to maintain discipline within the Jewish community and prevent resort to non-Jewish courts. Second, in the absence of an adequate number of persons knowledgeable in Jewish law, it was necessary to legitimatize the status of judges who were not experts and somehow integrate their legal creativity into the corpus of Jewish law. Third, business practices of the areas in which Jews lived may have been alien to the Jewish legal tradition. As in the case of the Law Merchant and English common law, it was important to incorporate these practices into the halakhic system. In other words there were factors within and without the Jewish community that might have made Jewish law non-viable. Then Jewish law would have been relegated long ago to the heap of antiquities for research by antiquarians. But somehow Jewish law coped with all the challenges. In great detail Professor Elon outlines the steps and cites the authorities pursuant to which all of this was accomplished. And what makes his presentation especially noteworthy—a quality to be found in all three volumes—is that his writing is so lucid that even one with no background whatever in Jewish law can follow each argument and understand every source. Aramaic words are translated into Hebrew in brackets and parentheses. Technical terms—terms of art—are also explained. He does not assume that his reader has any familiarity with, not to mention expertise in, talmudic literature.

In addition there are basic theoretical problems with which he had to deal. Every legal system has its ground norms. What is the source of its authority? Where does legislative power reside? For a people without a country, and with no sovereign other than God, these questions create a unique situation. Professor Elon does not evade them and as a result his volumes contain much that can be regarded as the political theory of Judaism. His presentation thus helps the untutored to become familiar with the essential character of the Jewish social order through the millennia. It is more than a treatise on Jewish law—it is an introduction to the political and legal theory of Judaism and the sociology of the Jewish people.

His third volume is a history of the legal literature that was created from the Bible to the present. Every work of importance is not only fully described but related to earlier works. The problems of codification are analyzed and a very correct comparison is made between such problems in other legal systems and their analogues in Jewish legal history. Indeed, all the volumes are replete with comparisons with Roman Law and Anglo-American law, and it is apparent that Professor Elon has mastered not only the Jewish sources but the fundamentals of general jurisprudence the world over.

With the advent of Emancipation in the last two centuries, a major revolution occurred in Jewish life. The scope of Jewish law in Jewish society was reduced radically. And with the establishment of the Jewish state there was hardly any restoration of the status that Jewish law enjoyed in antiquity and in the middle ages. Professor Elon cites all the data, and with remarkable objectivity, when one considers how deeply he feels personally about the change. He reports and rarely editorializes.

However, the report itself is, on the one hand, an indictment of those who failed to realize the centrality of the law for Jewish survival, and, on the other hand, a protest against the rabbis who were pathetically inert in the face of the challenges of the Emancipation period and especially with the establishment of the State of Israel. Indeed, there was more halakhic creativity by the Chief Rabbinate in Palestine prior to statehood than after 1948 (p. 83).

II.

Many popular misconceptions about Jewish law—most of which are deliberately propagated by those who want to relegate Jewish law to the realm of antiquities—are dealt with by Professor Elon. One cannot help but be impressed by the remarkably dispassionate and scholarly manner in which he does this. He does it not as a special pleader or an emotional controversialist but with the weight of historical facts and legal citations that simply overwhelm the reader who seeks the truth.

For example, the notion that traditional Jewish law permits very limited legislative creativity is proved to be utter nonsense. At great length Professor Elon discusses the concept of Mishpat ha-Melekh (The Law of the Sovereign) and how it made for the incorporation of new legislation into the frame of traditional Jewish law. This concept, first used to legitimatize the ordinances of Jewish monarchs, was used even in the Middle Ages to accomplish the same result for the legislation of democratically organized communities (p. 44). The concept also stimulated inquiry into, and analysis of, the basic contract between the ruler and the ruled, and Professor Elon cites Jewish authorities whose Hobbesian views antedate Hobbes by several centuries (p. 46, fn. 143).

Creativity in Jewish law, however, was not limited to the legislative power of the community. The "doctors of Jewish law," the rabbis, in their judicial capacity contributed as much or more. In his Chapter VII (pages 223—235) Elon discusses the role of human reason in the interpretation of revealed law and cites authorities from the second to the twentieth centuries who support the notion that human reason alone is definitive in the understanding, application, and development of legislation which was divine in origin.

Professor Elon does not deal with this problem. And understandably so. His purpose is not to help the religiously committed remain loyal to their legal heritage by undertaking to solve some of their problems with regard to it. He seeks rather to convince the secularist that there can be a renaissance of Jewish law without substantial diminution of the power of judges and the community to innovate and legislate within the frame of the tradition.

The doctrine of Mishpat ha-Melekh he discusses in connection with another important doctrine by means of which the creative process was magnified. That is the principle enunciated in the Talmud by the Babylonian Amora Samuel in the third century:

that the law of the state in which Jews reside is binding on Jews—at least in matters of finance and property, Without becoming involved in the controversy between Professors Leo Landman and Shmuel Shilo as to whether the two doctrines are one or even related, he does cite all the available sources. And that is another impressive aspect of his work, He does not let himself be distracted by scholarly controversies with regard to one minor point or an other but concentrates on his major objective—to overwhelm the reader with the abundance of legal creativity that there has been throughout the ages, and how the same principles that were used in the past to make Jewish law cope with new challenges are still available.

The distinguished Israeli jurist Haim H. Cohn cites at least three reasons why he does not share Elon's hopes for Jewish law in a Jewish state.[3] One is that most Israeli lawyers do not know Jewish law. But one might hope that as many of them mastered the tongue of the prophets, so the education of the growing number of law students in the land will include what the older lawyers did not see fit to master. A more cogent reason will be discussed in a subsequent section, but his main reason is that "many of the provisions to be found in the Jewish codes are nowadays anachronistic and obsolete; and it does in no way derogate from the beauty and progressiveness and wisdom of those laws in the times, places and communities in and for which they were created, that they cannot serve the purposes and requirements of a modern welfare state." Elon would not deny this. However, all legal systems have provisions in their codes which are "anachronistic and obsolete." The crucial question is whether the legal system contains within it the potential for growth and change. And that Jewish law has this potential is the thesis Elon has demonstrated. Moreover, his work is also a fine text to help Israel's lawyers who are untutored in Talmud to acquire basic information with regard to all the sources and principles of Jewish law.

III.

Justice Cohn's strongest argument against the reception of Jewish law by the Jewish state is that "the practical enforcement of the Jewish law of marriage and divorce by rabbinical courts has done very little, if anything, to encourage or justify" such a goal. Elon, too, is critical of Israel's rabbis today. But one of the most impressive features of Elon's work is his treatment of Jewish family law and

---

3. See his "The Spirit of Israel Law," *Israel Law Review*, 9:4 (1974), 460.

his proposal for the future. This merits special attention, for it presents a challenge.

Much of his second volume is devoted to the history of Jewish legislation, and many pages pertain precisely to the law of marriage and divorce and the principles by which extensive creativity was possible. He argues brilliantly that this creativity ceased in connection with the power to annul marriages when Jews lost all semblance of a central authority recognized by Jews all over the world. Since the legislation was usually of a local character, and Jews lived in countless countries and communities which had little or no contact with each other, rabbis hesitated to annul marriages on the basis of local legislation which might not be recognized elsewhere. While by the legislation of her community, a woman might be regarded as single because her marriage was annulled in accordance with the law of her residence, she might still be regarded in another community as wedded because the law of the other community did not have similar legislation. This would create bedlam in Jewish family law. But today with Israel as the center of world Jewry, and communication between Jewish communities easily available, that rationale to justify no annulment of marriages collapses, and powers exercised a thousand years ago can now be revived.[4]

Does Professor Elon suggest ways to cope with this new situation? He does not, and this prompts one to ask a basic question.

Professor Elon is of the opinion that though the Halakhah, which is the totality of Jewish law—religious, civil, criminal, public—must remain the preserve of scholars committed to the law, it is conceivable that much of it—under the rubric of Mishpat Ivri, Hebrew law—can be incorporated into the legislation of a democratically elected parliament of a secular Jewish state. It is also conceivable that this legislation may even become part of the Halakhah, if not because of Dina de-Malkhuta Dina, because it is a Jewish state and that principle may apply only to non-Jewish states, then at least by the principle of Mishpat ha-Melekh. Furthermore, Professor Elon is of the opinion that Jewish family law is in need of updating for many reasons. Would he then approve of action by Israel's democratically elected parliament to liberalize the traditional law of marriage and divorce in accordance with the very rules he describes so clearly ? Let one visualize that the legislation is drafted by men like himself—men committed to the

---

4. Vol. II, pages 711–712.

Halakhah. Let us also visualize that the administration of the law will be in the hands of courts (either existing ones or new ones to be constituted) whose judges are also masters of the Halakhah and committed to its ground norms, its methodology, and its spirit. The only difference between such judges and the judges of the present rabbinical courts is that the former will respect the new legislation while the latter will adjudicate without resort to the new techniques for conditional marriages or their annulment. The new legislation will be unmistakably in the spirit and within the letter of Mishpat Ivri—as Elon conceives of it. It will have been created by men who share his point of view, and it will have the approval of a majority of Israeli Jews as represented in their Knesset.

What ideological objection can one raise? Only that it will divide the Jewish community because a segment of the population will exercise their religious freedom not to take advantage of it. And in Israel one seeks less divisiveness, rather than more. But, by the same token, a very large number of Jews in Israel and in the Diaspora are committed to the Halakhah but crave the new legislation and do not want a continuance of that condition of which both Elon and Justice Cohn complain. Moreover, most Jews in Israel—even those not committed to the Halakhah—and most Jews the world over would be totally reconciled to having Mishpat Ivri as the basis for Jewish family law. This is no inconsiderable matter. As for the few who will resist, nothing in the legislation will affect their stricter standards which they may maintain in other areas of the Halakhah as well, as in dietary laws, or Sabbath and festival observance. The challenge to Professor Elon and those who share his views is simply whether they are prepared to act where others have failed to act. In Israel's Knesset it has already been proposed that those who cannot marry by rabbinical law shall have civil marriage available to them. There will be other proposals, more or less radical in nature to upset the status quo. One or more of them will ultimately pass. Would a love of Mishpat Ivri, therefore, not prompt those who are obsessed with it, to try an approach which will save it for Jewish family law in Israel and abroad?

Professor Elon does not hold with some purists in Israel that a secular legislature must keep hands completely off traditional Jewish law. On the other hand, he wants the legislature and the civil courts to make greater use of the legal heritage of Judaism. Unlike Justice Cohn he does not deem this a "secularization of divine law,"[5] because divine law itself allows for a secular legislature to have the status of a king, and its enactments would be incorporated into the very *corpus juris* of Judaism. Under these circumstances, then, he can do more than propose action by the rabbinical courts. He can help the legislature to solve a problem which plagues Jews everywhere.

IV.

Professor Elon's work, however, does more than simply familiarize the reader with the total legal literature of Judaism and its potential for future creativity in the new state. It also makes the reader aware of many unique features of Judaism's legal heritage.

For example, one discovers how resistant Mishpat Ivri is to undue formalism in legal procedure (p. 88). One also discovers that there were already in the Middle Ages what can be regarded as constitutional limitations on communal government.[6] This is a remarkable phenomenon and the hallmark of a theocentric law. A democratic community can enjoy legal autonomy but it is ever subject to a higher law.

Professor Elon deals extensively with many features which are common to many legal systems—such as the role of precedent and the roles of logic and experience. But he also demonstrates the importance in Jewish legal creativity of a literature which plays no part in other legal systems—the literature of the Aggada, which is the literature of Jewish ethics. The interrelationship between halakhic and aggadic literature is a field worthy of study.

If, for example, Jewish law in the first millennium of the Common Era was so empathic with debtors it was not only the biblical mandates that are responsible. It is also an aggadic concept that makes all of us aware of the fact that in the final analysis we are all debtors with God as our creditor, and as we seek His empathy, so we must be empathic with those who are our debtors.

The Bible orders the creditor each night to return to the debtor whatever night clothes the creditor has taken as security. They are to be returned to the creditor in the morning. And the Aggada

5. See Cohn, *Jewish Law in Ancient and Modern Israel* (New York: Ktav, 1971).

6. See Samuel Morell, "The Constitutional Limits of Communal Government in Rabbinic Law", *Jewish Social Studies* 33, Nos. 2–3 (April-June 1971), 87–119.

adds that the creditor must so act because God acts thusly toward him. Every day he inevitably commits sin against God and is therefore in God's debt. At night God takes his soul as security for the debt but restores it in the morning because the creditor has need of it. Consequently the creditor must do no less for his debtor with regard to those items that the debtor needs for subsistence or survival. If in the second millennium of the common era, Jewish law was more considerate of the creditor, and many earlier rules with regard to interest, and the debtor's immunity from search and seizure and imprisonment, were relaxed, it was probably because money-lending had taken on a different dimension in the economic life of Jews, and what the Bible envisioned as an ideal society was no more. However, who can gainsay that the aggadic conception of God as the creditor with every human being His debtor influenced the remarkable attitude of Jewish law toward debtors for many centuries!

Much of Professor Elon's third volume is devoted to the problem of the codification of Jewish law. In great detail he reports on the resistance to it, precisely as there was resistance to the codification of Anglo-American common law. The same arguments advanced in England and the United States were advanced centuries earlier by Jewish halakhic experts. Codification inevitably freezes the law and is an impediment to the freedom of judges in their legal creativity.

However, one unique aspect of Jewish law frequently eludes those who discuss this problem, and it is worthy of consideration. In most legal orders, codes, once prepared, are enacted by legislatures as statutes and as statutes are binding on courts whose latitude in decision-making as thereby proscribed. However, no legislature ever transformed a Jewish code into a statute. Moreover, the overwhelming content of Jewish codes are not for use by courts at all. They are for the guidance of individuals with respect to matters that will never require court action. And this also explains the tremendous diversity that is to be found among the authorities with respect to the preponderance of rulings that one finds in the codes.

A point which bears repeating because it is so often overlooked is that one of the distinguishing characteristics of the laws of modern states is their enforcability. Nowadays, when a law is not accompanied by sanctions it is seen as nothing more than an exhortation. Much of Jewish law is in fact exactly that because it so rarely envisages punishment meted out by a court. In this respect the concept underlying Jewish law goes far beyond that underlaying the law of a modern state because it attempts to embrace almost all the thoughts and deed of those who live by it.

Now, in a modern legal system which deals with matters that are resolved in courts there has to be a higher authority to ensure a degree of uniformity in the decisions taken by the different courts. Some control is necessary to prevent the injustice or even chaos that might ensue if different courts applied the same laws differently. Hence in the United States, for instance, there is the Supreme Court which hands down decisions binding on all courts and judges in the land. By contrast the Halakhah deals with so much that would never come before a court in some modern state. Since the domain of Halakhah covers so much more of the physical and mental behavior of human beings, it is almost impossible to impose any form of regulation or regimentation on the diversity of opinions that can arise within it. Furthermore, because these opinions so often exist without sanctions to impose them the individual is offered greater latitude than any modern legal system is likely to permit when it comes to following those opinions (or, in terms of a secular law code, of obeying the law).

The Halakhah, then produces a fascinating paradox: in scope it covers far more aspects of human behavior and is in a sense far more demanding and yet that very scope and the diversity that it produces has allowed the Halakhah to become the least monolithic of all the systems of law known to scholars in the western hemisphere.

For some the diversity of opinion that can be found in the halakhic system is not by any means a positive characteristic but is rather the unfortunate result of the fact that Jews in exile are scattered around the globe. This view would have it that the Halakhah, in some ideal form, calls for an ultimate authority, an halakhic Supreme Court, as it were, to determine all questions that fall within the purview of the Halakhah. If this ultimate authority were God, well and good. But this view assumes a human authority and that is surely out of keeping with the spirit of Halakhah. Even when there existed a Sanhedrin and it could issue a unanimous opinion the individual Jew was under no obligation to follow that opinion if he knew it to be wrong (Horayot 2a-3b). To be sure there were circumstances where obedience to authority was required despite substantive disagreement. For instance, to assist in maintaining the authority of the Sanhedrin at a time when it was under threat. But in matters of religious observance the obligation of the individual was not to submit to the authority of the Sanhedrin, but always to express his dissent if he knew that he was correct and the Sanhedrin wrong.

The individual Jew has complete freedom to be critical of many halakhic prohibitions. He can even disobey them with impunity. The Sanhedrin has no power to impose sanctions upon him. The question naturally arises, What do Orthodox Jews have in common? The answer is simple enough: they believe that the relationship between God and Israel requires obedience to divine Law—a Law, be it noted, that can change and evolve in its own terms. Dissenters have to base their dissent on that fundamental norm.

Under such circumstances the codification of Jewish law creates few, if any, of the dangers that one might expect in other legal systems The person committed to the law retains an enormous amount of autonomy. The code is at best a guide for the individual who cannot handle the source material while the scholar for himself and those who seek his guidance uses the code sparingly.

However, because of the tremendous diversity that prevails in Jewish law—within the codes and in spite of them—those who share Professor Elon's hope that the legal heritage of Judaism shall become the basis for law in modern Israel have a very difficult task. In the new state it is legislation that must be enacted. And in making choices from among the diverse rulings one must be guided by what is the spirit of Jewish law, or its philosophy, and to this challenge, Professor Elon's three volumes address themselves minimally. A few illustrations are cited, but to that task there must be directed the major effort of those who want to save Jewish law from the fate of antiquities.

V.

Does revealed law—or divine law—permit the exercise by human beings of their sense of justice in the interpretation of that which God had ordained? Professor Elon has demonstrated conclusively what an enormous role man can play in the application of the biblical legislation. But on what does man rely when he so acts? Does he rely on reason alone? To what extent can he act also because of his own conceptions of what is right—conceptions which have been variously called natural law or categorical imperatives or self-validating values?

In the view of some scholars Maimonides felt that only divine ordinance could be the basis for morality and justice. They also claim that Maimonides was unwilling to accept that basic moral principles could be derived autonomously.[7]

If such is the case, then one must inquire about the role of such moral imperatives in reinterpreting or even suspending revealed law. Professor Elon deals with the talmudic concept of Sevara—a conclusion dictated by pure reason with no need for revelation to promulgate it. However, he does not deal with conclusions which man's sense of justice would dictate as requiring a new look, at revealed law with an eye to revision either by reinterpretation or sometimes even suspension, solely on the ground that one's sense of the right cannot be reconciled with a heretofore acceptable interpretation of a biblical verse. For example, could God truly have meant that a childless widow shall have to wait a dozen years for a brother-in-law who is a minor to release her, or a brother-in-law who became an apostate, or a brother-in-law who without just cause seeks to extort money from her? True, Professor Elon indicates how many ways there may be available to prevent the incidence of such unfortunate cases, whether by conditions in the marriage or the exercise of rabbinic power to grant annulments. However, one does not enhance respect for revealed law by constantly seeking to correct it by legal fiction or legal contrivances. The very sense of justice which the Torah supports and seeks to sharpen and deepen requires that the Torah shall be understood in its light. And this is the area in which Jewish legal creativity has simply been deficient. Not enough has been done to analyze the basic mandates of the Torah with an eye to the discovery of their justice-content, their teleology, and the development of rules in the light of that discovery.

Chief Rabbi Kook once explained most impressively what kind of a family situation the Torah visualized for the operation of the levirate law in which situation the Torah's provisions were more than humane. When that situation changed, it was certainly the duty of the rabbis to take steps to prevent the law from working hardship on the very person it was designed to help. They did this in the past and can do it again.

However, in addition to legislation to modify the effects of a law that once was just and presently is unjust, students of Jewish law can undertake to interpret biblical mandates in the light of their sense of justice, which is as important as pure logic in the continuance of the partnership between God and man in the development of

---

7. See Marvin Fox, "Maimonides and Aquinas on Natural Law," *Dine Israel*, 3 (1972), v–xxxvi.

His Law. In at least one instance the talmudic sages did precisely that. They challenged the biblical mandate that required the killing of animals with whom human beings had committed sex offenses. "If a man did sin, how was the animal at fault?"[8] This query is not based on logic but rather on one's sense of right. Because of it the sages held that the animal is killed because, alas, she was the instrument for a man's execution; better yet, to prevent continuous comment by human beings—whenever they see the beast—that so and so was punished for a sin committed with her. The dignity of the offender, or his memory, was safeguard.

The Babylonian Talmud, in several folios in Sanhedrin,[9] analyzes this rationalization to ascertain how it would affect the rules of law. For example, should the animal be killed if a pagan committed the offense? He is punished but the second reason for killing the animal does not apply to him, for in pagan circles it is not humiliating to him to be known as one who engages in such sexual experiences.

One can appreciate the fact that with regard to rituals human beings hesitate to attribute their rationalization of the commandments to God and revise the mandates in the light of their own rationalization. However, to project the use of Jewish law for a modern state, with regard to matters civil, criminal, and public, requires that more work be done on the philosophical level to indicate that the traditional rules contain within them a more just approach to all problems of interhuman relationship. And this kind of research and analysis is not being done in adequate measure. The rabbis are so obsessed with fear of resorting to the so-called Ta-ama di-Kra (the rationale of the biblical verses) that their creativity is principally in the area of logical analysis of the precedents and the authorities. The values that Jewish law—civil, criminal, and public—are intended to conserve and promote receive little or no attention. These values are rarely articulated and used in judicial decision and still less in proposals for revision. In Professor Elon's monumental work there is also a minimum of material with regard to them. Yet this is precisely what is needed if one is to convince the non-committed that the renaissance of the Jewish people in Israel can be enriched by the revival of Jewish law.

---

8. San. 7:4.

9. 55a and b.

The Church Fathers and Hebrew Political Thought

For a quarter of a century I taught the history of political theory. During that period I used many different textbooks in order to force myself almost annually to revise my presentations to the students. In virtually no textbook that I used was reference ever made to the contribution of the Hebrew Bible to political and social thought. For almost all the writers, political thought begins with the Greeks and Romans; Christianity saved that heritage for the West and transmitted it to the modern world. It was as if there had been no Israelites and no Bible.

True, the Bible's contribution to political thought in Christianity's second millennium is well known. All theorists quoted Scripture either to conserve the status quo or to effect change or revolution. Similarly in American political and social thought the influence of the Bible was keenly felt. But why was the Bible of so little importance during the first millennium, especially during the first five or six centuries?

There was a time when I believed that the writers of the textbooks were responsible for ignoring the Jewish antecedents to Christianity and focusing only on the Greek and Roman sources. My research, however, now prompts me to place the blame on the Church Fathers themselves.

A.J. Carlyle in his *History of Medieval Political Theory in the West* also ignores the Hebrew Bible and deals only with the political theory of the New Testament. He concedes that "behind the New Testament there lies the literature of the Old Testament, whether belonging to the earlier history of Israel or to the period between the Exile and the advent of Jesus."

But certainly the Church Fathers had the Pentateuch before them and all of it, by any criterion, was written before the Common Era. How can anyone therefore gainsay its influence on the Church Fathers, who, wittingly or unwittingly, engaged in the controversies from which there ultimately emerged the fundamental ideas upon which democratic institutions were founded? Why their silence with respect to the Bible?

For example, at least three Church Fathers interpret a passage of the New Testament as supporting the view that Paul must have had some conception of natural law, since a few words in the New Testament allude to it. From Paul's words it appears that he may have held that there is a law written in men's hearts distinct from reason, and distinct from the positive law of the State and the law revealed by God. But why should any one have doubted Paul had such a conception? This view is abundantly clear in the Pentateuch itself. Carlyle too suggests that Paul might have entertained the conception because it was part of "the general stock of ideas current among the more educated Jews." But it was current among Jews because it is an authentic biblical idea.

In Genesis, Abraham is described as challenging God's plan to destroy the righteous with the wicked in the cities of Sodom and Gomorrah: "Will the judge of all the earth not do justice?" Is Abraham's argument not based on his heart and reason? Or take a passage in Deuteronomy in which we are told that fathers will not be executed for the sins of their sons or sons for the sins of their fathers but every man for his own crimes; or another passage in Deuteronomy in which Moses pleads with his people to appreciate the inherent righteousness of the laws given to them. The laws may have been divinely revealed, but their coming from God alone does not give them their validity—man's reason must vouchsafe how just they are. What better source for natural law than this! Or a passage in Exodus in which judges are told not to pervert justice by following a majority when it is wrong or favoring the poor in a lawsuit since justice must be blind.

It is my considered judgment that the failure of the Church Fathers to give the Hebrew Bible the attention it deserved caused a delay of at least 1,000 years in the advancement of human rights. In the second millennium, especially during the periods of the Renaissance and Reformation, a change took place, but during the first millennium it was reliance on the Greek and Roman sources instead of the Bible that impeded the march of mankind to greater freedom.

How does one explain the failure of the Church Fathers to make Hebraic political and social thought the basis for their own theories? There are several possibilities. It may be that the Christians were so intent upon establishing the superiority of the New Testament over the Hebrew Bible that they shut their eyes to the mine of material in the latter, and since they found very little in the New Testament that was relevant to political thought they preferred to link whatever ideas they expressed with the Greek and Roman heritage.

Or it may be—as many scholars now claim with respect to other fundamental notions—that the early Christians wanted a complete break with Judaism. They wanted to detach themselves from their roots and give the new faith a truly new image. They did this, for example, when they substituted a thoroughgoing universalism for Judaism's dialectical tension between particularism and universalism. Or it may be that they wanted to attract the intelligentsia of the pagan world by basing their ideas on Cicero and Seneca rather than on disdained Jewish sources. Stoicism was the delight of the then existing intelligentsia—the Bible was not. Or it may be that they so loathed the legalism of Judaism that they preferred to ignore all the biblical passages that are legal in character, and searched elsewhere for political ideas.

The neglect of the Hebrew Bible was especially detrimental to the cause of human freedom. Judaism, Stoicism, and Christianity were all committed to the doctrine of the equality of men. However, in Judaism the doctrine contributed not only to the principle of equality before the law but also to the value of personal freedom as distinguished from slavery. This was not true of Stoicism and Christianity.

The Church Fathers did find in the Hebrew Bible convincing justification for the equality of men—the fact that all human beings are descended from common ancestors—Adam and Eve. Augustine wrote:

> It was God's pleasure to propagate all men from one, both for the keeping of human nature in one social similitude, and also to make their unity of origin be the means of their concord in heart. Nor would any of this kind have died had not the first two (the one whereof was made from the other, and the other from nothing) incurred this punishment by their disobedience.

Parenthetically, I would like to point out here that even Tom Paine, in his classic Rights of Man, could find no better argument for the equality of man than that God created all of us from one Adam and Eve. He may have ridiculed the Bible but to prove his point he had to resort to the fact that while God created everything in the plural number, he created one Adam and since all of us have our origin in the one source, none can claim superiority in birth.

Judaism and Christianity were united in this conception. Christianity especially, in its commitment to a universal church for all mankind, had to stress the equality of men in the eyes of God for ultimate salvation. Judaism was not committed to a universal church. On the contrary, it preferred a multiplicity of nations and languages. And it saw in the enormous differences among people, despite the origin of all men in one man, an added reason for admiring God's creation.

What is surprising though is that the two faiths differed so radically on the issue of slavery, and it is especially surprising that Christianity was reconciled so easily to the existence of slavery despite the doctrine of equality.

Aristotle justified the existence of slavery by reasoning that by nature some men are born to be masters and others slaves. The equality of men was not for Aristotle a principle of natural law as it was for the Stoics and Christians. The Church Fathers, however, undertook to defend what they found to be a universal practice—the institution of slavery—and attributed its existence to man's sinfulness. Moreover, the slave was expected to accept his status as punishment and not seek to be free. For Stoics this was understandable. The Stoics believed every man should be totally indifferent to his physical condition; whether free or slave, only the soul mattered, and no man need feel that his soul was enslaved. But how did scholars, who presumably knew the Bible, ignore its preoccupation with freedom—its clear, unmistakable preference for the state of freedom from bondage to humans? Apart from the many references to the importance of freedom, the Pentateuch prohibits the return of a runaway slave to his master. Even the master's right to property—which according to some lawyers of the period was a principle of natural law—yielded in Judaism to the slave's right to seize his freedom.

As a matter of fact Augustine repudiates the notion that the precedent of the liberation of the Hebrew slaves in every seventh year (a misreading of the text on his part) might be applied to the case of the Christian slave. Slaves should obey their masters because it is God who has destined some to be masters and others to be their servants. In one of the canons of the Council of Gangrae (362) the anathema of the Church is laid upon anyone who under the pretense of Godliness teaches a slave to despise his master or to withdraw himself from the master's service.

The Church Fathers generally held that the law of Moses was given because men had failed to obey the natural law. Jerome, for example, held that the whole world received the natural law but the law of Moses was given because the natural law was neglected or destroyed. In connection with slavery, however, the law of Moses seemed to afford them no guidelines whatever. Instead, they accepted the Stoic doctrine, which in a way even glorified the lack of physical freedom because it creates more of a challenge for the cultivation of spiritual freedom. This is a far cry from the Hebraic view that a man in physical freedom shall exercise his free will to be God's servant. Without that physical freedom he may be free in his heart but he cannot prove his righteousness as a totally free, self-directing individual.

Once again, the Church Fathers abandoned the position of the mother faith, contributing immeasurably to the rise of slavery in the second millennium. That Judaism, which was committed to the doctrine of the equality of men, opted, unlike Christianity, for the elimination of slavery may be due to the fact that without so stating Judaism had a limited conception of natural law. It was humanity's loss that this Jewish perspective was not clearly stated and acted upon. In this respect the Jewish point of view was superior to that of the Greeks and Romans, although it later became the view of the Roman lawyers.

In Greek and Roman literature two sources for natural law are mentioned—man's reason and the universal practice of mankind. Aristotle specifically includes in natural justice "that which everywhere has the same force and does not exist by peoples thinking this or that." Roscue Pound speaks of the natural law that is based on pure reason as a priori while the natural law based on the universal practice of mankind is a posteriori. He further states that when legal development was based on the a priori—man's pure reason—it was progressive, liberal. When it was a posteriori, it was reactionary, conservative This was especially true in the United States. The Roman lawyers did finally differentiate between the ius naturale based on the human heart and human reason, and the ius gentium based on the universal practice of mankind. The institution of slavery was justified by the Church Fathers not on the basis of natural law but rather by reference to the ius gentium. As a result, the abolition of slavery was delayed for centuries. If Jewish sources, rather than Roman sources, had prevailed in Christian thought, the situation might have been quite different.

In Jewish law the ius gentium was of little, if any, importance. Consequently, and especially in connection with slavery, the natural law was all a priori.

The rabbis did not call it natural law but it appears again and again in the Hebrew Bible and in the Talmud in the form of a protest, as if asking, "Is that just?" The classic instance in the Bible, mentioned above, is Abraham's protest when God told him that he intended to destroy cities of iniquity.

In the Talmud natural law also appears in the form of a protest. "Will 'A' sin and the punishment be imposed upon 'B'?" The most moving instance involves the debate between the School of Shamai and the School of Hillel with regard to a man who is half slave and half free. This would come to pass, for example, when one of two partners or heirs emancipated the slave. He could do so only with respect to his half interest. As a result the slave was still bonded to the other partner or heir. The School of Hillel felt that this created no problem. The slave could work three days a week for himself and three days for his master. The School of Shamai protested: "You have provided for the master's interest. But what of the slave? A free woman he cannot marry because he is half slave. A slave woman he cannot marry because he is half free. How is he to fulfill God's will to populate the earth?" Needless to say, if his status does not allow him, because of divine law, to populate the earth, then he is under no obligation to do so. It is God's law that stops him. But the School of Shamai was concerned with the slave's natural right: he is not to be denied his humanity. And the School of Shamai ruled—with the concurrence of the School of Hillel—that the slave should be fully emancipated. He shall give the master who did not want to free him a promissory note to indemnify him for his loss, and repayment was to be made by the erstwhile slave—now a free man.

Why did Judaism accept only the a priori natural law while it never permitted the universal practice of mankind, the so-called a posteriori natural law, to play any role in its awareness of natural law? To me it seems that in Judaism there is such emphasis on being unlike the Gentiles that what the Gentiles did could never be a criterion for what is just. As everyone knows, the constant repetition in the Bible of the command to be different—never to practice what the neighbors practiced—made impossible resort to what was the prevailing usage in the world at large. In any event, in Judaism, natural law plays an important role but only the a priori type, based on the human heart and human reason. The Church Fathers could not possibly have been unaware of it, but it seems that they preferred to rely on the writings of pagans, especially the Roman ones. And instead of moving in the direction of the abolition of slavery as Judaism did, it gave Church support to the institution for more than a millennium.

It may be that if the Church Fathers in the first five centuries of the Common Era had embraced and propagated Jewish views on natural law and slavery, the institution would not have been eliminated anyway. However, I do not think that this can be said of their failure for a long time to appreciate two other biblical ideas that lie at the very heart of democratic institutions. One is the notion that may be called the right to question the legitimacy of the exercise of authority. The other may be called the need for the existence of two authorities in society—the temporal and the spiritual—in two distinctly separate persons or institutions. The first idea is fully presented in the chapter "Theocentricity in Jewish Law"

The net result of the biblical insistence that God is the one and only Sovereign is that the legitimacy of the exercise of authority by one man over another must always he questioned; the unlawful seizure of power must be prevented; power must be diffused; and to make possible the challenging of authority, temporal and spiritual powers must be kept separate from each other.

Why did the Church Fathers ignore these ideas and make total obedience to civil government a virtue even if that government is unjust? Why did they reconcile themselves to unjust government as punishment for sin? Of course, they found some biblical verses on which to rely, but the greater weight of the evidence favored Talmon's and Sibley's views as I have quoted them above.

One answer might be that they wanted to put an end to the anarchical proclivities of many Christian sects. This was a period when the Church was trying to become institutionalized, and it had to discourage any ideas that would be subversive of this goal.

The centuries that followed found the popes engaged in major, often bloody, conflicts with the kings. What the Bible had visualized was coexistence, with neither having ultimate sovereignty, which inheres only in God. Everyone else has only limited authority in a world in which power is diffused so that none will usurp God's role.

To document the theses of Talmon and Sibley would make this essay unduly long. Suffice it for me to submit only a few of the biblical ideas which support their conclusions.

1. The Bible is unequivocal that the establishment of any state—and even the very constituting of the nation—was the result of a covenant between the people and God. Each party to the covenant assumed obligations. As the rabbis of the Talmud, contemporaries

of the Church Fathers, understood it, the covenant obligated God to be bound by His own law. Professor Moshe Zilberg argued that this meant that God Himself was bound by the rule of law.

2. All authority was to be exercised pursuant to that law. A king, if appointed, was also subject to it. He was obliged to have a copy of the law with him all the time.

3. No king was to be appointed unless the people asked for one; this is crystal clear from the verses in Deuteronomy. And the people were to choose him. The qualifications were set forth in Scripture.

4. The law is exoteric. It must be promulgated and made known to everyone. Thus, all would be able to know on what basis to question the legitimacy of authority—all would be learned in the law.

5. Every person is capable of achieving the gift of prophecy and the people themselves are to judge who is a false prophet and who is a true one.

6. The people were to nominate the persons from among whom Moses was to pick the judges and administrators.

7. Those who rebelled for more authority than was permitted to them were severely punished.

8. Those to whom spiritual authority was delegated were to be landless.

9. Moses assigned the spiritual authority to the members of his tribe, but temporal authority was given to Joshua, who was of another tribe; in this way Moses divided the succession. In later Jewish history Joshua's authority passed to Saul and finally to the Davidic dynasty of the tribe of Judah. (The rabbis were critical of the Maccabees who arrogated to themselves both kingship and priesthood.)

All of these sources were sadly neglected by the Church Fathers. If they had gained an early acceptance humanity might have been spared much sorrow.

The Federal Constitution of the United States and the Jewish Heritage

The Bible did not play a significant role in the debates of the delegates who drafted the American constitution in 1787. A few references were made to it in connection with the issue of slavery, but John Rutledge, among others, rejected the idea that religion or humanity had anything to do with the importation of slaves. Nonetheless, it cannot be denied that the Bible was probably the one book about which the delegates would have said that it ranked first among the volumes that influenced their lives, and they were all familiar with biblical political thought. Therefore, one may properly speak of the Hebraic roots of the constitution even if one cannot prove that in the deliberations there was an awareness of the biblical sources upon which their fundamental notions and specific proposals were based. The Bible was a very important element in the delegates' cultural background, as was their colonial experience. And in the celebration of the two hundredth anniversary of their historic achievement one ought take a look at a number of its components which parallel Hebraic tradition and could easily have been derived from it.

As a matter of fact, the political writings of the colonists in both the seventeenth and eighteenth centuries were replete with references to the Bible. One discovers in the first two volumes of Vernon Parrington's "Main Currents in American Literature" that the literature of the period was principally political in nature with many of the clergy contributing to it even in their sermons. Needless to say, the Bible was a respected source to support many of the views advanced. Roger Williams had argued, for example, that all the citizens need not be of one faith which European states had learned belatedly. The Bible itself is unequivocally committed to the idea that in the Jewish state "the stranger and the citizen" (Lev. 24: 22) may reside, with equal protection of the law. Thomas Hooker relied on Deuteronomy (1:13) to support the democratic idea that the people nominate from among themselves their choices for the exercise of power, while Moses was to make the final choice.

I.

The basic ideas of freedom and equality figure as much in the American Declaration of Independence of 1776 as in the constitution of 1787, and the values are central in both documents.

The biblical notion of freedom includes personal freedom and national freedom. The state and its people are to cherish freedom from the exercise of foreign power and the individuals within each state were to enjoy maximum freedom from submission to others. True, in a limited way the Bible condoned slavery, and delegates from the southern states did not hesitate thus to argue. However, there is so much in the Bible and its commentaries to glorify freedom that in the constitution the delegates avoided use of the word "slaves" lest so important a document give recognition to the existence of the institution of slavery and by implication sanction it. The constitution speaks only of "free persons" and "all others".

It is too often overlooked that the notions of freedom and equality are essentially Hebraic and not Hellenic. Both Plato and Aristotle assumed that in nature there is a difference between those born to rule and those born to be ruled. (Plato perhaps, more than Aristotle, would have made the differentiation on the basis of one's education rather than one's endowments from birth.) The number of freemen in Athens was tiny by comparison with the number of slaves. With the advent of Christianity there was little change, and slavery was condoned as punishment for sin. Even the Stoics, for whom equality was as basic as it was in Judaism, urged slaves to be free in spirit and not be concerned with physical freedom, unlike the biblical point of view which stresses physical freedom as well. Furthermore, the Stoic notion of equality was attributed to the fact that all men are endowed with reason and that is the rationale for their equality, while Judaism, and subsequently Christianity, based the notion of equality on man's having been created in the divine image.

One passage in Tom Paine's "Rights of Man" affords us with some proof of the centrality of biblical thought even in such an iconoclast as he was. Certainly in the thought of his more devout contemporaries the Bible played a significant role. He was constrained to reply to Edmund Burke, who shared Aristotle's view that men are unequal by nature. On what basis, however, can one establish equality as a fact when the inequality about us is so overwhelming? Tom Paine cited Chapter 1 of Genesis. God had created only one man and one woman, unlike his performance in connection with the creation of all other living things whom He created in the plural number. Why? Simply to make it known that all humans are descended from one set of progenitors and, therefore, none can claim superiority over another. Paine may not have known of this argument because of its talmudic source (Sanh 4:5). He may have known of it because Augustine used it in his *City of God*. But who can deny that the idea is authentically biblical!

However, the biblical notion of equality did not imply sameness. In the same passage in which the argument for equality is brought the Talmud says that God is a remarkable King. Human kings mint coins from one die and all are identical. Yet God from one couple brought forth all kinds of human beings, different in many ways. He did not clone—He did the very opposite. No two are alike. And these differences are reflected in the legal system of Judaism as in all other legal systems. Yet, equality before the law is the ideal explicitly stated in Leviticus (24:2), "One law applies to all of you, to the stranger and citizen alike". Is this not the guarantee of "equal protection of the laws" which was finally included in the 14th amendment?

Almost everywhere equality is only a projected ideal, and States vary in the measure of their fulfillment of it. However, at least with respect to one matter the delegates were agreed. Whatever protection the constitution afforded was to "persons," not necessarily citizens. For some purposes, persons not free and Indians were excluded, but in most respects the law applied to the stranger and the citizen alike.

II.

The Constitution makes it very clear that those who wrote it feared too much government and had a negative attitude toward monarchy. The experience of the colonists with the kings of England was enough to evoke the latter attitude, but the resistance to monarchy also has biblical roots which were well known to all literate contemporaries of the delegates. The hostility finds expression in the constitutional prohibition against the granting of titles of nobility by States and providing that no one holding "office of profit or trust" shall accept such a title without the consent of Congress.

Furthermore, to protect the citizens against too powerful a government of any kind, the constitution provides for the separation of powers and checks and balances. No one had absolute power. There were constitutional restraints on all who exercised power—and there were even certain powers that were beyond the scope of government altogether. There was liberty against government or freedom from government, as one great scholar of constitutional law described it.

The Bible is quite emphatic that no king in Israel was to be an absolute monarch. He would be subject to law. The passage in Deuteronomy (17:14-20) may create ambivalence as to whether the appointment of a king was mandatory or optional. However, that his powers were limited was never questioned. Indeed, every king was to write for himself a new copy of the Torah which was always to be with him to remind him that there were restraints upon him. There is a Sovereign above him and he must never forget it. The dramatic tale of King Ahab and Naboth's vineyard not only illustrates the limitations on monarchial power, but the courageous words of the prophet Elijah have become part of the equity law of England and the United States, "Would you both murder and inherit (the victim)"? (I Kings 21) The law does not permit anyone to profit by his criminal deed.

In the talmudic period it was not uncommon for rabbis to read portions of the Bible to those appointed to public office that they too might be made aware of the fact they must serve according to the Law.

It should be of interest that in the Middle Ages, when Jewish communities enjoyed legal autonomy, the rabbis often held that even a majority among them were also limited in what they could do. There were so-called constitutional restraints upon majorities. And Hamilton, Madison and Jay were very aware of this Hebraic principle in the Book of Exodus. The verse in Exodus orders Jews not to follow a majority to do wrong (23:2).

One cannot be sure that the delegates knew that some of the restraints upon executive power for which they provided also existed in Jewish law and were derivative from the Rabbis' study of the Bible. A president in the United States, for example, cannot declare war without the consent of the Congress, as a king in Israel could not embark upon an offensive war without the consent of the Sanhedrin. Moreover, he must compensate the citizens for damage done to their property because of the exigencies of war. However, what is most important is that from the Bible one derives the insight that one may always challenge a person who seeks to exercise power over another and ask on what basis this is being sought to be done. What is the authority? What law, what customs, what tradition, justifies it?

The doctrine of judicial review derives directly from the assumption that one may challenge the legitimacy of the exercise of authority of one over another. It was a Hebrew slave, we are told in Exodus, (2:14) who challenged Moses' right to interfere in a dispute. He was asked who gave him that right or power. Later on in Moses' career, his disciple Joshua wanted to stop two prophets presumably from competing with Moses, and Moses refused to listen to him. On the other hand, he argued, would that all were similarly endowed. (Numbers 11:29) The only restraints upon people are those specified in the Law.

III.

Professor Talmon sees the permanent tension between Church and State as a derivative from the Jewish insistence that anyone exercising authority over another must legitimatize his act. This legitimacy can only come from God and/or His Law. But who speaks for God? This led to a bifurcation of authority on earth: spiritual authority resides in God's surrogates and temporal authority in the state. And this separation is indicated in biblical history. Moses himself, pursuant to God's command, divided the succession to himself. Priestly or spiritual authority was given to his brother Aaron, and executive power, or temporal authority, to Joshua, of another tribe. This tradition was maintained as kings came from one tribe while priests and levites were of another tribe. Only once in Jewish history were the two powers joined in one person. The Maccabees arrogated to themselves both kingship and priesthood and the rabbis frowned upon them for this, among other reasons.

Augustine recognized this unique feature of Judaism—the dual character of authority, spiritual and temporal, but cited Jesus as the only person entitled to exercise both.

Separation of church and state was discussed by political theorists in the Middle Ages, but its biblical roots should not be overlooked. And in connection with judicial review Jews had a very clearly articulated rule that a Jew could defy a king's order if it violated a command of the Torah. Such a person was not a rebel and his action was not treason. Therefore, he could not be punished.

IV.

One of the most important limitations on the monarch pertained to his exclusion from a judicial role. This is discussed at great length both in the Babylonian and Jerusalem Talmuds. Yet it was the Bible itself that precipitated the discussion in the Talmud, and even if the founding fathers did not know of the discussion in the Talmud they could fathom from the very text of Scripture itself how important it was to separate the judicial authority from the executive authority. The king had the latter authority but not the former. Witness, for example, the fact that King Ahab could not punish Naboth by his own decree. He had to establish a tribunal and suborn witnesses to convict him.

Needless to say, the Bible does cite one famous case brought before King Solomon, and his ascertaining who was the mother of the living child (I Kings 3:16-28). But his authority to judge as he did was questioned by later authorities. In his day much of the culture in the country was pagan and kings among pagans may have had the right to judge. David too offended in this way, and the rabbis sought justification for it. Perhaps he could be trusted because he would feel bound by the Law while other kings would not feel so bound. Nonetheless, it must be evident that the separation of the judicial power from executive power was not a biblical idea which was foreign to the founding fathers.

This was not true of legislative and judicial power—these powers did reside in one body according to the Bible. Their separation in the American constitution was due to other influences such as Montesquieu.

V.

Few biblical ideas have had more impact on western political thought than the idea of the covenant. For the framers of the constitution it was basic.

The constitution was to be a covenant between the states as the Mayflower Compact was a covenant between the Pilgrims. And it was to be irrevocable unless the revocation was bilateral. The biblical notion involved principally a covenant between the ruler and the ruled—God and His people. The American Constitution instead was a covenant between allegedly sovereign states. But it created a permanent relationship whose permanence the Civil War finally confirmed.

Moreover, it was a Covenant involving not only the states but also the citizens of each state—precisely as God's covenant with His people applied directly to individual Jews as it did to the organized Jewish people or state.

With hindsight one might say that it was unfortunate that while the Covenant idea was central in the thought of the founding fathers, another biblical idea, linked with it, was not included in the Constitution, and that idea is the responsibility of all those affected by it not only to support the covenant but also to be responsible for each other's support of it. Perhaps it was too early to think of national unity when only a federation was contemplated. Yet thus a later civil war might have been avoided and the welfare state would have encountered less resistance than it did a century or more later. In the Declaration of Independence both ideas were expressed. That document concluded with the words "we mutually pledge to each other our Lives, our Fortunes and our sacred Honor."

The "hidden" influence of the Bible did not cease with the adoption of the federal Constitution. As late as in Griswold v. Connecticut, the historic case which gave constitutional protection to the right to privacy, one finds echoes of the words of Scripture. In writing the majority opinions the judges did not quote the Bible. They relied principally on three paragraphs in the Bill of Rights, two of which have deep roots in the Bible, and provisions of Jewish law which were well known to common law lawyers because of their British heritage.

The judges argued that the right to privacy, though not explicit in the Constitution, is implicit in three of the amendments.

First, there is the protection against unlawful searches and seizures. The Bible protects the privacy of one's home, that a creditor may not enter to collect the debt due him. He can come to the door and no further. In the Talmud this protection was extended to include even the sheriff.

Second, there is the privilege against self-incrimination, which protects the privacy of one's doings. The Talmud deals with this extensively. Indeed, the privilege is a disability. It cannot be waived. It was a doctrine that British jurists were familiar with.

Third, one amendment precludes the imposition on citizens of hospitality in peacetime to soldiers. In Judaism this was unthinkable. No king, and no state, could exercise such a power and thus endanger the chastity of a woman in a household. Nothing was clearer in biblical law than the protection of women from even the remote possibility of sexual abuse. As a matter of fact the law of privacy with regard to one's religious behavior is derived from those passages. Whether husbands and wives observed the laws pertaining to ritual cleanness or uncleanness was a matter of honor; nevertheless their privacy was protected.

Indeed, biblical ideas and Jewish law enriched western political thought in the past and there is much reason to believe that there is an abundance of insights still available for the advancement of democratic thought and action in the present.

The Case of the Sotah in Jewish Law: Ordeal or Psychodrama?

Introduction

The rabbis of the talmudic period often differed with each other in interpreting Scripture, and many times arrived at mutually contradictory conclusions. Lex talionis is the best known example of the rabbis interpreting the Scripture in a manner inconsistent with its literal meaning. It was speculated that perhaps the biblical command of an "eye for an eye"[1] required exact retribution, but it was held that it called for monetary compensation.[2] It was even suggested that the offender choose which punishment he preferred.[3] Less known but no less sharp is the controversy with regard to the "beautiful captive".[4] A dispute existed as to the very nature and purpose of the law, which was only articulated clearly in its details. The rabbis differed on the issue of whether she was to cut her nails or let them grow. This minor dispute was fundamental in understanding whether the "beautiful captive" was to remain voluntarily in the home of her captor, or not. One rabbi held one view; another rabbi held the opposite.[5]

It is the thesis of this essay that the rabbis also held antithetical views regarding the ritual of the sotah,[6] the indiscreet wife. One group maintained that the ritual was an ordeal by which God's intervention proved her guilt or innocence. The other group did not clearly state its rejection of this view, but all its prescriptions indicate such a stance. This latter group of rabbis were not free to verbalize why they did not accept the supernatural approach for they feared that public criticism of the supernatural approach would

---

1. Exod. 21:24; Lev. 24:20; Deut. 19:21.

2. BK 83b–84a; *Encyclopedia Talmudit* 12 (1974), 695.

3. BK 83b.

4. Deut. 21:10–14.

5. Yeb. 48a.

6. Num. 5:11–31. The noun *sotah* is derived from the Hebrew verb *sth*, to deviate.

152

have vitiated the value of the sotah ceremony as they perceived it. Even for them, however, the ceremony had great probative and social significance. They instead adopted legislation which converted this apparent ordeal into a pseudojudicial event designed to extract a confession from the accused if she was guilty, whereupon she would be divorced and would only forfeit her monetary rights under her ketubah.[7] On the other hand, her innocence would be established if she was so, thus restoring her husband's erstwhile love and confidence. To this group of rabbis, the sotah procedure was designed to remove doubt in a framework where there was little penalty for honesty.

The existence of the implied latter view enables one to better understand the talmudic literature on the subject. It is also consistent with the general spirit of Jewish law. Furthermore, there is reason to believe that it is more in consonance with the original intent of the scriptural passages when read in the light of the Code of Hamurabi. The biblical intent would be, as is thought in many other cases, to protest against an ancient idolatrous practice by prescribing something similar in many ways, but diametrically opposite in purpose.[8]

The Ritual of Sotah

The biblical verses are relatively clear:[9] if a wife shall "go wrong" and be unfaithful to her husband without the presence of witnesses, the husband can bring her to the priest, taking along with him a

---

7. A ketubah is a prenuptial agreement authorized by the husband and wife establishing the rights of each party in cases of divorce or death. It can be forfeited upon misconduct. See Ket. 72a–b.

8. Another example of this phenomenon can be found in the interpretation of Exod. 21:31, where the Bible commands that the law shall be identical whether the negligence of a person kills the claimant or the claimant's children. This is in contrast to the Code of Hamurabi's decision that "if a builder build[s] a house for a man and do[es] not make its construction firm, and the house which he has built collapse[s] and cause[s] the death of the owner of the house, that builder shall be put to death. If it cause[s] the death of a son of the owner of the house, they shall put to death a son of that builder." The *Code of Hamurabi, King of Babylon* § 229–30 (R.F. Harper trans. 1904). See also G.R. Driver & J.C. Miles, *The Babylonian Laws* II (1952), 217, 282–83, 407–8, 439–40, 43–44, 95–96.

9. Num. 5:11–31.

very simple meal offering. The priest then places "holy water" in an earthen bowl and puts some earth from the floor of the tabernacle in it. As she thus stands before God, the priest dishevels[10] her hair and places the meal offering in her hands. An oath is then administered to the wife, who attests to her innocence[11] and says amen. The oath (or curse) is written on parchment and placed in the water so that the words are erased in the solution. The wife drinks the water and the priest performs a prescribed ritual with the meal offering. If she is innocent, nothing happens to her and she will even soon bear children.[12] If she is not innocent, the curse is fulfilled, and her thighs and stomach will provide evidence of her guilt.[13]

These verses inevitably create the impression that trial by ordeal was sanctioned by Judaism. Undoubtedly, many rabbis believed that the water was endowed with supernatural power. These rabbis maintained that if a guilty woman drank the water, not only would she die, but her illicit lover as well.[14] Moreover, some believed that a similar result was achieved by Moses after the Jews had made the golden calf.[15] The Midrash states that Moses ground the calf into a powder and forced the Jews to drink it. Those guilty of

---

10. Perhaps "uncovers" rather than dishevels; see Y. Weinberg, *Sredai Eish* III, 30. 11.

11. Num. 5:19–20. The priest shall administer an oath to the woman, saying to her, "If a man has not lain with you, and you have not committed adultery so as to be defiled to your husband, you shall be unharmed by this curse-bearing bitter water. But if you have committed adultery against your husband and have become defiled, and if a man other than your husband has had intercourse with you . . ." [At this point] the priest shall administer to the woman [the part of] the oath containing the curse. The priest shall say to the woman, "[in such a case], God will make you a curse and an oath among your people, causing your thighs to rupture and your belly to blow up." Translation from A. Kaplan, *The Living Torah* (1981), 396–98.

12. Num. 5:28.

13. Num. 5:27. (If the woman who drinks the water has been defiled and untrue to her husband, the curse-bearing water will enter her body to poison her, causing her belly to blow up and her thighs to rupture. Translation from A. Kaplan, above, note 11.)

14. Sotah 8:1.

15. Exod. 32:1–35.

idolatry perished while the innocent survived.[16] Yet, it is perplexing that in all of talmudic literature there is but one report of an actual case in which a woman drank the water or the ritual was used.[17] What happened to the woman is not stated and the entire passage is ambiguous.[18] Indeed, the propriety of giving her the water was questioned in a talmudic discussion, where one rabbi even suggested that it was all a hoax.[19] Certainly, one of the reasons to doubt that the ritual was regarded by many rabbis as one designed to prove guilt or innocence is the almost complete absence in Jewish literature of accounts of the use of this procedure.

First and foremost, the rabbis debated in the Talmud whether the ritual was mandatory or permissive.[20] The question arose as to when it was permissive for Jewish authorities to look the other way when the commission of a crime had been alleged. The majority may have held that it was a *mitzvah* (a religious duty and a legal obligation) to pursue this matter, like any other criminal prosecution.[21] However, the fact that some dissented from this view and believed that the ritual was permissive, proves that some authorities must have maintained that the purpose of the mission was not punishment but something else. These rabbis believed that the sotah proceeding served a didactic purpose—by teaching the sanctity of family life and the high cost of infidelity. Yet, the ritual was instituted not to gather judicial proof of the alleged infidelity, but to calm the husband and afford the wife with an opportunity to establish her innocence or confess her guilt with less than fatal consequences.[22]

Second, the Talmud's description of the effect of drinking the

16. Avodah Zara 44a.

17. Eduyot 5:6.

18. Id.

19. Id.

20. Sotah 3a.

21. The law is codified in accordance with this position. See Mishneh Torah, Hilkhot Sotah 4:18.

22. The problem confronted in these situations is simple: to design a process which not only establishes facts but also re-establishes confidence by both partners in each other by removing doubt.

water does not coincide with what the Bible predicts.[23] Some commentators try to reconcile this inconsistency by suggesting that the Talmud mentions ill effects that will follow those that the Bible mentions.[24] Yet, it is interesting that while the Mishnah does not mention the biblical effects at all, those which the Mishnah does mention could well follow any subjection to stress.[25] The same effects could even now accompany the application of a lie detector test.[26]

All of this is relevant to my thesis only insofar as it reveals the lack of evidence that the ritual was ever consummated to the very end. If a procedure actually existed which was regarded as capable of actually conclusively proving guilt or innocence, it would have certainly been resorted to with great frequency; rather, this Mishnah establishes that the rabbis were describing symptoms that they felt would occur after one was subjected to a stressful situation, such as the sotah procedure.

Third, the Code of Hamurabi states that a woman accused of adultery, but who has not been caught in the act "shall leap into the river for her husband."[27] This is the typical ordeal by water against which the more humane biblical ritual is to be understood. The Bible substitutes a drink of special water for the leap into the river. Usually when the Scripture orders, in a similar state of facts, something radically different from the Code of Hamurabi, the intention is to ameliorate rather than cause greater suffering.[28] Without a doubt, the immediate danger from drowning is greater than that of a drink whose ill effect only God could precipitate. Most significantly, the biblically mandated ritual required a miracle in order for harm to befall its victim; the Hamurabic Code required a miracle in order to survive. However important this difference is between these two apparently similar rituals, I believe it unlikely that the amelioration intended would be limited only to this. Although some rabbis have held this belief, others have seen in

---

23. Sotah 3:4. "She hardly finished drinking when her face turned sallow, her eyes burst and her veins swelled." See also Sotah 20a.

24. Mishneh Torah, Hilkhot Sotah 3:16, and commentaries ad loc.

25. L. Taylor, *Scientific Interrogation* 318–29 (1984) (stress as a form of interrogation).

26. Id.

27. Code of Hamurabi, above, note 8, at § 132.

28. See G.R. Driver, above, note 8.

the biblical prescriptions, as contrasted with that of Hamurabi, a design to give the proceeding a more radical departure from prevailing mores and methods of proof.

The Role of Reason in Jewish Law

What makes the literal view so untenable and what prompted rabbis to take another view without diminishing from the psychological value of the proceeding to accomplish what they thought it was intended to accomplish? The answers to this question are many. First, while the basic premise of Judaism is that its laws reflect the will of God, it is paradoxical that more than any other system of law in antiquity, Jewish law firmly denied God any role in its legislative and judicial processes. Legislators and judges were expected to fulfill God's will as revealed in His words and in the oral traditions which emanated from Him. God could not intervene by miracles, supernatural phenomena, dreams, or ordeals. Nor did the rabbis believe that God would ever appear again to modify his commandments. It was believed that human reason, experience, and thought alone determined the outcome, especially when establishing judicial proof. It was as if God had said to man, "I have given you enough guidelines to proceed on your own."

This should not come as a surprise to students of Jewish thought. The practice of any form of magic, sorcery, witchcraft, divination, and necromancy was forbidden in Judaism,[29] and in fact, the use of the urim and tumim[30] was abandoned early in Jewish history.[31] Maimonides disparaged those who took astrology seriously, even though he himself believed that the heavenly host possessed consciousness.[32] According to Jewish thought, humanity must rely only upon the faculties with which God blessed it, such as reason and sense experience. Even one's faith must be consistent with them. The goal of much of Jewish philosophy, particularly the

---

29. At least five verses in the Bible prohibit such practices: Exod. 22:17, Lev. 19:26 and 31, Lev. 20:27, and Deut. 18:14. These were prohibited according to some commentators even though they actually did work. See Nachmanides, commenting on Lev. 19:26.

30. The *urim* and *tumim* were used by the High Priest to communicate with God. See Encyclopedia Judaica 16, col. 8 (1972).

31. See Sotah 9:12; See also *Encyclopedia Talmudit* 1, col. 391–97 (1978).

32. Mishneh Torah, Hilkhot Avodah Zara 9:16.

Maimonidean tradition,[33] was to prove this theory. Most significantly, judges who had to determine guilt or innocence, the existence of obligation, and the measure of damage or punishment, were bound to disregard anything other than that which could be demonstrated by human faculties.[34] This was a major contribution of Judaism to western jurisprudential philosophy.

One of the most famous talmudic texts, in tractate Bava Metzia,[35] justifies the conclusion that God is estopped from intervening in debates between rabbis as to the meaning or application of biblical verses. In this famous case, Rabbi Eliezer called upon the heavens to provide proof of the authenticity of his position and the invalidity of the majority's approach. Although God provided confirmation supporting Rabbi Eliezer, the rabbis refused to change their position.[36] This incident demonstrated that once God gave the Bible to man, it became theirs to interpret without the assistance of heavenly signs or sounds. The Talmud concludes this incident with the classical statement: "It [the Bible or the commandment] is not in heaven" (*lo bashamayim he*).[37] Professor Moshe Silberg derives from this text the primacy of the rule of law in Judaism. Even God is bound by it. God is subjected to man's jurisdiction and their conception of his legislative intent is binding also on Him.[38]

---

33. See, e.g, J.B. Soloveitchik, *The Halachic Mind* (1986), 85–100.

34. San. 6b ("A judge only has that which his senses can use").

35. BM 59b.

36. Id. [R. Eliezer] said: Let this carob-tree prove that the Halakha prevails as I state, and the carob was . . . thrown off to a distance of one hundred amot. . . But they said: The carob proves nothing. He again said: "Let, then, the spring of water prove that so the Halakha prevails." The water then began to run backwards. . . He again said "Then, let the walls of the [Beit Medrash] prove that I am right." The walls were about to fall. . . . They did not fall for the honor of R. Joshua . . . He said again: "Let it be announced by the heavens that the Halakha prevails according to my statement," and a heavenly voice was heard, saying: "Why do you quarrel with R. Eliezer, who is always right in his decisions!" R. Joshua then arose and proclaimed (Deut. 30:12) "The law is not in the heavens." (M. Rodkinson trans. 1918)

37. Id.

38. M. Silberg, *Talmudic Law And The Modern State* (B. Bokser trans. 1973), p. 65; but see Drashot Ha Ran, derasha 11 (1973).

Another talmudic text[39] seems to say that a heavenly omen is accorded respect when it is supportive of the majority decision of the rabbis.[40] Needless to say, a majority must feel favored when, after reaching a decision, a voice from on high commends them. It is important to realize that although God may commend the majority for their decision, His opinion is not dispositive. This is dramatically demonstrated by the case of Rabbi Eliezer, discussed above, where a majority decision was not reversed even though God had intervened against them. The rabbis used God's own mandate to the effect that one must abide by the majority will, even when it is against God's own will.[41]

One of the assumptions of traditional Jewish law is that the legislation promulgated in the Pentateuch is divinely revealed and all that came after enjoyed a lesser status as rabbinical legislation. It appears from the Talmud that in rare instances God does communicate with the prophets in order to give new rituals to the Jewish people, and some of these rituals have virtually the status of the divine law contained in the Pentateuch.[42] For example, the prophets mandated a ritual observed on the seventh day of the Succot festival with willow branches.[43] These revelations, however, never involved matters that could result in litigation.

Undoubtedly, Jewish law allowed for the invocation of the divine in the area of ritual; it was only in the areas of law that involved man's relationship with his fellow man that divine intervention would not be sanctioned. In none of the sources discussing divine additions to the law does one find any discussion of topics involving areas where litigation is possible. Jewish law never resorted to anything other than reason and sense experience in the judicial

---

39. Yeb. 14a.

40. Tosafot, commenting on BM 59b (starting with the words *lo bashamayim he*) and Rabbenu Nissim, quoted in Shita Mekubezet, commenting on id. See also *Encyclopedia Talmudit* 5 (1986), col. 1.

41. BM 59b.

42. See Urbach, "HaHalakhah v'Nevuah," *Tarbiz* 18 (1947), 6-27. Professor A.J Heschel has assembled data trying to establish that even during the post-talmudic period much law was established by mystical experiences, messages from the Holy Spirit, and even dreams. Heschel, "Ruach HaKodesh Beyemai HaBainayim," *Sefer Hayovel Likhvod Alexander Marx* 175-208 (1950), 175-208 .

43. Urbach, above, note 42, at 10–14.

process. More significantly, the new rules of law or new interpretations which came from sources other than reason and sense experience never involved anything other than an individual's religious behavior vis-a-vis God, and not matters which could have precipitated a justiciable controversy in court.[44] Those areas where the implications from the prophets changed biblical law in relationships between persons were not followed.[45]

Another famous example, this time from the medieval period, of an attempt to resort to the divine to settle disputes, is the discussion regarding the use of a defective myrtle as one of the four species in the ritual of the festival of Tabernacles (Succot).[46] Maimonides deemed it usable.[47] Rabbi Abraham Ben David, on the other hand, did not, because "The Holy Spirit appeared in our house of learning years ago and we have rejected it as unusable."[48] What is of interest in this case, as in many others, is that not everyone in Israel was as impressed as Rabbi Abraham Ben David with the appearance of the Holy Spirit in his house of learning. Rabbi Caro, for example, defended the view of Maimonides and ignored the revelation to Maimonides' controversialist,[49] despite the fact that he was a mystic and cabalist.[50]

Jewish law did allow judges to use their own sense experience even in the face of contrary evidence. According to the Bible, at least two witnesses are required to establish any fact.[51] Yet, judges can be creative and establish facts by resorting to other means, such as intuition, and can resist uncontradicted, unimpeached testimony of two or more witnesses if they feel that a miscarriage

---

44. See id. for a complete list of the locations.

45. See Ezek. 44:22 for one example of a statement in the prophets which differed in a legally significant way from that of the Bible.

46. See J. Caro, Shulchan Aruch, Orach Chaim 645:1–4.

47. See Mishneh Torah, Hilkhot Lulav 8:5.

48. Abraham Ben David (Rabad), Hasagot; Mishneh Torah, Hilkhot Lulav 8:5.

49. See Shulchan Aruch, Orach Chaim 646:1; and glosses of M. Isserles on id. See also Don Vidal De Toulouse, Maggid Mishneh, commenting on Mishneh Torah, Hilkhot Lulav 8:5.

50. See J.R. Werblowsky, *Joseph Karo: Lawyer And Mystic* (1962), 148–69.

51. Deut. 17:6.

of justice might result.[52] While help from the supernatural is not permitted, intuition and creative discovery may be employed.

The classic case for judicial creativity (without regard to the biblical requirement that every issue shall be resolved by the testimony of at least two witnesses) is that of King Solomon and the two mothers who appeared before him; each had recently given birth and both claimed the surviving child as her own. Solomon ordered the child to be cut into two; a decision which evoked the immediate reaction of the real mother who waived her rights rather than see the child killed.[53] Solomon's decision was apparently not within a judge's power to make. The proper procedure was to seek witnesses to ascertain which child belonged to whom, or at least to discover other forms of testimony (visual, medical, etc.).[54]

Can any judge take it upon himself to act similarly? The Meiri, in his commentary on the Talmud,[55] says that only the very great may do so. The Talmud recounts a story about one such person—Rabbi Bana.[56] A man overheard his wife counseling her daughter to be more discreet in her promiscuous behavior. The mother said that she was sufficiently wise in her day to have had ten sons, only one of whom was her husband's. The husband, overhearing this, left his entire estate to his one and only son whose identity was unknown. When the case came before Rabbi Bana he ruled that the man's grave should be reopened for consultation. One son refused to participate in the procedure, since it would have been disrespectful to his father's remains. Rabbi Bana then ruled that this son was entitled to the entire estate. The other sons informed against him to the ruling authorities and accused the rabbi of expropriating heirs "without witnesses and without proof."[57] Although their complaint was well founded, the Talmud did not reject Rabbi Bana's verdict.

The Meiri maintained that only one who is endowed with exceptional wisdom and analytical skills greater than those of all

---

52. Shulchan Aruch, Hoshen Mishpat 16:3 and glosses of M. Isserles (Rema), on id.

53. I Kings 3:16–28.

54. For one example of the proper procedure of a court in such a case see Shulchan Aruch, Even Haezer 3:9 and commentaries ad loc.

55. M. Meiri, Beit Habechira, BB 58a.

56. BB 58a.

57. Id.

his contemporaries may resort to this type of proof.[58] Because the case is so exceptional, one commentator ventured the thought that the father knew who the real son was, and so did Rabbi Bana. The suggestion that the body be disinterred was only a device to make the verdict seem plausible.[59] While this type of adjudication is not in accordance with the classical rule of law, one cannot argue that it involved omens or the supernatural. One may argue that judges should not be allowed such latitude in the exercise of their judicial functions, though certainly it was clearly an exercise of reason that led Rabbi Bana to decide as he did. However, one should still ask whether a judge can legally ignore incontrovertible proof, oral or documentary, simply because he is not convinced that the case is free of deceit, fraud, conspiracy or the like. In talmudic literature, such a case is called *din merumeh*.[60] The judge may also feel that there is a great deal that is being concealed at the trial and for that reason is loath to render a verdict. In all such cases the judge may rely on his feelings, insight, and intuition. None of these can be equated precisely with reason or sense experience, but certainly all are related to such perceptions.

A judge can only rely on his instinct to a certain extent. According to some authorities, he may do no more than withdraw from the case and let another judge deal with it.[61] According to others, he may even make a final disposition of the case.[62] Still other authorities try to make a fine distinction as to when he may take one of the courses available to him.[63] Yet, the only cases in which he may so act, are cases that involve the suspicion that the parties are guilty of fraud, concealment, or similar offenses against the court. The judge may not so act because he has had visions, mystical experiences or heard voices from above guiding him in his decision.[64] Unfortunately, the sources do not reveal whether the judge must indicate in his decision that he decided on the basis of

---

58. M. Meiri, above, note 55.

59. See Commentary of the Geonim, commenting on Y. Habib, Ein Yakov. BB 58a.

60. San. 32b.

61. Mishneh Torah, Hilkhot Sanhedrin 24:3.

62. Beit Yosef, commenting on Tur, Hoshen Mishpat ch. 15.

63. Asher Ben Yechiel (Rosh), Responsa 68:20.

64. See Beit Yosef, commenting on Tur, Hoshen Mishpat Ch. 15; Shulchan Aruch, Hoshen Mishpat 15:3. and glosses of M. Isserles on id.

his suspicions when in fact that was the case. In any event, resort to the supernatural as a source for judicial decision in a litigated controversy was simply non-existent.[65]

Against the background of a logical, rational jurisprudential system, it is difficult to accept the possibility that the guilt or innocence of a woman would be predicated on a supernatural revelation. Even when debating legal issues, a rabbi was not permitted to summon a heavenly voice to prove that he was right.[66] In all of biblical and talmudic literature there is only this one procedure where apparently a court is to act (jointly with the High Priest) in arriving at a verdict and punishment by a method resembling witchcraft or sorcery. In no other cases, civil or criminal, is this allowed. Therefore, its anomalous character begs for another interpretation.

The Purpose of the Oath in the Law of Sotah

The second anomaly in the law of sotah is the unique type of oath used. While oaths are generally regarded by legal historians as partaking of the character of ordeals in other cultures,[67] they played quite a different role in Jewish judicial procedure. Their role was not to establish facts or constitute proof. The only purpose they served was to clear one of suspicion.[68] That is all. It is difficult to reconcile the fact that while so little probative value is accorded to oaths generally, the oath of the sotah would be designed literally as a procedure to ascertain guilt or innocence.

If one assumes that the procedure was indeed an ordeal with metaphysical intervention to establish guilt or innocence, there was no need for a long period of importuning by the presiding officials to the woman to confess.[69] It was unnecessary then to plead with her that if guilty she need only say so and all that would happen would be that she would forfeit her ketubah and

---

65. See also Temurah 16a (supernatural cannot even be used to re-learn that which had been forgotten).

66. See text accompanying notes 35–41.

67. See, e.g., Code of Hamurabi, above, note 8, at § 131. See also Anderson, "Oaths as Old as a Belief in God," 61 *L. Inst J.* 502 (1987); Levinson, "Constituting Communities Through Words that Bind; Reflections on Loyalty Oaths," 81 *Mich. L. Rev.* 1410, 1447–48, 461–62 (1986).

68. Shulchan Aruch, Hoshen Mishpat 34:5. See also below, notes 88–89.

69. Sotah 8a–b.

be divorced.[70] If she was guilty, was it not their duty to see that she received the appropriate punishment? Rather, this is an indication of a more humane purpose to the law.

In all of Jewish law the anomaly of judges pleading for a confession does not exist. Witnesses in a capital case were often urged to tell the truth and not cause an innocent person to suffer the death penalty.[71] The judges never pleaded with the accused. It is hard to believe that they urged the woman to confess because they wanted her to be spared the writing of God's name on parchment and its erasure in the prescribed waters.[72] The Bible ordered this procedure to be done[73] and there is no reason why they would want to avoid it. Furthermore, at least on a superficial level, the Bible ordered it because it wanted to punish a guilty woman. This is an important mandate of the Bible "to exorcise the evil" from amongst us.[74] Why then this hesitancy to conform to the ritual? In addition, since Jewish law did not accept the validity of confessions as part of the criminal process[75] it is difficult to understand why they should do so here. Yet, precisely in this instance, the cardinal feature of the ritual was to elicit the confession.

It was well established in the Talmud and Mishnah that even if the woman had already drunk the water and presumably established her innocence by surviving it, she could still be proved guilty at trial through the judicial process.[76] It is hard to explain the fact that more credibility was given to human testimony than to what was a divinely established fact. In order to sustain belief in the supernatural power of the waters it was then necessary to argue that the waters only established facts when there were no witnesses on earth who could tell the tale.[77] However, if this is so, the rabbis made the ceremony quite useless. The husband will hardly deem her innocent; if nothing happens to her he will assume that there are witnesses somewhere on earth who will one day

---

70. Sotah 8a–b.

71. Shulchan Aruch, Hoshen Mishpat 28:7–8.

72. Sotah 8b.

73. Num. 5:23.

74. Ps. 104:35.

75. See A. Kirschenbaum, *Self Incrimination in Jewish Law* (1970), 3–25.

76. Sotah 26a–b.

77. Sotah 28a–b.

establish guilt. If so, the ritual prescribed by the Bible is even more cruel than that of Hamurabi's Code. Since it can only establish guilt and never innocence, it is unlikely that the Bible would mandate this ritual.

Additional problems abound: if the ritual had probative value, the guilty man should have been punished too—his identity was known.[78] The Talmud states that he would be punished by God,[79] but if the rabbis had faith in the ritual's efficacy, why did they not rely upon it to pursue the punishment themselves? Also, if there were witnesses to the act of adultery, there was no ritual even if the witnesses' testimony failed to accomplish its purpose.[80] This is true even if the testimony would not be admissible in court.[81] The Talmud also lays much emphasis on the fact that God wanted His name to be erased (after it was written on parchment) to restore domestic peace.[82] Perhaps His name was to be used to establish guilt. The assumption of the law appears to be that, typically, nothing would ever happen to the woman and she would be restored to her husband who would have at least some assurance of her innocence. Even if there might be witnesses elsewhere, the mere fact that she resisted the enormous pressure to confess would give him peace of mind.

Sotah as a Psychological Proceeding

For the above reasons, I submit that many of the rabbis saw in the ritual a sophisticated psychological device—virtually a drama to reconcile a suspicious, jealous husband to his indiscreet, but innocent wife. In this connection, one must bear in mind that if there was a charge of adultery by witnesses who saw the act, there was no ritual, even if the witnesses were finally discredited, since, at that point, it was appropriate to run a judicial, not a psychological, hearing. Proof adequate for the criminal punishment of adultery was therefore rare, since adulterers do not usually cohabit before witnesses and such evidence was a prerequisite to punishment.[83]

---

78. The sotah ritual mandated that the husband warn her against isolation with a particular person. Sotah 2b–3a. Hence, his identity must be known.

79. Sotah 27b–28a.

80. Sotah 31b.

81. Id. See also Mishneh Torah, Hilkhot Sotah 1:16.

82. Sotah 18a.

83. There is a dispute in the Talmud as to what precisely the witnesses

As a matter of fact, the witnesses were required not only to see the act of adultery with their own eyes, but also to warn the offenders in advance of the gravity of the offense they were about to commit,[84] an unlikely situation. If witnesses claimed that they saw an adulterous act, the ritual was not applicable even if punishment could not occur. The husband might divorce his wife,[85] but there was no activity before a priest.

The ritual applied only when the husband had suspicions but no proof. He ordered the wife not to be alone with a particular man and witnesses saw her flouting his will. She was disobedient but there was no proof of adultery. In such a case, how does one reassure a husband who, in his fury, might resort to violence or divorce? The rabbis saw in the biblical mandate a readiness on God's part to let His name be erased for the sake of restoring domestic tranquility by certifying to the woman's innocence, or on rare occasions producing a confession. The woman drank water in which was placed a piece of parchment with verses and God's name among them. Before she drank she was urged, if guilty, not to drink, but to confess and forfeit her ketubah and nothing more. There was no criminal punishment based on her confession. If she was innocent she was urged to drink the water and be reconciled to her husband.

Of course, the ritual could only achieve its purpose as long as people believed that it was in fact a means of establishing the truth. In actuality, it required a miracle to punish her as the mixture was medically harmless.[86] Nothing was ever established from a judicial point of view—if the woman confessed, the court did not punish her. If she drank and nothing happened to her, she was assumed innocent and reconciled to her husband.

I am driven to the conclusion that the sotah ritual was a psychological proceeding and not an ordeal. First, because of the

---

must see, and this dispute is not resolved by the decisors of Jewish law. Some authorities maintain that the intercourse itself must be seen; others maintain that circumstantial evidence of actual intercourse may be used. See Makot 7a, and the commentaries ad loc.

84. San. 8b.

85. It is possible that she will also suffer certain monetary penalties. See Shulchan Aruch, Even Haezer 116:2–4.

86. The mixture consists only of water, dust, wormwood (or any other bitter, but not poisonous substance), ink, and paper. Mishneh Torah, Hilkhot Sotah 3:9–10.

accent in talmudic literature on the fact that the rabbis praised God for having permitted His holy name to be used for the purpose of restoring domestic tranquility in a troubled home.[87] They did not say that God is to be praised because He permitted the use of His name to establish the guilt of a woman. The guilt established by eliciting a confession involved no punishment other than the termination of the marriage and the forfeiture of the ketubah.

Second, proof that the ritual was essentially a psychological technique for establishing innocence rather than guilt can also be gleaned from the fact that some of the principal rules pertaining to oaths in Jewish law are derived from this law of the oath of the indiscreet wife. All oaths exacted from parties in accordance with biblical provisions were exculpatory, designed to clear a defendant of guilt. If a defendant denied the claim of a plaintiff, the plaintiff maintained the burden of proof and the defendant did nothing. However, if there was one witness to the claim instead of the required two,[88] or if the defendant made a partial admission of the claim,[89] then—since he was already under some cloud of suspicion because of his own admission or the testimony of the one witness—he took the oath and cleared himself. This, says the Talmud, is the nature of all biblical oaths: the defendant swears and does not have to pay.[90]

The Talmud's generalization that all biblical oaths were for the sake of clearing defendants from suspicion and its linking of all oaths with the oath administered in this so-called "ordeal of jealousy" warrants the assumption that the wife's oath is also for the sake of clearing her of suspicion.[91] Indeed, the alleged male adulterer is not at all involved, though by Jewish law, if he is guilty, the death penalty is due him as much as to the married woman with whom he cohabited.[92] Yet, the court ignores the charges against him. It is true, however, that in the time of the Mishnah, oaths had a purpose beyond that of clearing a defendant of suspicion. For instance, under rabbinic legislation, some claimants

---

87. Sotah 18a.

88. Shevuot 40a.

89. Shavuot 7:1.

90. Id. at 8:1.

91. The use of the sotah procedure as a paradigm of oaths is common in the Talmud. See, e.g, Shavuot 29b, 32a–b, 33b, 36a.

92. Mishneh Torah, Sefer Kedushah, Hilkhot Isurai Biah 1:1, 6.

were given the privilege of proving their case by simply taking an oath that money was due them.[93] Yet, from the point of view of the court, it simply meant that in a particular kind of case, the burden of proof shifted from the plaintiff to the defendant, and the plaintiff could make out a case by simply taking an oath that money was due him.[94]

One thing is clear however, oaths cannot serve to prove facts. Pressure could be put, by means of an oath, on a reluctant witness to testify.[95] People respected the oath and were hesitant to abuse it, not only because perjury might result in punishment.[96] If a man was a proven perjurer, he would be denied the option of taking the oath in any lawsuit in which he might be obligated to take one. Instead, his adversary would be privileged to take the oath instead of proving his case by witnesses or documents. The plaintiff would then recover the amount alleged to be due.[97] Thus, anyone who would be reckless with oaths made litigation more

---

93. Various categories of people were allowed to swear and collect according to rabbinic law. See Tur, Hoshen Mishpat ch. 89 for a complete list.

94. For example, a daily worker may claim his pay at the end of the day. If the employer claims that payment was already made, what is the legal result? How can the plaintiff in such a case prove that he was not paid? The rabbis decreed that the employee should take an oath that he was not paid, and, in the absence of any other proof, it would be sufficient. In such a case, one can hardly call the use of the oath a form of proof which is beyond the exercise of reason and sense experience. The rabbis shifted the burden because the employer was better able to protect himself against a false claim by demanding a receipt from the worker. See Shulchan Aruch, Hoshen Mishpat 89:1–3.

Another example is a claim by a widow for payment of the ketubah due her. In this case there is no shift of the burden of proof. It is sufficient that she has written evidence of the claim while the heirs cannot prove payment. Yet, it might be that, during the marriage, the husband had made payment and did not disclose it to anyone. Therefore, as added reassurance to the heirs, the widow takes an oath that she was not paid. See Ketubot 9:7, Mishnah Shavuot 7:7.

95. This was already clearly realized in tannaitic times; see Shavuot ch. 5 for various scenarios where swearing could be a tactical strategy.

96. Tosefta, Makot 4:5.

97. Shavuot 7:1, 4, Shulchan Aruch, Hoshen Mishpat 89:1.

difficult for himself. He placed himself at the mercy of unscrupulous claimants who, with proof adequate only to place upon him the burden of an oath, would prevail in their causes merely by taking oaths themselves, since their victim had been precluded from clearing himself.[98]

The talmudic association of the law of oaths with the ritual of the indiscreet wife yields a common denominator. In both cases, the objective was to clear the suspicions that attached either to an accused woman or a defendant against whom a monetary claim was made. This association is suggestive of how rabbis must have regarded the so-called ordeal of the indiscreet wife.

The fact that the woman was not forced to drink the water after she confessed her guilt is virtually conclusive proof that what was sought was not punishment. If punishment was regarded as the objective, the water would have been administered once she confessed, or, at the very least, some other significant criminal action would have been instituted. The rule, however, was precisely the reverse. Once there was a confession, no further action was taken. Additionally, if the goal was either a confession or the restoration of domestic tranquility, one can understand why it was that the Talmud states that there was no proceeding if her husband and she cohabited after he had accused her.[99] It was apparent in that case that a reconciliation was achieved and there was no reason for any thing further. In addition, the danger that the husband might harm his wife while in a rage was now greatly reduced. The ritual was therefore not needed.

Since the principal objective was either a confession of guilt or the restoration of peace to the home, it is understandable why in the course of the ritual so many things were done to induce a psychological drama: excessive walking up and down the mountain,[100] carrying a load,[101] and seeing with her own eyes how the potion was being prepared for her to drink.[102] All of these rituals can only be explained if the objective was to create a

---

98. See Rackman, "Legal Sanctions for Moral Obligations," in *Justice, Justice Shalt Thou Pursue* (1975), 151–53.

99. Sotah 7a. If he divorced her after they had cohabited, she received all the financial rights associated with divorce. Id.

100. Sotah 7b; Mishneh Torah, Hilkhot Sotah 3:3.

101. Sotah 7b.

102. Id.

psychological drama rather than a judicial proceeding and punishment. If my thesis is correct, the ritual of sotah does not constitute an anomaly in Jewish law and is not a judicial procedure to establish facts by appealing to divine intervention. If anything, it stands in beautiful contrast to the true ordeal mandated by the Hamurabic Code. It is a brilliant libretto to evoke a confession or establish domestic peace by removing psychological uncertainty. If witnesses were available at any time before or after the ritual, then, of course, a judicial proceeding occurred. But in the absence of witnesses, the goal was divorce or reconciliation, not punishment.

After this analysis, one must inevitably ask if the biblical verses provide any justification for some rabbis' radical re-interpretation of the simple meaning of the verses. I submit that they do. The most obvious hint that the ceremony was designed to evoke a confession and not to try the accused and punish her, is the uniqueness of the oath which was administered. It was unlike any other oath in the Bible. Normally, one swears in order to establish a fact, and in the absence of any contradictory evidence, it is final. In the instant case, however, the oath established no fact—it was nothing more that a dramatic statement of the ritual's nature.[103]

The anomalous character of the oath, therefore, suggests the interpretation that I maintain. It was in this spirit that the rabbis drafted the text to be read to the woman who hesitated to drink although she protested her innocence: "Our daughter, if you are sure that you are innocent, drink, because the waters are like a dry poison placed on live flesh. If there is a wound, it will penetrate the body, but if there is no wound, it accomplishes naught."[104] Thus, as much as she was urged to confess if guilty, so she was urged not to fear the waters, if innocent.

Conclusion

It is a fact that the biblical verses regarding lex talionis are ambiguous. Dr. Joseph B. Soloveitchik has stated that many times the Bible deliberately states the "ought" even if that "ought" is difficult or impossible to enforce. He who removes the limb of another deserves to have his limb removed, but, since precise, exact retribution is never possible, the courts can do no more than force him to pay for the injury he caused.[105]

---

103. Num. 5:19–22.

104. Tosefta, Sotah 1:3.

105. Most likely, Rabbi Soloveitchik was trying to explain the position

The biblical verses regarding the sotah are also ambiguous. One can see in them the typical ancient middle eastern ordeal. One can also interpret them as mandating a psychological drama designed to either evoke a confession or reinvigorate a marriage plagued with doubt, but not as a prescription for an ordeal. It is obvious that here the ambiguity was necessary. The ritual would have no value if the latter interpretation became publicly known. Yet, certainly it is the latter interpretation that is consonant with all of Jewish law and philosophy while the alternative view makes it an anomaly in Jewish jurisprudence.

The Kuzari states that the Bible was given at Mount Sinai to hundreds of thousands of people openly and without any secrecy.[106] Judaism must always be exoteric and not esoteric. Judaism relies only on what was available to all—reason and sense experience. Furthermore, Jewish law invites all to judge for themselves how just are God's laws.[107] This is an appeal to reason and sense experience. The Law can only be appreciated in this way. Indeed, to effectively transmit the Law to succeeding generations one appeals to them on the basis of those faculties available to everyone. The Jewish faith requires none to believe in the absurd. The faith itself rejects the irrational. The processes of the law must be similarly rational and natural.[108]

---

taken by Maimonides in his *Guide To The Perplexed* where he maintains that ideally, retribution should be the law. See Maimonides, *Guide to the Perplexed* III, ch. 43 § 3 (S. Pines trans. 1963). The position of Rabbi Soloveitchik can be found in a taped lecture, see Rabbi J B. Soloveitchik, *Taped Lecture On Parshat Korach* (available on file at the Nat'l Jewish L. Rev.).

106. Y. Halevi, *Kuzari* 87:1 (Y.E. Shmuel trans. 1973).

107. Deut. 4:8.

108. The author graciously acknowledges the invaluable assistance of Michael J. Broyde

A Jewish Philosophy of Property: Rabbinic Insights on Intestate Succession

There is only one small paragraph in the Bible that deals exclusively with the Jewish law of inheritance. Yet talmudic literature on the subject is vast. One might have expected this. There are many owners of property and they too must die. Their property must be disposed of in an orderly fashion if there is not to be a disruption of the social order by an unbridled "grab" of the deceased's assets by everyone present at the time of death. Moreover, the law must provide for the satisfaction of whatever obligations the deceased had. His death must not cause his creditors to sustain loss.

This paper will undertake to interpret several aspects of the Jewish law of intestate succession. An attempt will be made to glean ethical insights from the Talmud's treatment of the subject. The Talmud does not explicate these ethical considerations, but they are implicit in the rules. Whether or not the rabbis had them in mind may be questioned. Therefore, what is here offered is more a Midrash on the applicable rules of law than a scholarly analysis of rabbinic teleology.

While the rules are no longer applicable to the estates of most Jews, they are a part of Torah and for those who deem Torah the will of God, it is important that they try to fathom that will and see how Jewish sages coped with it through the ages—sometimes supportively and at other times manipulatively. The least that the study will yield is another instance of a biblical ideal that was compromised radically in the course of Jewish history. How this was done in connection with testate succession Professor Solomon Zeitlin has already demonstrated.[1]

But the biblical pattern and the early talmudic views merit more analysis and rationalization than they have heretofore received. This is the burden of this paper.

---

1. See his "Testamentary Succession: A Study in Tannaitic Jurisprudence," *JQR* (75th Anniversary Volume, 1967), pp. 574–581.

I.

The one basic norm of the Jewish law of property is that the earth is the Lord's. While a man lives, God indulges him some power over things, especially their use and enjoyment. However, after his death his power to dispose must revert to the Master. That is why it was held in the Talmud that the laws of inheritance as set forth in the Bible must be obeyed.[2] An owner of property has no control over the manner in which his belongings shall be distributed after his demise. That is up to God, the ultimate Owner.

This position is in bold contrast to that of Roman law, which had a deep-rooted dislike of intestate succession.[3] Roman law preferred wills even though a will may be—in the words of one of its critics—the expression of the will of a man who no longer has any will, respecting property which is no longer his property, and the act of a man no longer accountable for his acts to mankind. Yet Roman law was very much private property oriented, and it was inevitable that the champions of private property should aggrandize man's control over that which he acquires in his lifetime so that he can retain control even after his death.

Jewish law in time succumbed to the same pressures, and many ways were devised to enable an owner to dictate how his estate shall be divided. The most commonly used technique was to make gifts during one's lifetime to take effect upon death.[4] Human nature being what it is, one could have expected that this would come to pass. People crave economic power and relish the exercise of that power even from the grave. However, the spirit of the biblical and talmudic position ought not to be forgotten. That position clearly held that a man is without power over his assets after his death. That decision God makes. He decrees who are heirs, and in what proportion. And even a written document altering the biblical pattern was deemed a nullity.[5]

This position also eliminated the possibility that heirs would quarrel with each other and charge fraud or undue influence on

---

2. BB 130a האומר האיש פלוני יירשני במקום שיש בת, בתי תירשני במקום שיש בן לא אמר כלום שהתנה על מה שכתוב בתורה.

3. See Carl Salkowski, *Institutes and History of Roman Private Law*, trans. E. E. Whitefield (London: Stevens and Haynes), 1886, p. 770.

4. See Zeitlin, above, note 1.

5. Mishneh Torah, Nahalot 6:1, . . . אין אדם יכל להוריש למי שאינו ראוי ליורשו בין על פה בין בכתב.

the testator. They could complain only against God for that which they failed to receive or received in inadequate measure. The fixity, or immutability, of the pattern of inheritance never threatened family solidarity, as so often do the patterns presently prevailing.

Yet there was a more basic reason for the rule against altering the biblical pattern. When it was impossible for owners of land to dispose of their holdings in accordance with their own desires and only lawful heirs could get it, one could more readily hope that the laws of the Jubilee year would be respected. Their observance would create minimum economic upheaval.

Thus, if one's lands had never been sold to anyone at all, then the redistribution of land in the Jubilee year would affect no one other than heirs, who in any event were in possession of the land. Perhaps there would be some change insofar as some would lose or gain a fraction. However, it was unlikely that there would be strong resistance on their part to the turn-over, which would result in the expropriation of no one.

If one's lands had been alienated, then resistance to the redistribution could be expected from those who purchased the fields before the Jubilee. But if the Torah had in addition permitted owners to bequeath their holdings to anyone they chose, including non-heirs, then resistance would also come from those persons who benefited from such bequests. Not only would the resistance be compounded by the fact that more people would be adversely affected but the resulting economic upheaval would exacerbate social tensions and hostilities. More people would have to give up altogether what they had learned to cherish and the entire biblical plan for a redistribution of the land every half century would be in greater jeopardy of non-fulfillment because of the wider circle of people resenting it.

It was when the laws of the Jubilee were no longer practiced or enforced that the biblical pattern of inheritance could also be altered.

The first major deviation from the biblical pattern came when the Talmud permitted a man to prefer one heir to another.[6] True he was limited to the class of heirs who, according to the Bible, would be entitled to take. If he had sons, who, according to the Bible, were the first group entitled to inherit, he could prefer one to another (except for the share of the first-born) but he could not

6. BB 130a . . . ר׳ יוחנן בן ברוקה אומר אם אמר על מי שראוי ליורשו דבריו קיימין

אמר רבא מאי טעמא דרבי יוחנן בן ברוקה אמר קרא והיה ביום הנחילו את בניו התורה נתנה רשות לאב להנחיל לכל מי שירצה.

prefer his daughters to his sons since daughters had no share in the estate if sons survived.

Not all the sages of the Talmud agreed with this deviation. But it finally prevailed. Nonetheless, the Talmud urged fathers not to disinherit their children. Their rationale was based on the religious concept of penitence. One should not expropriate a child in anger or resentment, for the child might repent. Or the child's offspring may prove worthy of the estate. Saints are often born to parents who are villains.[7]

However, a deviation that was limited to preferences among those whom the Bible deemed heirs anyway would not complicate the redistribution of land in the Jubilee year. At least it would not increase the number of people affected, and thus the number of resisters to the great upheaval of the Jubilee was not enlarged. In this instance too, no one would suffer total expropriation which would have been the case if one could skip heirs altogether or an entire generation of them.

II.

According to the Bible sons inherit their fathers.[8] This appears natural enough and was taken for granted in all the biblical narratives dealing with the patriarchs. However, in all those instances it was assumed that the deceased was not survived by his own father. But if a man was survived by his father and his sons, it was not apparent that the sons had a right prior to that of the father. The Talmud suggests the possibility that the father may come first and rejects it.[9] Why was the hypothesis even considered?

One must understand that in a patriarchal society the patriarch virtually owns his offspring and certainly their belongings. If the patriarch died he would be succeeded by his son, but until that time neither sons nor grandsons had private property. This was true in the Roman law of paterfamilias, unless the paterfamilias had emancipated the filiusfamilias. By the Roman system the clan's property was kept intact. Moreover, the family as a unit would continue its religious rites as a family. There was a religious basis for the patriarchal system.

Yet despite the fact that Jewish law was certainly religio-centered,

---

7. Ibid. 133b הכותב את נכסיו לאחרים והניחם את בניו מה שעשה עשוי אלא אין רוח חכמים נוחה הימנו.

8. Num. 27:8 איש כי ימות ובן אין לו והעברתם את נחלתו.

9. BB 108b . . . שהאב קודם לאחיו יכול יהא קודם לבן ת״ל הקרוב קרוב קודם קרוב קודם.

it upset the patriarchal system by denying the father any power whatever over the life and death of his sons and daughters and they enjoyed separate property rights which upon their death passed to their issue—and not to the deceased's father. Only if there were no descendants whatever did the father have any rights in the estate of his child. If he had predeceased his son or daughter, his other sons would succeed to his rights. But the descendants of the deceased always had priority.

The Bible, surprisingly enough, makes no mention whatever of the rights of a father to his offspring's estate even when the offspring had no descendants. Perhaps this is too tragic an eventuality for Moses to have referred to it. Indeed, it is not pleasant to contemplate the death of a child before the parents. Yet the Bible does not hesitate to refer to an even more tragic situation in which the parent is responsible for the child's execution.[10] Therefore, the more reasonable explanation of the omission is to assume that the Bible sought to place the accent where it was needed in ancient times—on the rights of descendants rather than ascendants. Only when there were neither sons nor daughters, nor grandchildren nor great-grandchildren, could the father or the brothers of the deceased take the estate.

III.

The Bible itself acknowledged that its law of inheritance disadvantaged women, and it gives us one of the earliest accounts in history of a protest by women with regard to their status. The daughters of Zelafhad complained that they saw no reason why their father's share in the land of Canaan should be denied them simply because their father had no sons. Apparently they would not have complained if there were sons. This would indicate that when there were sons to take the father's estate there was adequate provision for the needs of the daughters. This was certainly the case according to later talmudic law[11] which probably gave expression to what had been the custom in Jewish society almost from the beginning. In any event, as a result of the protest of the daughters of Zelafhad, it was ordained that when there are no sons, daughters will inherit their father. However, the Bible and

---

10. Deut. 21:18–21 כי יהיה לאיש בן סורר ומורה . . . ותפשו בו אביו ואמו והוציאו אותו . . . ורגמוהו כל אנשי עירו . . .

11. Ket. 4:11 בנן נקבן דיהוין ליכי מנאי יהוין יתבן בביתי ומתזנן מנכסי עד דיתנסבן לגברין חיב שהוא תנאי בית דין.

Talmud shed much light on why it is that the males enjoy the preference. Apparently it was the tribal form of social organization from which there was derived the maxim that only "the father's family is deemed family."

The people of Israel were divided into tribes, and as tribes they divided the land of Canaan among themselves. When a woman married a man of a different tribe, she and her children became a part of the husband's tribe. In early Jewish history the areas belonging to the twelve tribes were like states or provinces. Even for military recruitment, judges and kings called upon tribes to furnish manpower. Thus the tribal form of organization had military and economic significance. National solidarity was slow in coming and was not achieved for many centuries.

To maintain the integrity of the areas allocated to the tribes, it was necessary that upon the death of a person his land should go to males who belonged to the same tribe. If a female took the land by inheritance, she might, as a result of marriage to a man of another tribe, cause the land to be transferred to the tribe of her husband—if he inherited her estate—or to the tribe of her children, whose tribal affiliation was their father's tribe.

Even Moses faced this problem. Indeed, the pattern of land distribution was upset whenever a woman inherited from her parent and her estate passed to husband or children who were identified with a tribe not hers or her father's. When Moses confronted the problem it was ordained that all women who inherit estates from their fathers must marry within their father's tribe.[12]

One of the boldest instances of rabbinic legislation was the ruling that this mandate of Moses was limited to his generation. It would not be applicable thereafter. The freedom of Jewish women to marry any Jewish male was more important than the preservation of tribal solidarity and the integrity of the tribe's land holdings.[13]

So important was this decision to the development of national unity that the day the decision was made became a national holiday, the fifteenth of Av, and it was celebrated especially with an eye to "boy meets girl"—the "Sadie Hawkins" day of Jewish history.[14]

---

12. Num. 36:6. אך למשפחת מטה אביהם תהיינה לנשים.

13. BB 121a . . . אמר שמואל יום שהותרו שבטים לבא זה בזה מאי דרוש זה הדבר דבר זה לא יהא נהוג אלא בדור זה.

14. Ibid. תנן התם אמר רשב״ג לא היו ימים טובים לישראל כחמשה עשר באב וכיום הכפורים שבהן בנות ירושלים יוצאות בכלי לבן . . . חמשה עשר באב מאי היא אמר רב יהודה אמר שמואל יום שהותרו שבטים לבא זה בזה.

The prior right of males to inherit was not disturbed. Family and tribal association was determined by the fathers. Mothers and daughters were to be protected in other ways, although daughters would take in the absence of sons. But national unity was not to be placed in jeopardy and the intermarriage of Jews with each other was safeguarded.

IV.

An important assumption of Jewish law—implied in the concern of the Rabbis that daughters who inherit from their fathers may be responsible for the transfer of land from one tribe to another—is the rule that sons inherit from their mothers as well as from their fathers. The Talmud expresses concern that the transfer of land from one tribe to another may come to pass in one of two ways.[15] A daughter may marry a man of another tribe, and if he inherits from her, his sons—who belong to his tribe—will ultimately inherit from him. However, after her marriage, her husband may predecease her, but her sons by that husband—who are members of their father's tribe—may also inherit from her directly. This too would result in the alienation of holdings from one tribe to another.

This right of a son to inherit from his mother is not specifically mentioned in the Bible, although there is an allusion to the daughter inheriting from her mother.[16] The Rabbis ignored a third possibility that a woman's heirs shall be limited to her family—her father and her brothers. Early Roman law subscribed to this view. A son was the agnate of his father and not of his mother and the right of succession was limited to agnates. Here, as in so many other instances, Anglo-American law followed the pattern of Jewish law and the same law of succession that applies to a man's estate applies to a woman's estate. One Rabbi did hold that in a mother's estate all children should share equally—sons and daughters alike.[17] His view did not prevail. The first-born son was denied any right of primogeniture in his mother's estate. This will he discussed

---

15. Ibid. 112b–113a תניא בסבת הבן ותניא בסבת הבעל תהיא בסבת הבן לא תסוב
נחלה לבני ישראל ממטה אל מטה בסבת הבן הכתוב מדבר . . . תניא אידך ולא תסוב נחלה
ממטה למטה אחר בסבת הבעל הכתוב מדבר . . .

16. Num. 36:8 and BB 111a תנו רבנן "וכל בת יורשת נחלה ממטות בני ישראל" היאך
בת יורשת שני מטות אלא שאביה משבט אחד ואמה משבט אחר ומתו וירשתן.

17. BB 111a ר' יוסי בר' יבודה ור"א בר' יוסי אמרו משום רבי זכריה בן הקצב אחד הבן
ואחד הבת שוין בנכסי האם.

more fully in a subsequent section. But what emerges from the talmudic discussion is that the unity and solidarity of the conjugal family unit was to be protected. What property both parents acquired would pass to heirs virtually the same way. The mother's tribal affiliation was to vanish. Even when she inherited from her parents of another tribe, her gains became a part of the new family unit which she had helped to form. We have come to take this for granted in modern western society, but this is part of the Jewish heritage—and not that of the Romans.

V.

A husband inherits his wife, although she does not inherit him. Her very substantial rights against his estate derive from her ketubah—or more accurately from the law pertaining to marriage rather than the law of inheritance. If her husband predeceased her she took from the estate all the property she had acquired by gift or inheritance during the marriage and all the property which constituted her dowry as appraised at the time of the wedding and stipulated in the ketubah (plus some appreciation in value). Until her remarriage she also received a domicile and maintenance both of which were charged against the estate. But she was never an heir.

The husband, on the other hand, was her heir. The Bible does not mention this at all. And the talmudic discussion on the subject[18] indicates how hard put the rabbis were to justify this legislation by reference to biblical texts. Their interpretation of the cited passages is both strained and unconvincing. That is why some sages later held that the rule is wholly rabbinic and not biblical.[19] Indeed, in Roman law there was no inheritance whatever of spouses from each other.

Why were the rabbis so determined to establish the rights of the husband to inherit his wife and even give it the force of a biblical ordinance ? Would such a rule not deter the wife's father, for example, from making gifts which would ultimately pass to a son-in-law ? And was it fair to give the husband a right which was not reciprocated—since the wife never inherited from him?

The rabbis were not oblivious of these considerations. However, one must visualize how much healthier it is for a marital relationship

---

18. Ibid. 111b

19. Mishneh Torah, Nahalot, 1:8 והבעל יורש את נכסי אשתו מדברי סופרים and Meiri, BB 112a.

that the husband be generous with his wife and be spared continuing concern that what he gives her may not revert to him if she predeceases him. The rabbinic legislation (to which, as already noted, many rabbis even sought to give the status of a biblical enactment) was designed to promote a more relaxed and expansive attitude on the part of husbands in making assets available to their wives without the strain of a careful accounting as to what is his and what is hers. In the final analysis, he would get everything back if she did not survive him. And as for that which her father wanted to make available to her as a dowry, he could rest assured—because of an implied term of every ketubah—that it would first go to her children and not to her husband.

In the hope that in the relationship of husband and wife there would be joint use and enjoyment of the family property, the rabbis also ruled that neither husband nor wife could ever acquire presumptive rights of ownership (*hazakah*) because of their use of the assets in togetherness.[20]

Imagine how domestic tranquility would be adversely affected if husbands and wives had to be continuously on guard lest their spouses hold on to property for too long a time and thereby acquire a title belonging to the other!

Furthermore, if the parties did not approve of the rabbinic rule they could stipulate in advance of the marriage, or during the coverture, that they do not want the rule to apply.[21] Even though the biblical laws of inheritance were ever applicable—and never subject to change by a testator—this rigid limitation did not apply to the husband's right to inherit. He could waive it.

Moreover, the husband's right to inherit applied only to such property as the wife had reduced to possession at the time of her death. It did not apply to expectancies or choices in action.

In addition it must be noted that if the husband predeceased his wife, not only did he lose his right to her estate but his heirs too would not succeed to it. His children might, if they were also her children. But her estate reverted to her heirs, not his, according to the exact same rules applicable to his estate, first, her issue; then her father, and then her father's heirs. Indeed, if the mother had children who predeceased her, her estate did not pass to the children's father and his family, but rather to her family—to her

---

20. BB 42a לא לאיש חזקה בנכסי אשתו ולא לאשה חזקה בהכסי בעלה.

21. Ket. 83a כתב לה דין ודברים אין לי בנכסיך ובפירותיהן ובפירי פירותיהן בחייך ובמותך אינו אוכל פירות בחייו ואם מתה אימו יורשה.

father and his issue, her brothers, sisters, nephews, or nieces. In the language of the Talmud, a son in the grave inherits his father to transmit to his heirs (his father's family) but a mother's son does not inherit his mother in his grave to transmit to his heirs because that would mean that his father's family would take.[22] Instead it reverted to his mother's family.

VI.

One of the most important differences between the Roman law of succession and talmudic law—and here too Anglo-American common law adopted the Jewish position—pertains to the doctrine of universal succession. According to Roman law the heir or heirs succeeded to the estate of the deceased as his complete replacement and were responsible for all the assets and liabilities as if the deceased were alive.[23] If more than one heir took, then the assets and liabilities were shared in the proportion that they took. And it mattered not that the assets may not have been adequate to pay the liabilities. The heir or heirs paid the difference out of their own property. Because it would have been improvident for the heir or heirs to incur such a responsibility, or risk it when they did not know how solvent the deceased was, Roman law later invented sundry devices by which heirs might protect themselves. However, for religious reasons it was thought that the heir or heirs should enter as if into the very shoes of the deceased as extensions or prolongations of his legal personality. It was as if this were the deceased's way of continuing to live.

Despite the fact that Jewish law was so much more religio-centered than Roman law, this doctrine of universal succession was never a part of Jewish law. Heirs were responsible for the debts of the deceased only in the measure that they acquired assets.[24] When their father's reputation was at stake—as in the case of a theft—the heirs were urged to redeem their father's reputation and make restitution even if the estate's assets were inadequate for the purpose.[25] But this was moral exhortation—not strict law, nor

22. BB 114b. אף אשה את בנה אין הבן יורש את אמו בקבר להנחיל לאחין מן האב.

23. Salkowski, op. cit., p. 768.

24. BK 111b הגוזל ומאכיל את בניו והניח לפניהם פטורין מלשלם ואם היה דבר שיש בו אחריות חייבין לשלם.

25. Ibid. 94b הניח להם אביהם פרה וטלית וכל דבר המסויים חייבין להחזיר מפני כבוד אביהם.

even equity. With regard to debts that involved no moral turpitude, the obligation of heirs was not only limited to the assets but the court pleaded for them all available defenses and made the plaintiff bear the burden of proof.[26]

One can very readily see in this major difference between the two legal systems a reflection of another important difference. With regard to the law of agency it took Roman law many years to develop the notion that an agent is the representative of his principal and not an extension of his person. For that reason, Roman law regarded the heir as a substitute for the deceased—the visible manifestation of the prolongation of the deceased's life beyond the grave. Jewish law, on the other hand, maintained very early that an agent is only a representative and not an extension of the person of the principal. Thus, for example, an agent was competent to testify with regard to the terms and fulfillment of the agency. He was not regarded as identical with the principal so that he would be disqualified as a witness as one who was a party to the action.[27]

It might be that Jewish law developed so advanced a notion of agency precisely because of its religious roots. In connection with the work of the priests in the temple the Talmud ponders whether the priests are God's agents or the people's agents. The conclusion is that they are God's agents.[28] Especially would this be so when they bless the people or make available forgiveness for sin. Yet if they are God's agents, how can one possibly regard them as substitutes for God ? This was unthinkable in Judaism. The most that they could be is representatives with no identification of their personalities with that of God. And thus agency generally came to mean that. Heirs too were representatives, and no more, in connection with the estates of the deceased. They paid the debts of the deceased out of the deceased's assets and the remainder they took as heirs.

VII.

The early insistence of the Rabbis that the distribution of the estate shall be in accordance with God's will—and not the deceased's—led to some anomalies. This is usually the case in a theocentric legal system. It is by respecting the anomaly and fulfilling it that we

---

26. BB 41a הבא משום ירושה אינו צריך טענה.

27. Kid. 43a והלכתא שליח נעשה עד.

28. Ned. 35b הני כהני שלוחי דידן הוו או שלוחי דשמיא.

prove that we are obeying God rather than a rational or natural impulse. We yield to the divine mandate. In this way we reaffirm that all worldly goods are His and not man's.

One such anomaly was the subject of controversy between Pharisees and Sadducees. If a son predeceased his father, but was survived by a daughter, she took the estate ahead of the father's surviving daughter.[29]

From the point of view of the descendant it would appear to be absurd that his son's daughter shall take his assets and not his own daughter. But the pattern of succession was fixed and unalterable. Sons and their issue came first; daughters took only when there were no sons.

The Sadducces felt that the two groups of women should share the estate—the deceased's daughters and granddaughters (by a son). This seemed reasonable. But the biblical mandate was unequivocal. The Pharisees made a holiday of the day when they prevailed in their debate with the Sadducees.[30]

The emphasis in Jewish law on God's ultimate ownership of all property so that man deals with property, as God willed it and not as man sees fit—can be gleaned from still another anomaly. Jewish law did not approve of escheat whereby the king or state takes all property for which there are no heirs. The king or state enjoyed no special status in this connection. Indeed, it is inconceivable according to Jewish law that a Jew shall have no heirs. He can always trace heirs back as far as the patriarchs, Abraham, Isaac and Jacob. But what of a convert to Judaism? If he weds and has children, he too has heirs. But if he should die before acquiring heirs, his forbears cannot be traced back to the patriarch Jacob and his non-Jewish kin are no longer his relatives by Jewish law since his adoption of the faith constitutes a rebirth and he is regarded as a spiritual son of the patriarch Abraham. In such circumstances one would have expected that his estate might escheat to the king or state. But it did not. It was regarded as ownerless and anyone could seize it as one could any other ownerless property.[31]

The Bible does not specifically mention this but one elusive passage leads to the conclusion. It deals with a thief who had

---

29. BB 115b אמר רב אמר רב הונא אמר רב כל האומר תירש בת עם בת הבן אפילו נשיא שבישראל אין שומעין לו שאינן אלא מעשה צדוקין.

30. Megillat Taanit and B. ibid. בעשרין וארבעה ביה (=אב) תבנא לדיננא

31. Mishneh Torah, Zekhiyah, 1:6.

stolen from a convert and then compounded his theft by taking an oath to the convert denying the theft. If the theft were from a person other than a convert the thief would make restitution with some additional penalty and he would also bring an offering to the temple to atone for his perjury. However, if the offense was committed against a convert who is now dead without heirs there is no one to whom he can make restitution. Having compounded his original crime of theft with perjury, he must bring the offering to atone but the offering without restitution does not bring forgiveness. He therefore, makes restitution to the priests who succeed to the convert's rights. Yet since it is only when perjury too is involved that the priests take, it appears that otherwise the thief could keep what he had stolen because the estate of the convert is regarded as ownerless when the convert dies. Thus we deduce that whatever a convert had when he died can be seized by anyone at all. Neither the state nor the priests are the heirs. This is another illustration of theocentric law stripping the state of power. God is the Sovereign over property, and not the state. The state too must yield to God's will.

Even as Jewish law placed so much emphasis on God's ultimate ownership of all the earth, so that heirs in essence took from Him and not from the deceased, so did Jewish law seek to impress heirs with their sense of debt not only to immediate forebears but also to all their people, past and present, without whom they would have had no sense of Jewish identification, no awareness of their history, and no opportunity to enjoy God's bounty as Jews. It is virtually impossible for a legal system to incorporate this kind of mood in rules of law. But the study of the Jewish law of inheritance was to induce it.

This is the philosophy underlying a most difficult talmudic passage in which the sages essay to become historians and ponder a purely historical question: When Joshua divided the land of Israel among his people who conquered it, how did he make the division? Equal it was, but was it distributed among those who were the conquerors or rather among those who were emancipated from bondage in Egypt ? On its face this question would appear to be most academic. Only two people who left Egypt were alive when Joshua made the distribution. What then is the point of the query? It becomes clear that what is meant is whether those who received portions of the land from Joshua took equal portions as conquerors, or rather whether the land was assigned theoretically, in equal portions, to those who were emancipated from Egypt, while those who actually took the land, received portions as heirs of those who had been slaves? The almost unanimous conclusion was—and it matters not what actually happened or how material it was in talmudic times—that Joshua made the division taking into account both the present conquerors and the rights of those who were in Egypt to a share in the land. The details of the computation would have baffled a computer, but what emerges is the ethic of Judaism: Whoever took a portion of the land of Israel in Joshua's time did so not only as a conqueror or settler, but also as an heir of those to whom the promise of the Promised Land had been made. They took not only in their own right but as the heirs of those who suffered the bondage in Egypt and the trials and tribulations of the Exodus.[32]

So relevant is this mood to our own day. Does the land and state of Israel belong only to those who in 1948 and subsequent wars made possible its restoration or does it belong to all who identified with the ebb and flow of Jewish fortunes in the past ? Does it belong to Klal Yisrael—the collectivity of Israel—past and present? The unavoidable conclusion of the Talmud is that the latter is the proper attitude. That mood cannot be incorporated into many rules of law, but at least the state of Israel has incorporated it into one—"The Law of Return." The land, and citizenship in the state, are available to every Jew who identifies with his people and wants to share their destiny in the new republic.

Thus while it is God's will that makes an inheritance available to an heir when the land of Israel is involved, the heir takes not simply as a son or daughter of a deceased, but as the heir of generations that came before, with whose fate and destiny he must identify. His economic gain is the bounty of history, as well as God's gift.

VIII.

In a patriarchal system the eldest son usually succeeds to the status and rights of the deceased head of the family or clan. Far less frequently does one find the youngest son enjoying this privilege. The Bible too gave recognition to the special status of the first-born but denied him the right to take the entire estate. He would get more than the others but not all. This biblical limitation on an almost universal practice may have inspired the sages of the Talmud

---

32. BB 117a–b דתניא ר׳ יאשיה אומר ליוצאי מצרים נתחלקה הארץ . . . ר׳ יונתן אומר
לבאי הארץ נתחלקה הארץ . . . רבי שמעון בן אלעזר אומר לאלו ולאלו נתחלקה הארץ.

to add many other limitations which they discussed at length. Indeed it appears that as time passed the legal development was continuously in the direction of limitation.

The institution of primogeniture has much to commend it. One head of family succeeds one head of family. He keeps the property intact; creditors can easily identify the one person who is accountable for debts of the deceased; the king can look to one heir to fulfill military or tax obligations—all in all, the problem of succession is simplified. In addition, the first born is the family's religious functionary. However, the younger children are certainly disadvantaged; democracy within the family is hardly achieved as the eldest virtually becomes the family's dictator; and untold damage is done to the personality development of all the constituents of a tightly knit family unit, all of whom are dependent on the largesse of one eldest son. Moreover, the religious functions are better performed for a community or nation rather than for each family by itself. In that way religion makes for greater social and national solidarity.

Perhaps the talmudic sages were right in implicitly assuming in their dialectic that the Bible frowned upon the almost omnipresent institution of primogeniture and gave it only token recognition, as the Torah so often does when it wants to abolish a social pattern. It proceeds not by social revolution but by a slow process of limitation and regulation. This also happened with the institution of human slavery until it was virtually abolished. Perhaps—as Philo says—the first born was to be given more than his brothers because the father owed him a debt of gratitude—in the final analysis it was he who made the father a father. Yet the narratives in the book of Genesis reveal how much grief resulted from the deeply entrenched preference for the first-born—the rivalry between Ishmael and Isaac, Esau and Jacob, Reuben and Joseph. The Midrash also dwells upon these rivalries, and one wonders whether the famous psychoanalyst Alfred Adler did not rely heavily on this background for many of his theories. But whatever the reason, the Talmud progressively reduced the right of the first-born.

First, it gave the most restricted interpretation it could to the biblical phrase "a double portion." Did that mean two thirds of the estate in every case, or two portions of the estate after it is divided by the total number of sons, plus one ? The latter interpretation was upheld.[33]

---

33. BB 22a–b ת״ר לתת לו פי שנים פי שנים כאחד. אתה אומר פי שנים כאחד או אינו

Second, he received this double portion only with respect to such property as the deceased had reduced to possession at the time of his death.[34] They denied his special privilege with respect to expectancies, debts, and even that appreciation in the value of the property after the death of the deceased which required no effort on anyone's part. If the buds on the trees became fruit, that natural gain was not an asset with regard to which the first-born could claim a double portion. Indeed, in cases cited in the Talmud the most innocuous act by the first-born—such as his making an equal distribution of the produce of a field among his brothers and himself—might constitute a waiver of his right to a double portion in that field.[35]

And that was not all. He must be the first-born of his father beyond the shadow of a doubt and he must have survived his father.[36] He must have been born naturally and not by Caesarean surgery.[37] If his older brother died immediately after birth he lost his special privilege.[38] Nor does he have it if he was born after his father died.[39] His twin brother born minutes after him is an equal heir in such a case, because as a foetus he does not acquire special privileges, although generally in Jewish law a foetus does inherit the father who predeceased him.

The Rabbis' strict construction also limited the right of the first-born to the father's estate—it did not apply to the mother's estate.[40] What rationalization can one discover other than that the institution was frowned upon, and while one does not blithely ignore a biblical provision, one seeks to fathom its direction—and the biblical direction was understood by the sages to be restrictive, but

---

See R. אלא פי שנים בכל הנכסים . . . אין עליך לדון כלשון האחרון אלא כלשון הראשון. Gordis, "The Ethical Dimension in the Halakhah," *Conservative Judaism* 26, no. 3 (Spring 1972), pp. 71–72.

34. Bekh. 51b הבכור נוטל פי שנים בנכסי האב . . . ואינו נוטל בשבח ולא בראוי כבמוחזק.

35. BB 126a אמר רב אסי בכור שנטל חלק בפשוט ויתר.

36. Ibid. 127a. אמר רבא תניא כוותיה דר׳ אמי . . . בכור ולא ספק.

37. Bekh. 47b יוצא דופן והבא אחריו שניהן אינן בכור לא לנחלה ולא לכהן

38. Mishneh Torah, Nahalot, 2:10 בן תשעה שהוציא רוב ראשו חי הבא אחריו אינו בכור.

39. BB 142b אמר מר בריה דרב יוסף משמיה דרבא בכור שנולד לאחר מיתת אביו אינו נוטל פי שנים . . . והלכתא ככל הני לישני דאמר מר בריה דרב יוסף משמיה דרבא

40. Bekh. 51b הבכור נוטל פי שנים בנכסי האב ואינו נוטל פי שנים בנכסי האם

expansive.

Nonetheless the Rabbis refused to apply their restrictive approach to the bastard and deny the first-born who was a bastard his special privilege. This was a masterpiece of equity at work![41]

A recent decision by the United States Supreme Court adversely affected the rights of illegitimate children to inherit from their natural fathers. Perhaps from the point of view of constitutional law the decision was a proper one. However, the position of Jewish law stands in bold contrast to that of Anglo-American common law and even statutory provisions which sought to correct the harshncss of earlier rules.

First it must be noted that according to Jewish law a child born out of wedlock is not illegitimate.[42] Only a child born of an adulterous or incestuous relationship has any stigma attached to it. This limitation by itself almost completely eliminates the incidence of illegitimacy. If the offspring of unwed Jewish mothers suffer no legal disabilities, then they are already spared the indignity which the common law accorded the progeny of the unwed mothers subject to its jurisdiction. Furthermore, when the status of illegitimacy attaches only to children born of an adulterous or incestuous relationship, the difficulty of proof is an almost insuperable impediment to bastardy. How does one prove whose sperm caused the pregnancy? The presumptions are always in favor of the innocent infant.

According to common-law the child born out of wedlock was not only illegitimate but was also regarded as the "child of no one." He was not entitled to any of the rights and duties existent between parents and legitimate children. By statutes subsequently enacted the bastard was made the heir of the mother if the mother left no will. However, when she left a will and bequeathed property to her "children," it was not universally assumed that her intention was to include the illegitimate child. Most courts were sympathetic enough to so hold. Yet fewer courts were inclined to permit an

---

41. Yeb. 22b. ממזר לאתויי יהודה רב אמר מאי לאתויי מקום מכל . . . בן לו שיש מי.
Sifre on Deut. 2:15 ת"ל שמים בידי כרת עליהן שחייבין העריות את ארבה לא ועדיין
Mishneh Torah, Nahalot, שמים בידי כרת עליהן שחייבין העריות את ריבה שנואה שנושא.
2:13 יכיר. השנואה בן הבכור את כי שנאמר שנים פי נוטל ממזר הבכור היה. B. Epstein, Torah Temimah, on Deut. 21:15, n. 107

42. Kid. 66b ממזר הולד קידושין אחרים על לה יש אבל קידושין עליו לה שאין מי וכל
שבתורה העריות מכל אחת על הבא זה ואיזה

illegitimate child to share in benefits recovered in an action for causing the death of the parent responsible for its support. They interpreted relevant statutes much more strictly. Perhaps it was prejudice against the mulatto child that made American courts so cruel.

Jewish law starts with the assumption that everything must be done to ameliorate the lot of even the relatively few illegitimate children that there could possibly be. This attitude was the prevailing one throughout Jewish history, including the period when the late Isaac Halevi Herzog was Chief Rabbi of Israel. When illegitimacy was due to an unequivocally proved adulterous relationship, the rabbis were even bold enough to annul the earlier marriage of the mother so that her child by the second mate would be legitimate. They retroactively made the mother an unmarried woman.

However, as to the right of the *mamzer*—the unequivocal bastard—to inherit both father and mother there was never any doubt. And if the child was the father's first-born he even had the right of primogeniture. The Bible, it would appear, had limited his competency to marry. And the rabbis saw no reason for worsening his status by economic privation. If his parents sinned, why should his suffering be aggravated? On the other hand, from biblical sources they derived his right to inherit.

Thus we read in Maimonides' code: (Mishneh Torah: Hilkhot Nahalot, 1:7).

> All who are related (even) as a result of the commission of a sin inherit as do the legitimate. How? If a man had a son who was illegitimate or a brother who was illegitimate they are like other sons and the other brothers insofar as inheritance is concerned.

And in the second chapter (see 13) he adds that if the first-born is illegitimate he, nonetheless, takes a double portion, for the Pentateuch denied the father the right to prefer one child to another even if the child whom the father wants to disadvantage is one of whose conception God had disapproved.

To this very liberal interpretation at least one of Maimonides' commentators raised an objection. He claimed that it has no source in talmudic literature. However, Rabbi Boruch Epstein in his "Torah Tmimah" (Deut. 21:n. 107) found the source in the Tannaitic Sifre.

IX.

As already noted, it appears that one of the aims of the biblical and talmudic law of succession was to eliminate all uncertainty with regard to the succession at the very moment of the death of the decedent. Professor Moshe Silberg, in his book *This Is The Way of Talmud*, makes the point that talmudic law generally sought to minimize the incidence of litigation and even make unnecessary resort to "doctors of the law" for the resolution of halakhic questions. The rules were to be formulated with such precision that their application was comparatively easy even for the layman. Especially was this true of the rules pertaining to inheritance. And one maxim makes this abundantly clear.

Certain heirs always took to the exclusion of doubtful heirs. If a man was survived by a son and a hermaphrodite the son took as sole heir because the sex of the hermaphrodite was doubtful (Baba Batra 140b). Similarly, if a father and his son perish in a common disaster, the father's estate goes to those coming after the son according to the law of succession since they certainly survived the father. If the son had issue, they would receive a share as heirs of their father's father but the son himself received nothing that would be subject to claims of his creditors or even his widow. They would have to collect their claims from assets that he personally had at the time of his death. In either of the aforementioned cases the court would accept conclusive proof that the hermaphrodite was a male or that the father predeceased the son. But as long as there was doubt, heirs who were certain heirs enjoyed priority.

In at least two cases that the Talmud cites, the rule protected the interests of women. If a widow and her son die together, her family takes her estate. If she had died first, then the estate would have passed to her son's heirs and thus to his father's family. Similarly, if a father and his married daughter perish in a common disaster (and the father had no sons), it is her husband who loses. If her father were deemed to have died first, the estate would have passed to the daughter and from her to her husband. But if it is deemed that she died first then her issue, who are the issue of her father, take directly from him.

The rule that heirs who are certain enjoy priority over those who are doubtful thus promoted not only the value of certainty but protected estates from being alienated to kin that are more remote from the circle of affection and sense of beholdenness of the decedent.

The quest for the immediate and certain vesting of the inheritance in the appropriate heirs might have precipitated the disinheritance of the posthumous child because the delay in his birth means that in the interval between the death of the decedent and the birth of his youngest child it will not be known how many will share the estate. Perhaps to encourage the first-born to proceed diligently with the administration of the estate and the conservation of the assets, it was decided that his share shall not be diminished by the birth of the posthumous child. However, the posthumous child of a son among sons, or of a daughter when there are no sons, was also assured his or her share with those in his or her class. And because the right of the first-born was fixed as of the date of the father's death, he did not enjoy the right of primogeniture with respect to the shares of brothers who died without issue before the division of the estate. These shares were divided equally among all the brothers.

Though the Bible envisioned only intestate succession, and the Talmud sought to safeguard the biblical pattern with repeated affirmations that the biblical mandates are unalterable, the last two thousand years yielded a tremendous amount of legal creativity to make possible last wills and testaments and a greater control by their authors of the disposition of their estates after their death. Of course the development was an aggrandizement of the notion of private property and a partial negation of the biblical conception that all property is the Lord's with the right in mortals to enjoy and control it during their lifetime and to surrender control when they breathe their last. What the Rabbis did in the last two thousand years is indeed proof of the fact that Jewish law is by no means rigid. It has always been amended, and resistance to change today is due to the intransigence of those who are presently the oracles of the law and not the fault of the Halakhah itself.

While a full discussion of the legal development in the last two thousand years is far beyond the scope of this essay, a few observations are relevant. Most of the changes——wrought by judicial interpretation, legislation, and the creation of new legal devices, such as revocable gifts to take effect a moment prior to death—were not made to give a property owner more power than the Bible had allowed him. Often this was an indirect result of the legal development. What was sought principally, however, was a correction of the shortcomings of the biblical pattern—especially in connection with women's rights to share in the estate.

Fathers wanted their wed and unwed daughters to share with their sons in greater measure than the Bible had ordained. Husbands also wanted to provide for their wives even more abundantly than the ketubah did. By the same token, there was a concerted effort to reduce the rights of husbands to inherit their wives—and this was due to the desire of the wives' fathers to give more to their daughters and yet not lose too much if the marriages did not endure long because of the early death of the women.

Fathers also wanted to make their children more attentive to their mothers by making them dependent upon her during her widowhood, and yet guaranteeing that there would be a remainder for them.

Much of the motivation for rabbinic creativity in the law of testamentary succession was noble. The certainty of the patterns of intestate succession was sacrificed; testators were accorded more economic power, and the incidence of litigation increased. However, among the devotees of the law there persisted the desire to fulfill some of the biblical patterns and thus perform the *mitzvah* of "Yerushah de'Oraitah" (Inheritance according to the Torah's mandate). In this way one would ever be conscious that one ought to dispose of one's earthly possessions as God had willed it.

Index